ללמד וללמד
STUDIES IN JEWISH EDUCATION AND JUDAICA IN HONOR OF LOUIS NEWMAN

ללמד וללמד
STUDIES IN JEWISH EDUCATION AND JUDAICA IN HONOR OF LOUIS NEWMAN

Edited by
ALEXANDER M. SHAPIRO
and
BURTON I. COHEN

KTAV PUBLISHING HOUSE, INC.
NEW YORK

Library of Congress Cataloging in Publication Data
Main entry under title:

Studies in Jewish education and Judaica in honor of
    Louis Newman = [Li-lemod ule-lamed]

    In English; one article in Hebrew.
    Includes bibliographical references.
    1. Jewish religious education—United States—Ad-
dresses, essays, lectures. 2. Bible. O.T.—Criticism,
interpretation, etc.—Addresses, essays, lectures.
3. Newman, Louis—Addresses, essays, lectures.
I. Newman, Louis. II. Shapiro, Alexander M. III. Cohen,
Burton I. IV. Title: Li-lemod ule-lamed.
BM103.S78   1984   296'.07'073   83-23903
ISBN 0-88125-038-4

The editors wish to acknowledge with gratefulness the
contributions of the following individuals and institutions which helped make possible the publication of this
volume:

Rabbi and Mrs. Kassel Abelson
Janet and Dr. Bernard Aserkoff
Jacob Behrman
Anne and Dr. Jacob J. Freedman
Melton Research Center
Rabbi and Mrs. Alexander Shapiro
Ruth and N. Ronald Silberstein
Dr. Susan and Norman Krinsky
Rabbi and Mrs. Chaim Rogoff
Louis Winer
Rabbi Bernard Lipnick
Rabbi Jehiel Orenstein

CONTENTS

INTRODUCTION AND MEMOIR

The essays in this *Festschrift* represent, far more than is usual in similar scholarly volumes, an expression of love. They were written to honor a man who has had the utmost influence on many who have devoted their lives to Jewish education. Unfortunately, however, he has never written extensively, nor have his insights and understanding ever been systematized into an imposing academic structure. Yet, the wonder of it all is that he has so touched the lives of men and women, particularly in the field of Jewish education, that his intellectual sagacity and the inspiration of his life has remained a source of strength many years after daily, intimate contact with Louis Newman as mentor and guide has ceased.

Lou was the consummate teacher, a model of what he sought to develop in others, probing, searching for the inner spirit of human beings, and then carefully and decisively helping them bring that spirit to the surface in their relationships with others. It was often extremely frustrating to work under his supervision, for one waited in vain for the nod of the supervisor, the sign that one had done well or poorly. How anxious I remember being, hoping for an objective evaluation of my work, one that would establish a clear, unequivocal view of the rights and wrongs of my own early fumbling attempts to work with American-Jewish teenagers. For Lou, however, an entirely different mode of supervision was far more appropriate.

Dr. Alexander M. Shapiro is rabbi of Oheb Shalom Congregation in South Orange, New Jersey. He has taught at Ben Gurion University of the Negev, Beersheba, Israel, and in the Department of Religion at Temple University. Rabbi Shapiro has spent twenty years in the Ramah movement including a period as Director of Camp Ramah in the Poconos in 1969–70.

It was one, I began to realize later, that was more preoccupied with individual growth than with professional judgments; judgment ultimately was to come from within, not from without.

I had come to know Lou at one of the most exciting and creative times in his life. It was also one of the most exciting periods in Jewish education and group work. We were all terribly young and untried; yet we had the feeling that we were at the cutting edge of a whole new point of view, a whole new way of seeing the educational process. To many of us who had been given traditional educations and who were exposed to a lockstep approach to formal and informal education, Lou's notions of a child's involvement in his own educational destiny came as something revolutionary. This was particularly so because the discovery of new dimensions in the lives of our children coincided with significant self-discovery for us as well. In part, our own naivete and unsophistication led us to the rather remarkable feeling that we all shared. We believed deeply that we were changing the lives of human beings, and through them, that we were literally changing the world. Strangely enough, inspired in an altogether unorthodox fashion by one man, our own belief in ourselves struck a responsive chord in the children entrusted to our care. They, too, came to believe in themselves and in the community of which they were a part. While in some ways it is very strange, it is nonetheless true that the memory of it all remains as fresh now as it was then, more than thirty years ago. We worked in a relatively small summer camp, much smaller than the large, much more complex camp populations of a later time. Yet, the camp of Wisconsin Ramah in 1951 considered itself to be a utopian community in the making. Over the course of a very short period of time, everyone in the community, from the youngest child to the oldest member of the professional staff, considered himself to be part of the community. I remember well the meetings of the entire camp community that were called each week to talk of the problems that we shared. How well I remember the intensity of those meetings! How well I recollect the marvel of one of the youngest children in camp addressing Lou, and having his questions answered seriously and patiently by the director while the exchange was heard without condescension by the child's older campmates as well as by his counselors.

The simple truth is that Lou's admonition to be receptive to the life of the child and his needs was remote from a call for permissiveness. Quite to the contrary, I am hard put to remember another educational endeavor that had quite as much preoccupation with moral issues and with the moral responsibility of children. It extended into every single area of the camp community, from the cleanup of the grounds to the impassioned debates on the morality of color-wars. We were then but dimly conscious of the fact that we were engaged in the kind of serious educational experiment that was ultimately to have a significant impact on others. How far-reaching that influence was to be we could not possibly imagine. What we all knew was that it was far more than a summer job that drew us together. We seriously debated whether it was a moral act for us to take a day off once a week. After all, the children were put in our charge for twenty-four hours a day. Is it not irresponsible, we seriously asked, to leave even for awhile? Those of us who had the temerity to take the day off came rushing back at the end of the day to discover what new development we had missed. Yet, we had no sense that we were extreme in any way, nor were there exhortations from above to spur us on to particular ideological loyalties. Quite to the contrary. Lou's approach was entirely that of stimulating within the individual group worker his own overwhelming sense of responsibility for what transpired in camp, one that tended to be much more far-reaching than any set of demands put forward by any camp administrator. What made the entire experience unique from the perspective of later educational endeavors was that the conditions under which all of us worked were totally primitive. The camp grounds were indifferently maintained, sports equipment minimal, food indifferent at best, and housing conditions terrible! Moreover, every single one of us could have earned significantly more than the pitiful salaries we were paid in any one of a number of other institutions. Yet, all of that faded into insignificance in comparison to the enterprise of which we were a part.

What was even more fascinating was that our own commitments, youthful and naive as they were, were miraculously transmitted to the young people in our charge. Over the years I have had the good fortune of working with many young people whose intellectual attainments and abilities were certainly comparable to those of the teenagers with whom I worked during the years of the Newman Revolution. Later generations of teens within a camp setting were far more preoccupied with rebellion against adult authority, and indeed with the variety of personal areas of growth and social maturation characteristic of adolescence. Yet, somehow, that particular group of teenagers was radically different. They came to share the vision of the members of the staff and were able to harness themselves to the ideal of creating their own just society. The memory is all the more poignant because of the distance between the generations so clearly evident in the sixties, when young people often took angry, radical positions of confrontation because they did not discern that they had a stake in society. The environment that we were creating under Lou's direction, more than anything else, was probably comparable to that of a kibbutz, a cooperative, supportive environment, minus the umbrella of Zionist ideology but with intense religious concern. It was not accidental perhaps that a significant proportion of the staff people had been deeply influenced by the liberal and radical ideologies of the old left of the forties. Those very ideologies had profound effects on other experimental educational structures, some of which were models for the Ramah program.

What was, in fact, unknown to me and to the others was that our beloved director was under rather consistent attack from the backers of the camp for his radical ideas about education as well as for insufficient attention to the physical plant and to the other issues that were of significance to them. It was always my impression that Lou did much better with those with whom he worked directly and with the children whom he loved so much than with public relations, which is always necessary to wielders of power within the community. It is of more than passing interest, however, that conflicts with the Camp Committee and with others concerned about the camp were never directly communicated to us. Unfortunately, we never adequately enough described to laymen the nature of our educational endeavors.

What must also be understood is that unlike later developments in the far more radical sixties, the intellectual environment of the camp never suffered because of our preoccupation with the issues of individual growth. The professor of the camp was in those years exactly what he was meant to be, namely, the ideal, the model of wisdom in whom were to be found for young and old alike the secrets of understanding the tradition that ultimately was the repository of the answers to the perplexing issues of our lives. In fact, Ramah represented the first serious attempt I had ever encountered to apply religion to life, not in the abstract but in the very concrete. All of the years that I spent in Orthodox institutions were never oriented in that way at all. Religion in my training had to do solely with the understanding of classical texts and classical formulations. The possibility that its insights could be applied to the world of children and, in fact, to the world of adults, too, in the context of the daily life of a society came as a revolutionary idea in those days. The intensity of religious concern was overwhelming, particularly since it did not stimulate simply the fulfillment of mitzvah but rather the deepest possible understanding of what was behind the ethical command.

In those days I literally saw with my own eyes the conversion to Judaism of young people raised in rather indifferent middle western Jewish surroundings. It was the first generation of the young Jewish religious revolutionary who returned home to upset rabbis, parents, friends by the very intensity of his religious belief and commitment. Even more significant with the passing of years has been the recognition that in both staff and campers of those days were to be found personalities who later became the leading exponents of Jewish education in some of its most creative forms across the length and breadth of the country. Moreover, when you add to those who were present then, those whom they themselves later were to train, the extent of the Newman influence is overwhelming. I am, of course, aware of the fact that in later years Lou Newman hurled himself at other educational establishments, sometimes with greater and sometimes with lesser success. Yet in all of his work, the honesty and integrity of the positions he took and the brilliance of his philosophical insights deeply affected all those with whom he came in contact.

In looking back on the early days, more than thirty years ago, one has to be careful lest one is afflicted with nostalgia and over-romanticization. There were failures as well as successes, and, of course, there were the usual excesses of unbridled youthful enthusiasm. Nonetheless, after discounting the aberrations of memory, it seems to me that what was present then was an interesting model for the present as well. We live in a far less ideological age, and some see far less commitment on the part of young and old alike than seemed to be the case then. I would hold, nonetheless, that the Lou Newmans of the future remain to be discovered and put to work on the educational issues of our own time. The fact that one human being had such a deep and overwhelming impact on so many is an indication that it is possible to do far more than we are currently doing. It is possible for us to influence the younger generation of our time and the generations to come if only we can summon the kind of belief, the kind of commitment, and the kind of readiness to sacrifice that was so fundamental to the vision that Lou sought to inspire in us.

It is within the pages of this *Festschrift* that some of Lou Newman's contributions will be discussed, analyzed, and evaluated so that the impact of his professional life will not be lost on the generations yet to come. In addition, scholars and colleagues have added contributions of their own fields allied with Jewish education. It is to be hoped that unlike many

Festschrift volumes whose fate is to gather dust on the shelves of scholars, these essays will stimulate long-needed study of many of the educational issues Lou Newman addressed during his long and productive career that remain central for our lives as well. There could be no more fitting way to repay the debt we all owe him.

Dr. Alexander M. Shapiro, Rabbi

October 28, 1982

OF PRIMARY FAITH AND RICES: A PORTRAIT OF MY FATHER

MORDECAI NEWMAN

Hanging in my parents' living room is a gift they received a few years ago from an artist friend. It is an oil painting done in the form of a *ketubah* for their marriage. The artist chose to illustrate the *ketubah* with images from his own memory, recollections of the period—more than thirty years ago—when, a young immigrant from Morocco, he lived for some months with my family. Prominent among these images is a representation of a man in an armchair. He has a *kipah* on his head, a book held open with one hand. The other hand is occupied with supporting a small girl, who clings to his arm like a koala bear on a branch. His arm cradling the girl, the man gazes over her head into the book. He does not appear at all put out or distracted by the child. Indeed, the girl and the book seem to be twin elements in a natural equilibrium. The girl is my sister, Miriam. The man who holds her is my father, sitting at home as he prays the *Kabbalat Shabbat* service to himself from an open Siddur.

The painter of this vignette had a stern and demanding father, and the sight of my father at prayer, welcoming little Miriam to him on her own childish terms, was for this artist, a startling and unaccustomed demonstration of paternal tolerance. Here was a man who held the affection, however undisciplined, of a small daughter to be perfectly consonant with the

Mordecai Newman is editor of *Young Judaean* and assistant editor of *Jewish Frontier,* for which he also serves as film critic. His freelance writing has included film and theater criticism, radio plays for "The Eternal Light," scripts for audio-visual presentation, and the libretto of a forthcoming opera *Dreyfus.*

1

formal act of welcoming the Shabbat, a father at ease with a
child's need to be a child. What the painter perceived is what
Louis Newman's three children have experienced. Nothing is
more central to Abba's style as a parent than his regard for our
own idiosyncratic selves. He has never tried to bend or twist us
against our own true natures. Instead, he has been content,
even eager, to discover us.

Not that anyone would confuse Abba with a laid-back,
"value-free" parent. From the time of our earliest moral awareness, none of his children has ever doubted his commitment to
a fundamental standard of decency. And we came to understand his devotion to Jewish tradition as a reflection of that
same standard. Judaism would, I believe, be worthless to Abba
if he did not find within it a system of mechanisms for promoting and perpetuating decent behavior among people. His primary faith, his basic axiom, is that nothing is more worthy than
an ethical life. And while I confess to some disagreement with
him over the nature of halacha as an educational device and a
social tool, I and my siblings are heirs to his primary faith.
Whatever else he taught us, that faith has been his greatest
lesson. He instructed us in it without harangues and without
authoritarian insistence. He nurtured our gentleness by being
gentle, our kindness by being kind, our empathy by being
empathic. The qualities that made us love him became the ones
we wanted to emulate. We felt that in being like him we were
unearthing some of the finest aspects of ourselves—and we
were right. Learning values from him was a process of self-
discovery, not of submitting to coercion. Believing that his
children's best selves are their truest selves, he gave us rein to
be who we were without abdicating his role as an exemplar and
guide.

It happens, however, that the tactics of stern discipline rest
secure within Abba's repertoire of educational maneuvers,
waiting to be called upon when needed. Knowing as we did
the depth of his tolerance and understanding, his children
rarely confronted him with open rebelliousness. His capacity
for quelling youthful insubordination was not a familiar part of

our home life. Things were different, I discovered, at Akiba Hebrew Academy. Abba was principal of the school during my first three years in attendance, while I was in grades six through eight. The man who skillfully wielded a more-than-slightly-forbidding presence to bring school assemblies to order, who could squelch rowdiness with a withering glare, was a different human being from the one I knew at home. Those students who didn't know that Mr. Newman was my father were not about to learn that embarrassing secret from my lips. On more than one occasion, some student ignorant of my parental lineage would, in my presence, vent his displeasure at the malign individual who was our principal. If called upon for my opinion, I would usually pretend to concur.

In later years, I was to learn more about Louis Newman the disciplinarian from anecdotes that he himself told. There was the time when, as a young Hebrew teacher, he was bitten by a student. It took virtually no time for Abba to devise a punishment that fit the crime. He bit the student back. There was also the threat my father made to an Akiba student who had been tormenting a female classmate not distinguished by her physical adorability. Summoning what must have been his full, and long dormant, store of machismo, Abba made a promise—that if the boy didn't leave the girl alone, he would knock his teeth out and string them on a necklace. Abba would not have spoken that way to a student who cut classes, neglected his homework, or threw food in the lunchroom. It was a mode of expression he reserved for dealing with cruelty. In this instance, at least, it worked. The student stopped bullying the girl. But there is more. Years later, this same student became an annual guest at our family Seder. My father rarely bears a grudge. Nor does he behave in a way that invites a grudge to be borne against him.

Abba is a master teacher, and not only of values. His ability as a teacher is the only thing I have ever heard him boast about (although rarely). I once heard him say that anything he knows, he can teach. He's probably right. His love of teaching is inseparable from his love of learning. Abba regards the

transmission of knowledge and insight as a thoroughly marvel-
ous process, no matter which side of that process he is on. One
of the great frustrations of his professional life has been that it
has left him little time to read for pleasure. Such reading, were
he free to pursue it, would probably consist of a list of works
something like the University of Chicago Great Books syllabus.
The perceptions of a scrupulously rational mind, expressed
with grace and clarity, are for Abba a source of manifest
delight. Profoundly devoted as he is to the conviction that the
universe is not absurd, that system and order are essential
aspects of the world and apply to our lives, it is his great
pleasure to encounter that order under the tutelage of brilliant
minds past and present. An intricate mathematical solution, a
closely reasoned and lucidly rendered passage of philosophical
thought, a meticulously devised piece of scientific investigation, a rigorous analysis of biblical text—from these Abba
draws as much entertainment as edification.

Moreover, matters of great intellectual consequence elicit
from Abba an eloquence that he lacks with regard to mundane
affairs. A paradox of his habits of speech is that his articulacy
rises in direct proportion to the difficulty of what he intends to
express. He can expound abstract theory with utter clarity. It is
when he recounts what happened at the supermarket or in the
street that his verbal ability runs into trouble. An incident that
has entrenched itself into our family lore occurred at a dinner
my parents attended at the home of friends. Over the meal, my
father turned to compliment the hostess with the observation,
"These rices are delicious." Graciously ignoring the collective
nature of rice, the hostess replied with something along the
lines of "Yes they are, aren't they." My mother, whose syntax is
impeccable, later reported that she felt tempted to kick my
father under the table. At any rate, the Newman family no
longer eats rice. We eat rices.

But no matter. Abba has no trouble conveying the things that
count. And the example of his personal qualities, his unwaver-
ing embodiment of a standard of goodness and decency, is
more compelling than any well-turned phrase. To Hillel, Mi-

riam, and me, he (together with my mother) has given unstinting love. And he has inspired us with his absolute faith that there are things worth knowing and ways worth being. There is no greater legacy.

RAMAH PHILOSOPHY AND THE NEWMAN REVOLUTION

SHULY RUBIN SCHWARTZ

A new chapter in the history of the Conservative movement began in 1947 with the founding of Camp Ramah.[1] What started as a modest venture in response to the specific needs of various groups within the movement eventually became a major innovative educational institution with a far-reaching impact that is still evident today. Certainly, the motivation for its establishment lay in the mood and priorities of American Jewry in the postwar period. In the wake of the Holocaust, American Jews were painfully aware that they were the last Jewish community of any sizable proportions. With this knowledge foremost in their minds, the preservation of the Jewishness of their community became a vital necessity. Yet the means for ensuring the future of Judaism in this country were sorely lacking.

The Conservative movement, in particular, suffered from a dearth of rabbis, educators, synagogues, and schools. Camp Ramah was one answer to these various needs. Ramah would be a laboratory for the leadership training of high school youth. It would provide the Jewish Theological Seminary of America with a pool of potential students who could then be trained to serve the Jewish community as rabbis and educators. At the same time, Ramah would partially solve the problems of Jew-

Shuly Rubin Schwartz is a Ph.D. candidate at the Jewish Theological Seminary of America. She is currently writing her dissertation, entitled "The Coming of Age of Jewish Scholarship in America: The Publication of the *Jewish Encyclopedia.*"

ish educators who were struggling with the lack of time for Jewish education. By utilizing the summer months, these educators hoped to intensify the level of Jewish education received by American Jewish youth. Of course, Ramah was established also to provide members of the Conservative movement with a Jewish summer camp for their children. It was this final reason which motivated the Chicago Council of Conservative Synagogues to support the venture.[2]

Though Ramah grew out of a unique combination of factors which came together in the postwar period, it drew heavily on earlier models of Jewish educational camping in the United States. Camp Achvah, founded by Samson Benderly, was a camp with classes as its essence and Hebrew as its official language. Established by the Central Jewish Institute, Cejwin Camps combined recreation with communal Jewish living. Camp Massad, directed by Shlomo Shulsinger, was a camp with Hebrew and Zionism at its core. These three camps in particular deeply influenced the founders and staff of Ramah, for many of them had worked at or attended one or more of these camps.[3]

The original philosophy of Ramah, then, was developed in response to the pragmatic needs of the Conservative movement and in light of the experience of other Jewish educational camps. In 1947, three values stood out above all others as the pillars of the Ramah philosophy: Hebrew, study, and Jewish living. All three would be emphasized in a total camp setting consisting of adventure, sports, and games.

First and foremost, Ramah would allow a child to live Jewishly. Most children whose families were affiliated with Conservative synagogues had never experienced intensive Jewish living. Ramah would supply that atmosphere for them. As Ralph Simon, one of the key figures in the establishment of Camp Ramah in Wisconsin in 1947, explained:

> It put a child in a total Jewish environment and enabled him to live the so-called ideal Jewish life from the time he got up until he went to bed. . . . And that was of tremendous

value. Most children had never lived a complete Jewish life. Here they not only lived it, but they lived it without tension. It was the normal way.[4]

For the architects of the Ramah philosophy—Moshe Davis, Sylvia Ettenberg, Henry Goldberg, and others—Jewish living meant both ritual observance like Kashrut, daily prayer, and Shabbat observance, and moral behavior. They believed that Jewish living implied a certain sensitivity to the needs of others.

Conservative Jewish living was the facet of this concept stressed by those whose previous experience had been shaped by Massad. They wanted Ramah to be distinguished by a specifically Conservative religious practice, which for them included tolerance of those whose observance level was different from the camp's norm. By *Conservative*, these ideologues also had in mind a camp that would successfully accomplish the synthesis of the American and the Jewish environments. Ramah would not be a European-run or Palestine-directed venture but, rather, an American camp with American staff and campers who chose to live Jewishly together.[5]

In order to understand the key position given to the Hebrew language at Ramah, one must recall the needs of Jewish educators at that time. Striving to capture more time for Jewish education, they hoped Ramah would become a summer arm of Jewish education, not a camp alone. Since Hebrew was central to the curricula of the afternoon schools, it naturally assumed a role in their summer counterpart. Yet, Hebrew in Ramah was to do more than this. Educators were convinced that Hebrew would be learned much more easily in a camp setting. By creating a Hebrew-speaking camp, these ideologues had in mind the improvement of both the level of the campers' Hebrew and the quality of the supplementary schools as a result of the higher Hebrew level of the returning students. In addition to these pragmatic reasons, Hebrew speaking was crucial in yet another way: A grasp of the language was considered to be a fundamental part of the background of any knowledgable Jew. Since knowledge was a prerequisite for leadership, Hebrew would have to play an important role at Ramah.

Study, the third pillar of Ramah's philosophy, was also rooted in the reality of Ramah's potential constituency. The need for study in camp originated from two practical considerations. First, study was the only way in which Hebrew could be firmly established. Since the potential campers would not be fluent in Hebrew, formal study was essential to teach them the language. In class, campers could first learn the basic vocabulary without which a Hebrew-speaking environment could not succeed. Moreover, many campers lacked a basic knowledge of Judaism. In order to live a Jewish life, they would first have to learn some fundamental skills and concepts. Finally, on a theoretical level, the importance of study was firmly rooted in traditional Jewish values. Thus, at Ramah everyone—staff as well as campers, teachers as well as those deficient in Jewish knowledge—would study on a regular basis. The camp would have a professor-in-residence whose very presence would symbolize the importance of study.

There was general agreement on the importance of these values to Ramah. Yet, different people stressed one or another of the values based on their individual philosophies. Conservative rabbis stressed the fact that Ramah would be "Conservative in conception and in execution, and it would be open to anyone who shared our point-of-view." Educators, on the other hand, were not so concerned about the religious ideology of the camp. For them, Ramah would be first and foremost a place to teach children a maximum of Judaism. A small though influential group of committed Hebraists hoped that the camp would teach youngsters enough Hebrew to create a vibrant Hebrew atmosphere. Through this they would keep alive the Hebrew movement in America.[6]

Not to be forgotten amidst this emphasis on Ramah's unique philosophy are the general aspects of summer camps which were also important to Ramah ideologues. Their philosophy did not preclude swimming, physical exercise, adventure, sports, and games. On the contrary, they firmly held that Ramah's ideology would best flourish in a total camp setting.

The camp's actual program in the summer of 1947 closely reflected its goals. Mornings were devoted to prayer, breakfast, cleanup, study, and a general swim. In the afternoon, campers went by bunks to various activities, including arts and crafts, sports, and music. Evening activities consisted of programs like campfires, social dancing, and movies. Hebrew was central to camp activities, and both public announcements and camp routine were conducted primarily in Hebrew.[7]

The first Ramah camp season was an undeniable success, and the Jewish Theological Seminary saw the opportunity for expansion. Camp Ramah in Maine was opened in 1948, and Ramah in the Poconos in 1950. During these subsequent years, the 1947 summer remained the model, and the Ramah philosophy was essentially unchanged, though individual directors left their personal imprint on the camps they ran. It was not until Louis Newman assumed the directorship of Ramah in Wisconsin in 1951 that the ideological revolution began.[8]

Newman was seen as the perfect person for the position. He was a man with deep Jewish commitment who spoke Hebrew fluently and had a background in camping—all important qualities for a Ramah director. During the year, Newman had been teaching psychology at the Herzliah Teachers Seminary and had expressed an interest in buying a camp where he could try out some of his educational ideas. When this became known, he was offered the directorship of Camp Ramah in Wisconsin.

Though Lou Newman had never before run a camp, he had some highly developed theories of education to guide his new undertaking. His ideas were strongly influenced by those of John Dewey, and the progressive approach to education affected his thinking profoundly. Since Newman believed that a camp experience could affect a person's character, he wanted to create an atmosphere that would build character, not merely one which would focus on teaching skills and Hebrew and providing a good time. Newman became the first person to introduce this approach to the Ramah movement, attempting a synthesis of progressive educational ideology and traditional Ramah philosophy. So devoted was he to both sets of goals that he was often depicted as the director with "Torah in one hand and Dewey in the other." Though he rarely put his ideas on paper, Newman did write one statement on his thoughts in June 1951. In it, he included his vision of the aims of Ramah.

> In camp, we want (1) to create living situations through which all people, campers, counselors, and all workers will become better human beings. . . . We want (2) to transmit to our campers the knowledge of traditional Jewish values. . . . We believe that the experiences of our people as a whole, and of outstanding Jews individually, offer criteria to aid anyone choosing among alternative ways of behaving. (3) to teach a working knowledge of the Hebrew language, both in reading and conversation.[9]

This stress on growth as a person, while understood by each of the preceding directors as being part of the growth of a Jew, had never before occupied so prominent a place in the Ramah philosophy.

One of the major problems Newman faced in attempting to implement his ideal was the lack of available models. No other Jewish camp in which Newman had been had tried this synthesis. Thus, Newman was motivated primarily by the many negative aspects of camping which he hoped to change: he was disturbed by the realization that the child's welfare was often neglected in camp. He had seen too many activities which were managed from above by staff and which ended up highlighting the talents of the leaders at the expense of the campers. Furthermore, not only were the child's needs often neglected but also, Newman felt, certain areas of camp were patently harmful to the child, for example, raids, stealing food, competition, and prizes. That a child enjoys such activities was not sufficient criterion for encouraging their continuation. They were anathema to Newman, and he believed that it was necessary to structure an environment which would remove from campers the need to perform useless or destructive acts. Newman also knew that he did not want immature staff as role models. He was convinced of the necessity of hiring older, mature, preferably married staff who could better deal with the emotional problems of children and adolescents. He felt that younger staff who had not yet found their emotional—particularly sexual—identities could not properly guide their young, impressionable campers.

The closest Newman could get to a successful camping model from which to learn was the National Experimental Camp of Pioneer Youth of America. A record of its first six summers was published as a book, *Creative Camping*, by Joshua Lieberman, the Pioneer camp director.[10] It describes Lieberman's experiment in realizing progressive ideology, and Newman was deeply affected by it. Newman had even considered working at the Pioneer camp and had met with Lieberman. However, while *Creative Camping* was an excellent guide for Newman, it was an incomplete one, for the book did not, of course, incorporate the traditional elements of a Ramah camp—study, Hebrew, and intensive Jewish living. By attempting this integration of traditional Ramah values and progressive ideology, Newman was embarking on his own pioneer adventure.

Newman understood both his strengths and his weaknesses. While a good theoretician, he was limited as an actualizer of ideas. Therefore, in choosing a head counselor, he selected Bernard Lipnick, someone who Newman felt possessed this necessary quality. The two met regularly on weekends during the winter and spring of 1950–51. Lipnick would read and listen as Newman filled him with his ideas; Lipnick became persuaded by the approach. The two were well-suited complements to each other—Newman the idea-man and Lipnick the implementer.[11]

Most other members of the staff met with Newman individually once during the year when he came to Chicago. There, he sounded them out with several of his ideas. While they expected the summer to be different, no one, including Newman himself, knew exactly how it would differ.[12]

The beginning of the summer of 1951 was extremely difficult. Newman created a furor by announcing that there was to be no schedule. No longer would campers go by bunks to a pre-scribed number of activities. It was now up to the individual camper to design his own program. Specialists and counselors were available and eager to help out, but staff would not enforce a schedule nor push campers to participate in an activity. Their example and not their directive would be their chief avenue of guiding the campers.

The first week was chaos. Campers wandered around doing very little. Slowly, though, things began to take shape. Formal study marked one definite period of the day. Since classes were required by the Seminary, they remained a fixed part of the morning. Campers chose their own activities for the afternoon; it was Bernard Lipnick who devised the system whereby individuals would create their own weekly schedules based on their interests. In working out the mechanism, Lipnick had to reconcile the theory of giving children a truly free choice with the reality of scheduling activities. The availability of facilities, the number of participants required for team sports, and the age and sex of the campers involved were just a few of the variables that he had to build into a schedule of free choice, and this schedule changed weekly so that no one would be boxed into an activity that he no longer wanted. The campers were offered a wide range of activities, including sports, arts and crafts, music, drama, and even more study. Lipnick made it possible for the campers to choose any of these and also to schedule a free period during the day if they so desired.

Scheduling difficulties, however, were only half of the re-sponsibility placed upon the staff by this new arrangement. The other part, more subtle, was in a sense also more demand-ing. First, it was the counselor's obligation to meet with each camper to determine his needs and help him make the choices which would be best for him. A child could conceivably spend the whole day in arts and crafts and never engage in sports activities. In general, such a child would be encouraged to diversify his interests, but there were situations when such a program would be considered right for a given camper. Only personal contact with and concern for the individual child could determine which was indeed the case. Second, counselors had to keep abreast of their campers' weekly schedules in order to know if the children were participating in activities. Clearly, this need to know each camper and his personalized weekly program placed an enormous burden upon the staff.

Other areas of camp life were equally affected by the new philosophy: since campers spent most of their day pursuing individual interests, a conscious effort was made to encourage bunk projects at other times in order to foster group feeling. There were frequent bunk meetings and votes to decide what to do and how to do it. This democratic process was extended to the camp as a whole on the controversial issue of the Maccabiah, a highlight of the summer in previous seasons. When the time for the Maccabiah arrived, Newman put the question of whether or not to have this "color-war" up for a vote. Newman was very much opposed to having a Maccabiah; the competitive spirit and adult management of the event ran counter to everything for which he stood. Yet, Newman felt that to impose his own bias, however strong, upon the group would cause hostility and anger. Newman feared that he would lose in the long run, though he might attain his immediate goal: "There are many cases where when you win you lose." Newman announced to both campers and staff in advance that he would abide by the outcome; it would not be an empty vote. Everyone in camp, including the director, had one vote. A majority did vote to eliminate color-war. Newman had gambled and won.

Social dancing was another controversial issue for Newman. Held on Saturday nights for the older campers and enthusiastically supported by the more popular among them, dances were often devastating for those who felt socially ill at ease. Newman and his staff were sensitively attuned to those shy campers for whom the activity was a potentially humiliating experience. In this case, though, the issue was not put up for a vote. First, it did not affect the whole camp. Second, Newman knew that there was nothing inherently wrong with dancing; the problem lay in the social pressure accompanying such an activity. It was decided by the staff to undermine this Saturday night ritual by offering a choice of other activities at the same time. Alternatives were emphasized, draining campers from the socials. Slowly, the strategy began to work, until the socials were no longer held.

Newman's ideas changed other aspects of camp as well. In keeping with the emphasis on individual needs, the bugle was eliminated, and counselors began to wake their campers individually. Group-interaction problems also received special attention as staff strove to talk openly and resolve difficulties with their campers.

By remaining true to his philosophy, Newman ended up eliminating many of the traditional, adventurous summer-camp activities. Color-war was one example; another was "raids." Newman and his staff believed that raids were dangerous, antisocial, and unethical. When a group did go on a raid, Newman would be furious, saying, "The camp is yours. From whom are you stealing?" Yet, he was keenly aware of the potential problems posed by eliminating these events, and he knew that he consciously had to program other exciting and adventurous activities. Because of this belief, Newman invested in canoes, ping-pong tables, and power equipment for woodworking. He also introduced overnight outings into the program. Conselors suggested and encouraged activities that would be challenging, useful, and real. For example, one bunk built steps from the lake to the dining hall. To the surprise of the camp, the library was painted pink one night by a group of campers. Newman, ever-aware of the potential dangers that could result from undirected adolescent energy and emotion, encouraged healthy, constructive projects to channel these feelings.

The Judaic part of the program was not fundamentally altered by this new educational philosophy, and its structure remained unchanged. Formal classes continued. Hebrew speaking remained important to the staff, and much effort was devoted to planning special programs and exciting ways to improve everyone's Hebrew level. In addition, the staff hoped to provide meaningful religious experiences, standardize the melodies and structure of religious services, and teach ritual skills to the campers. Most important, they tried to serve as models of committed, observant Jews who were themselves improving their knowledge of Judaism, for they believed this to be a primary way of deepening the campers' commitment to Judaism.

This emphasis on Judaica at Ramah tied in with Newman's philosophy in two ways. First, his focus on the needs of the child was seen as an expression of the ethical dimension in Judaism and thus in harmony with Jewish educational goals. A potential Jewish leader, in additional to being knowledgable and observant, also had to be a sensitive and mature individual. It was the recognition of the need consciously to foster this aspect of development that Newman brought to Ramah. Second, Newman's philosophy helped legitimize differences in Conservative practice. Variations in religious observance posed difficult problems at Ramah as the Teachers Institute sought to set policy and establish norms, especially for prayer and Shabbat observance.[13] By stressing individual choice and responsibility, Newman transformed the reality of Conservative diversity into a matter of principle.

Newman attracted a core of talented young people to his camp. Believing that some people's personalities clashed with the camp's ideology, Newman attempted to screen his staff by choosing mature, nonauthoritarian people who could work under his system. He also tried to provide housing for married couples in order to be able realistically to hire the mature staff he wanted. Newman worked closely with his staff and trained a group of young people who would later join him in having a major impact on Ramah and Jewish education in general. Some of these people are: Dr. Burton Cohen, national Ramah director; Rabbi Jerome Abrams, director, Camp Ramah in the Berkshires; Dr. Seymour Fox, director, School of Education of the Hebrew University; Dr. Joseph Lukinsky, associate professor of education at the Jewish Theological Seminary; the late Rabbi David Mogilner, former national Ramah director; and Rabbi Alexander Shapiro, spiritual leader of Oheb Shalom Congregation, South Orange, New Jersey. All of these men worked with Newman in Wisconsin, and all served at one time or another as Ramah directors. They and others who worked in camp were profoundly influenced by Newman.

Nevertheless, some people—staff, local rabbis, and laypeople—were not so enthusiastic about Newman's innovations. Several staff members opposed any change, and others merely preferred the camp as it was before 1951. Outsiders, on the other hand, opposed Newman because of his lack of formalism and his inexperience with public relations. This discontent eventually focused on the issue of cleanliness, for opponents were distressed by the dirty condition of some of the bunks and were furious that Newman would not force the children to clean them.[14] Apparently, approval of Newman outweighed complaints, for he remained director of Ramah in Wisconsin for three years. Newman also served as director of Camp Ramah in Connecticut in 1955. He later worked for Ramah in other capacities, particularly as director of the Mador–National Camp Leadership Institute.

Newman and his staff were so steeped in Hebrew, Jewish learning, and Jewish living that they were able to synthesize the original with the "Newman philosophy" and implement both in camp. However, the potential for conflict between the traditional Ramah values and the progressive educational philosophy was always there. For example, stress on discussing problems and group decision-making undermined the goal of speaking Hebrew. As one staff member put it: "As long as we didn't talk about anything, we could talk Hebrew, but when we started to talk about serious matters, then it became a problem."[15] Tensions such as these surfaced during the Newman years and have vexed Ramah to varying degrees ever since.

Despite the difficulties, Louis Newman made a profound contribution to the Ramah movement, and Ramah was permanently changed because of his efforts. While other Ramah camps remained basically unaffected by this new philosophy for many years, all eventually incorporated Newman's innovations, though with modifications. The junior-counselor training program instituted by Newman was strengthened and expanded. Courses in education as well as those in Judaica were taught to staff. The practice of campers' choosing activities was introduced to the other camps, though in modified form, since choices were offered less often than the original once a week. Color-war, Saturday-night socials, and bugles eventually disappeared from every Ramah camp. So pervasive was Newman's impact that contemporary Ramah staff find it almost impossible to believe that Ramah ever condoned such activities. Thus, Newman's philosophy became a crucial part of what has become known as the uniqueness of the "Ramah experience." Yet his influence extended beyond Ramah as well, since so many of the people who worked with him in Ramah in those years were inspired by him to continue his work in other spheres. Many of them went on to become prominent Jewish educators who themselves have made significant, original contributions to the field of Jewish education. As one of the many people who worked with Lou Newman commented almost thirty years later: "He is one of the great educators of American Jewish life. . . . Everybody who ever worked with him owes him more than can ever be said."[16]

Notes

1. For a complete review of the founding of Camp Ramah, see Shuly Rubin Schwartz, "Ramah—The Early Years, 1947–52" (M.A. thesis, Jewish Theological Seminary of America, 1976).

2. The needs and concerns of the Conservative movement after World War II are evident in the many publications of that period. Some of them are: *Proceedings of the Second Annual Rabbinical Assembly Conference on Jewish Education*, December 22–23, 1947, especially papers by Moshe Davis and Henry Goldberg; *Proceedings of the Rabbinical Assembly*, 1944–47, especially Mordecai Kaplan, "The Training of Teaching and Leadership Personnel," *Proceedings* 8 (1944): 348–360, including the responses to Kaplan's address; and Simon Greenberg, "Basic Problems and a Proposed Structure for Jewish Education in America," *Conservative Judaism* 3, no. 2 (February 1947): 86–88. Also helpful to me were taped interviews with Gerson D. Cohen, March 24, 1976, and Moshe Davis, April 2, 1976.

3. The beginnings of Jewish camping in America were reviewed by Beverly Gribetz, "The Rise of Jewish Educational Camping," April 6, 1974, mimeographed. Also useful is Shlomo Shulsinger, "Hebrew Camping—Five Years of Massad (1941–45)," *Jewish Education* 17, no. 3 (June 1946): 16–23. Taped interviews with Gerson D. Cohen; Sylvia Ettenberg, February 16, 1976; Louis Newman, March 25, 1976; Alexander Shapiro, March 9, 1976; and the taped response of Levi Soshuk, received April 23, 1976, illuminated the effect that these camps had on the founders and staff of Ramah. Less influential but nevertheless important in shaping the ideals of Ramah staff were Sharon, the school-camp of the College of Jewish Studies in Chicago; Sollel, a camp for teenagers sponsored by the Histadruth Ivrith of America; and Yavneh, the school-camp of Boston's Hebrew Teachers College.

4. Taped interview with Ralph Simon, March 29, 1976.

5. Taped interviews with Gerson D. Cohen and David Goldstein, March 15, 1976.

6. Taped interviews with Simon; Solomon Feffer, March 11, 1976; and Ettenberg.

7. Henry Goldberg, "Report on Camp Ramah—1947," files, Camp Ramah in the Poconos office, Philadelphia; taped interview with Burton Cohen, March 9, 1976.

8. Information on Newman's educational background and philosophy, unless otherwise noted, is based on taped interviews with Newman.

9. Louis Newman, "My Reflections on Counselorship," June 1951, personal files of Louis Newman, Boston, p. 1.

10. Joshua Lieberman, *Creative Camping: A Coeducational Experiment in Personality Development and Social Living, Being the Record of Six Summers of the National Experimental Camp of Pioneer Youth of America* (New York: Association Press, 1931).

11. Taped interview with Bernard Lipnick, March 29, 1976.

12. The description of the camp season under Newman's directorship is based on taped interviews with Newman; Lipnick; Shapiro; Burton Cohen; and Joseph Lukinsky, March 11, 1976.

13. Controversy over variations in observance focused on the issue of the use of electricity on Shabbat. The Teachers Institute decided that the camp should officially refrain from using electric lights on Shabbat, though individuals could turn lights on and off if they wished. Not everyone agreed with this decision, and the issue became symbolic of the difficulty of defining normative Conservative Jewish practice.

14. Taped interview with Simon.

15. Taped interview with Burton Cohen.

16. Taped interview with Lukinsky.

LOUIS NEWMAN'S WISCONSIN INNOVATIONS AND THEIR EFFECT UPON THE RAMAH CAMPING MOVEMENT

BURTON I. COHEN

The Problem of Educational Innovation

Over the past decade, one of the recurrent thrusts in educational literature has been the attempt to arrive at an effective theory of educational innovation.[1] This theorizing has been accompanied by detailed descriptions of successful and unsuccessful attempts at innovation.[2] Among the key questions which researchers in the field of educational innovation have sought to answer are the following:

1. Researchers have found that many well-meaning attempts at innovation fail because the innovators neglect to consider the possible wider effects of an innovation upon the total institutional setting. A successful innovation must both (a) achieve the particular narrow objectives for which it is designed, and (b) at the same time further, or at least not disrupt, the achievement of the overall objectives of the institution. This dual concern has required researchers working in the field of innovation to concern themselves with the question of what means of making

Burton I. Cohen is Assistant Professor of Education at the Jewish Theological Seminary of America and National Director of the Ramah Camps and Programs. Dr. Cohen was a camper at Camp Ramah in Wisconsin in 1947, the first Ramah camping season, and with the exception of two summers served continuously on the staff of that camp from 1948 through 1974; during the last fifteen summers, he served as camp director.

innovations are less disruptive to educational settings
than others?
2. What qualities of an educational innovation influence its
becoming a more or less permanent feature of the educational setting?
3. When an innovation is successfully diffused to other,
similar educational settings, (a) by what means did this
diffusion occur, and (b) what qualities of the innovation
facilitated its being replicated?

Researchers have asserted that finding the answers to these
questions could be helpful to efforts at school improvement.

There is no question in my mind that the educational leadership exercised by Louis Newman at Camp Ramah in Wisconsin
during the summers of 1951—53 represents one of the most
successful and far-reaching instances of educational innovation
in the history of Jewish education in the United States. Hope-
fully, a review of what Newman accomplished in this short
period in Wisconsin and its long-range impact can be of help to
educators seeking the answers to some of the questions posed
above.

Newman Undertakes to Revolutionize Ramah

Educational innovations are usually undertaken in response to
problems. This was not the case, however, with Newman's
work at Camp Ramah. The "revolution" which he conceived
and implemented did not come in response to some crisis at
the camp.[3] Though the founders of the camp had built an
educational institution on rather unique premises, the idea had
quickly caught the imagination of rabbis, educators, lay leaders, and parents. Newman was not brought to Wisconsin to
bolster a tottering institution, but to lead what was already,
after only four years, a successful, if not quite yet flourishing,
educational endeavor.

Newman's predecessors at Camp Ramah in Wisconsin were
two very capable Jewish educators. The founding director of
the camp, serving for the 1947 and 1948 camp seasons was

Henry R. Goldberg, the educational director of the East Midwood Jewish Center (Brooklyn N.Y.), one of the foremost educators in the Conservative movement. Goldberg was succeeded in 1949 and 1950 by Rabbi Hillel Silverman, who had served as head counselor under Goldberg in 1948. Silverman, who was ordained at the Jewish Theological Seminary of America in June 1948, possessed great charisma, had a very strong Hebraic background, and had considerable experience in the field of Jewish camping.

Goldberg and Silverman enthusiastically and successfully implemented the newly designed camp program, emphasizing spoken Hebrew, formal Hebrew classes, religious observance, and athletic and artistic activity, which had been put together by Dr. Moshe Davis and Sylvia Ettenberg on behalf of the Teachers Institute of the Seminary.[4] When Newman was hired to direct the camp for the 1951 season, there was nothing in the educational or recreational program that required change or innovation—yet Newman undertook to create the revolution which Schwartz describes for us.[5] Why did Newman do away with the activity schedule, change the nature of the counselor's role, do away with social dancing, etc? What was it that influenced Newman to devote countless hours and tremendous energy to pursuing educational objectives far beyond the requirements of his position as Ramah camp director?

The problems to which Newman was responding may not have loomed large before Goldberg and Silverman, but Newman saw them as widespread, insidious, and threatening to undermine the efforts of all Jewish educators. His grasp of these problems and his perception of the urgent need to find solutions to them had been sharpened by his experience on the staffs of Camp Massad and Camp Yavneh,[6] his employment as a synagogue-school teacher and principal; and most of all, by his conviction of the need for Jewish educational enterprises to have strong moral purpose and to be consciously and deliberately guided by a philosophy and psychology of education which was in harmony with the nature of the child as revealed by contemporary educational and psychological research.

For Newman, then, Camp Ramah, as successful as it may have been by accepted standards, was still heir to the plethora of educational defects which afflicted virtually all Jewish educational endeavors. When he was invited to assume the directorship of Camp Ramah in Wisconsin, he decided to seize the opportunity to build a new type of Jewish educational institution, free from those defects.

How Newman Made His Innovations

We will not go into the details of Newman's revolution here. Its salient features are well described in Schwartz's article.[7] What we want to do here is to try to analyze what Newman did in the light of the questions relating to educational innovation which are posed at the beginning of this article.

The first question which we posed asked how successful innovations are made. Newman's innovations were made in two very straightforward ways: either by imposition from above, or through a process of group deliberation and decision. The decision to do away with the structured activity program was imposed by Newman from above; the decision to continue or discontinue the very popular tradition of a Maccabiah (color-war) he gave to the camp community to decide. Possibly Newman's most important quality of educational leadership, at least that first summer, was his skill in distinguishing between decisions that he himself could make for the camp community and decisions that he needed to allow the community to make for itself.

Newman made his positions on the issues that the camp community would decide for itself quite clear, but when the campers and staff were together deliberating about the issues, it was in an atmosphere of free-for-all discussion and open debate. While Newman made his views known, his efforts and those of his chief aide, Bernard Lipnick, to sell them to the community were surely rather subtle and by no means could be characterized as politicking or "arm-twisting."

As for the changes which he imposed from above, Newman, like many other educators, felt that it was the prerogative and obligation of the director of an educational institution to order the program so as to fit the objectives.[8] He did not hesitate to impose his educational convictions upon the community, presumably because he readily exposed them to public examination and was prepared to defend them at any time in debate with campers, staff members, or lay committee people.

How did Newman "get away" with this? Why didn't the staff rebel against his impositions? After all, the Rand Report tells us that the truly successful educational innovations are those which germinate and are implemented through the joint efforts of a school's leadership and faculty.[9] Why did this staff of bright, articulate, well-educated college and graduate students "buy" what Newman, a stranger from the East, had to offer?

Part of the answer, it seems to us, is that in the camp setting Newman proved to be a charismatic leader who was able to have a profound influence upon many of his staff members. This charisma did not flow from Newman's personal "style"— he was not an exciting speaker or a glamorous personality. The source of that charisma lay in the recognition on the part of the staff of Newman's deep dedication to a series of Jewish religious and ethical ideals *and* in his ability to communicate many of these abstract ideals to many members of the staff. (The previous Ramah directors were also thoughtful and articulate individuals but were probably not as successful as Newman in inspiring staff members through their words and deeds.) Everyone felt that they knew where Newman stood. Consequently, no one could accuse him of having ulterior motives, of seeking self-aggrandizement, or of trying to undermine the established commitment of Ramah to Jewish religious practice, Jewish study, and the Jewish people. In a very real sense, Newman may have epitomized for many of the staff members the quality of "fidelity" which, according to Erikson, is the value most highly prized at the end of adolescence.[10]

Another part of the answer to our question would seem to be that Newman had the ability to attract and select potential staff members who would help him to implement his new program.

Like any good camp director or school principal, Newman did
not hire new staff members until he was able to have a long
conversation with them to determine whether they were well
suited to the role that he had in mind. Since, aside from some
rare exceptions, he could not find potential staff members who
were already educating young Jews in the style that he was
advocating, it appears that he tried, by and large, to find
people whose inclinations he felt he could trust, and who
seemed to possess the potential for guiding children and youth
on the basis of newly learned principle rather than rigid
adherence to the methods by which they themselves had been
previously treated by counselors or teachers at Ramah and in
similar educational settings.

The Lasting Impact of Newman's Innovations

Many of the specific changes initiated by Louis Newman are
characteristic of the Ramah camps to this day, thirty years after
they were first implemented: the color-war was never reinstitu-
ted; campers still move from activity to activity without bugles
or loudspeaker announcements; prizes are not awarded for
Hebrew-speaking, cleanliness, or atheltic prowess; etc. Some
of Newman's specific changes were not retained, yet they left
an imprint on the life of the camps; e.g., social dancing never
returned as a weekly activity, as it had been prior to Newman's
arrival in Wisconsin, but today there is not a Ramah camp in
which social dancing will not be scheduled for the older camper units sometime during the summer—though always being
sure that the staff pays attention to those who do not dance,
and that entertainment and refreshments are incorporated into
the program so that even the nondancers can enjoy the activity. Newman required that campwide and unitwide programs
be planned and carried out by the campers who were going to
participate in them. If they were unwilling to get together and
do the required work, there would be no program. Newman
also set aside time in the daily program for each cabin group to
program for itself a certain period of the day (*peulat tzrif*). The
campers could call upon staff members, such as specialists

(sports, arts and crafts, etc.) or teachers, to help with the implementation of the activity, but the nitty-gritty of preparing the activity was to be done by the campers themselves with the advice of their counselors. This daily, ongoing self-programming activity gave all campers the experience of being program planners, program implementers, and program evaluators. Early on, the campers recognized that the enjoyment and satisfaction produced by an activity was often directly proportional to the effort invested in it.

Today at Ramah, such cooperative or democratic group programming as exists is much more limited in its extent than it was at the time that Newman introduced it to Ramah. *Peulat tzrif* is to be found on the schedule of all camps, though possibly only for several hours a week. Additionally, cabin groups often plan parties, hikes, or other types of activities for themselves. Such campwide or unitwide programming as exists at Ramah today is largely limited to cross-camp committees which are formed to plan special days or events, but not to deal with ongoing day-to-day events, as in Newman's time. Many of the functions of the camper *vaadot* that flourished under Newman in Wisconsin, and subsequently in other Ramah camps as well (the *vaad peulat erev*—the committee for planning evening activities, was probably the most successful of these committees), are today handled by the Ramah counselors. Possible reasons for the fading away of this key Newman innovation are the lack of patience of current Ramah staff members to lead youngsters through the laborious process of planning and implementing activities, without a Newman to goad them on; and the discomfort of camp directors (and lay committees?) with the "messiness" which camper-centered programming introduces into various aspects of camp administration.

Undoubtedly Newman's major and longest-lasting contribution to Ramah was in introducing the psychological dimension—the dimension of concern for the individual camper—and bringing it to the forefront of the attention of the Ramah staff. Henceforth, every child would be treated as an individual, possessing different interests and needs. Except for those areas specified as mandatory,[11] campers would be allowed and even encouraged to design their own programs. Rather than being programmed together with the other members of their bunk or unit, all the campers were able to choose individually those activities which were of greatest interest to themselves. The counselors were obliged to review the choices of the campers and to encourage a "rounded" selection (e.g., aesthetic as well as athletic activity), but ultimately, the choice was left up to the camper to make. Newman's head counselor, Bernard Lipnick, worked out a complex system to reduce time and facility conflicts between the choices of campers in different age groups, so as to guarantee that each child would receive as many of his/her choices as possible. Staff members spent many sleepless nights working out the camper programs.

Today, all Ramah camps still offer campers a choice of activities. Most Ramah campers attend camp for an eight-week session, and the choice is usually made twice, at the beginning of the first week and the end of the fourth week. Newman had begun with a daily choice of activities but had quickly moved to a weekly choice when the daily choice proved too unwieldy for the staff to implement. Later Ramah directors decided that the value of making a choice was often nullified by the short period for which the choice was made and, therefore, little by little lengthened the period for which a camper was obligated to abide by the choice.

In Newman and Lipnick's system, campers chose from an otherwise unstructured list of possible activities. The campers were required to make ten or twelve choices, assigning an order of preference to each choice as it was made. When the staff sat down to work out the program, the camper choices were "weighted" according to the order of preference. All of the weighted choices for each particular activity were added together, and listed by total from highest to lowest. Then, going in order from highest to lowest, the activities were placed on the schedule by the staff, taking care that none of the most popular activities (i.e., those receiving the highest weighted totals) conflicted with one another on the schedule. When one activity had been placed in each of the time slots, then a second and third activity with lower totals could be placed in them. The Newman-Lipnick system allowed the most popular choices for boys, such as baseball, basketball, and tennis, to "smother" less popular choices, such as drama and choir, since they were entitled to nonconflicting positions in the schedule. This is not to say that there were not outstanding choir and drama programs under Newman's directorship—it was just very hard to schedule such activities so that boys who wanted to play baseball would also be free to participate in drama. To some extent Newman ameliorated this situation by attracting to his specialty staff outstanding artist-educators who could develop unusual enthusiasm for participating in the arts among typical middle-class American-Jewish teenagers, without the usual Ramah incentives of the color-war.

In more recent seasons, Ramah directors decided that a degree of structure should be built into the list from which campers made their choices so that camper needs and not just camper interests would determine which activities were scheduled against one another. In the newer system, when a camper chooses activities, he/she *is* creating a personal schedule, but not helping to determine which activities receive more or less desirable slots in the program schedule, as in the Newman-Lipnick system. In the youngest campers' unit, for example, there might be a time slot for sports activities three times a week and a time slot for arts activities three times a week, leaving the choice of the specific sports and arts activities to the campers, but guaranteeing that these campers would participate in both types of activities.

A second aspect of the psychological dimension which Newman brought to Ramah was his conviction that the camp program must respond to the maturing interests of teenagers. Newman's position was that if the camp did not provide these campers with a program of activities which was exciting and challenging, then they would create their own activities, probably of a destructive character, which would provide that excitement and challenge. Chief among such potential destructive activities were the intercabin "raids" which Newman had observed first-hand in the other camps at which he had worked, and which were known to Ramah staff and campers to be an accepted part of life at virtually every summer camp. Newman tabooed raids at Ramah, and when they did occur, he made use of the occasion as a major opportunity to educate campers about the Jewish tradition of respect for one's fellow man. This is what led Newman, at the very start, to purchase canoes, camping equipment, and power tools for the carpentry shop in Wisconsin. It also led Newman to encourage counselors of adolescent cabin groups to develop meaningful work projects for the campers within the camp. To this day, after thirty years, campers still use the steps which Alexander Shapiro built with his campers in front of the Wisconsin dining hall. When Joseph Lukinsky was appointed director of the Ramah American Seminar, he built the entire program around such service activities, both inside and outside the camp; most of the camps have, for many years, maintained an ongoing program of such activities. Over the years, all of the camps purchased the types of equipment that Newman purchased in 1951, as well as the equipment required to offer such activities as radio, electronics, rocketry, bicycling, and computer.

Finally, as a third aspect of the psychological dimension which Newman brought to Ramah, we would point out that Newman was very knowledgeable about the pathology of psychological illness and sensitized his staff members to the possibility that these pathologies might be present among the camper and staff population. Moreover, in response to the accusation that the Ramah director should not be so concerned with psychopathology, Newman never tired of pointing out that it was only by gaining an understanding of psychological illness that one gains an accurate picture of psychological health. Newman was the first Ramah director to introduce a staff psychologist into a Ramah camp.[12] While he did not propose to offer psychological therapy at Ramah, he felt that the psychologist could be of great help in identifying serious problems as such, and in helping counselors to better deal with campers who exhibited less serious psychological irregularities. Over the past thirty years, most of the Ramah camps have added to their staffs psychologists or social workers to do what Newman had in mind when he brought the first psychologist to Wisconsin.

Henry Goldberg and Hillel Silverman, the directors who preceded Louis Newman at Camp Ramah in Wisconsin, were both broadly educated and extremely dedicated to their roles as Jewish educators. That they did not emphasize the psychological dimension of the task along with the Jewish dimension, as did Newman, may have been more a function of the times and the pressures under which they worked than of their personalities or of instructions which they received from the Seminary, which gave them guidance. In the period of the founding of Ramah, it may have been necessary to work with the strongest resolve to establish the Jewish aspects of the program. Newman added a new dimension to the camp program his predecessors had successfully established. They had firmly placed Ramah within the rubric of Jewish education; Newman took the Jewish educational institution to which he came and moved it to the much broader rubric of general education—exploiting the fruits of contemporary educational research and thought to enrich and strengthen the Jewish educational program which Ramah offered.

Newman also provided the model for most of the Ramah directors who would follow him; in addition to camp experience, they would possess academic training both in Judaica and in education/psychology/social work. Training in the latter fields was essential in order to maintain the broad educational focus which Newman had brought to Ramah.

How Newman's Innovations Were Diffused Through the Ramah Movement

We have already indicated that many of Newman's specific innovations at Camp Ramah in Wisconsin, and especially his

emphasis upon serving the needs, interests, and problems of
the individual camper, sooner or later became characteristic of
all the Ramah camps which were then in existence or were later
opened: Poconos, Berkshires, Nyack, Glen Spey, Connecticut,
New England, California, and Canada. Those other camps
may also have had their own unique dimensions due to the
geographic location (e.g., the large-scale canoeing/sailing/trip-
ping program in Canada) or programmatic thrusts initiated by
a particular director; but in addition to everything else, the
impact of Newman's work in Wisconsin in the years 1951–53
was to be found in every Ramah camp, throughout the movement. How did it happen?

Basically it happened because Newman, during his three
summers in Wisconsin, built an unusually strong institutional
base for spreading the ideas which he introduced and translated into camp program in Wisconsin. The backbone of that
institutional base was a cadre of young future Jewish educators
who were recruited by Newman to work with him on the
Wisconsin staff during those three years and who, later on,
themselves served as Ramah directors in Wisconsin, and/or in
other Ramah camps and programs: Jerome Abrams, Burton
Cohen, Seymour Fox, Joseph Lukinsky, David Mogilner, and
Alexander Shapiro. For twenty years after Newman's departure from Wisconsin, the Wisconsin directors were men who
had worked at Wisconsin with Newman. A telling proof of
how thoroughly Newman's innovations had suffused the Ramah movement came in 1974, twenty-one years after Newman's departure, when David Soloff, the first post-Newman
director in Wisconsin who was not a member of Newman's
Wisconsin staff, arrived from Camp Ramah in the Berkshires
and felt perfectly at home!

Camp Ramah in Wisconsin served as both a hospitable
institutional base for Newman's ideas and as a "hothouse" for
training new Ramah camp directors from among Newman's
best staff members. Seymour Fox served in Wisconsin as advi-
sor and teacher to the junior counselors in 1952 and 1953 and
then followed Newman as Wisconsin camp director in 1954 and

1955. Subsequently, Fox served as dean of the Teachers Institute of the Seminary, which exercised educational and religious supervision over the Ramah camps. Fox was followed as Wisconsin director for the 1956 and 1957 camp seasons by Jerome Abrams, who had come to Wisconsin to work for Newman as a counselor in 1952. Subsequently, Abrams directed the Nyack, Connecticut, and Berkshires Ramah camps.[13] David Mogilner succeeded Abrams as Wisconsin director in 1958 and 1959. Subsequently Mogilner directed Poconos and Mador (the National Ramah Counselor Training Institute), and served as national Ramah director. He had come to Wisconsin to work for Newman as a counselor in 1951. Burton Cohen followed Mogilner as Wisconsin director and served for fifteen summers beginning in 1960. Cohen had been a camper in Wisconsin in 1947, the first camp season, and beginning in 1948 served as a staff member under all of the directors previously mentioned. Alexander Shapiro directed Poconos for two summers, and Joseph Lukinsky directed the Ramah American Seminar, an innovative work/study program for Ramah graduates offered at the Nyack camp. Both served as counselors in Wisconsin during the Newman years.

While the men who served in leadership roles at Ramah described above had dissimilar backgrounds and personalities, what they have in common is that all of them worked closely with Newman during the period 1951–1953; and that the Ramah camps which they directed were characterized by many of the "revolutionary" features which Newman had introduced in Wisconsin.

Our first answer, then, to the question of how Newman's ideas were diffused throughout the Ramah movement is that by the time he left Wisconsin after three summers, the educational leadership of the camp was firmly established in the hands of men who, if not Newman's "disciples," surely felt very comfortable with the new approaches that he had brought to the camp. They would all add their own wrinkles to what Newman had wrought; however, Newman's imprint had been firmly placed onto the camp. The six summers following Newman's tenure were a period in which three new camp directors from among the above-named group served two-year terms as Wisconsin director and then went forth to serve Ramah in other roles, in other places. Newman had created not only an ideological institutional base, but he had created an ideological training base for the leadership personnel of Ramah. Significantly, those directors who had worked with Newman themselves soon became the mentors of other young people who would serve after them as Ramah camp directors, creating a new "generation" of Ramah directors fully informed with Newman's ideas though never having worked with him at Ramah. Interestingly, because of Newman's subsequent significant activity in the field of Jewish education, most members of this younger group ultimately came to know him, but under very different circumstances than the earlier group.

Another factor which fostered the diffusion of Newman's approach to camping throughout the Ramah movement was the centralized character of the Ramah movement: (1) educational and religious supervision of all the camps was in the hands of the Seminary faculty and administration; (2) camp directors met frequently with Seminary representatives to review policies and programs; (3) key members of the camp staffs studied together at the Seminary and spent many hours sharing and discussing their experiences at the various Ramah camps; and (4) campers from the various camps came to know one another and learn about each other's camps through participation in the National Ramah Israel and American Seminars and the Mador–National Ramah Counselor Training Institute. All of this bringing together of staff and campers from throughout the movement had the effect of formally and informally providing the vehicles for diffusing throughout the movement Newman's ideas and programs which had become so firmly established in Wisconsin.

Of special importance in spreading throughout the Ramah movement the thrust which Newman had initiated in Wisconsin were two year-long seminars for key Ramah staff at all camps, led by Seymour Fox, at the Jewish Theological Seminary of America during the 1956–57 and 1957–58 academic years. Fox had already completed most of the requirements for a Ph.D. degree in education at the University of Chicago when he came to Wisconsin to work with Newman. Fox gave the seminar participants an intensive basic education along the lines of the psychological, philosophical, and group-work approaches that Newman had introduced into Ramah. All the seminar participants were paid stipends and required to write "term papers" that would be of practical use to their co-workers at Ramah; some of the papers produced in the seminars became key educational documents in Ramah for years afterward.

This, then, was the way that Newman's innovations were diffused throughout the Ramah movement: (1) by the establishment of a strong ideological base in Wisconsin; (2) through the presence in Wisconsin and elsewhere in the Ramah movement of a cadre of young Jewish educators who had worked with Newman in Wisconsin and were committed to implementing throughout the Ramah movement what he had innovated there; (3) through the formal and informal centralized character of the Ramah movement; and (4) through the efforts made at the Seminary to train key Ramah personnel between summers along the lines of the new educational thrusts brought to Ramah by Newman.

Newman's Enduring Contribution

In the course of this paper, we have tried to detail the process by which Newman's innovations were made at Ramah, how they stood the test of time, and how they were diffused throughout the Ramah camping movement. Newman's impact surely went far beyond anything that Newman himself or his co-workers could foresee at the time that they were working in Wisconsin in the summers of 1951–53. Certainly, the way in which the entire process was initiated by one man represents a signal achievement in the history of American-Jewish education. Moreover, it seems to us that what we have described is worthy of serious scrutiny by all who are concerned or involved with the problems of educational innovation in an open society.

Notes

1. See Milbrey Wallin McLaughlin and David D. Marsh, "Staff Development and School Change," in *Staff Development,* ed. Ann Lieberman and Lynne Miller (New York: Teachers College Press, 1979), pp. 69–94.

2. See Seymour Sarason, *The Culture of the Schools and the Problem of Change* (Boston: Allyn & Bacon, 1971).

3. See Shuly Rubin Schwartz, "Ramah Philosophy and the Newman Revolution," in this book, p. 7.

4. Davis and Ettenberg had been active in the founding of Camp Massad, the well-known Hebrew-speaking camp, several years previously, and many features of the Massad program were incorporated into the Ramah program.

5. Schwartz, op. cit.

6. These were both Jewish educational summer camps: Massad was founded by the American movement for the propagation of the modern Hebrew language, and Yavneh by the Boston Hebrew College. Among the aspects of the Massad program which Newman felt were miseducative were its rigidity, its insistence upon the speaking of Hebrew as an ultimate value, the prizes which were given for "right" behavior, and the Maccabiah, which forced campers to participate in "cut-throat competition" in activities which by their nature were irenic.

7. Schwartz, op. cit.

8. See Robert M. Hutchins, "The Administrator," in *Works of the Mind,* ed. Robert Heywood (Chicago: University of Chicago Press, 1971), pp. 135–156.

9. McLaughlin and Marsh, op. cit.

10. Erik H. Erikson, "Youth: Fidelity and Diversity," *Daedalus* 91, (1962): 5–27.

11. Mandatory areas included attendance at formal Hebrew classes and religious services as well as cabin clean-up and curfew.

12. Mrs. Rebecca Imber, practicing clinical psychologist in New York City, with a strong Jewish background, was invited to Wisconsin to serve in this position.

13. Newman himself served as Connecticut Ramah director in the summer of 1955, enlisting a few of the Wisconsin staff people to work with him there, and introducing his Wisconsin innovations himself.

LOUIS NEWMAN AND THE IDEA OF AKIBA HEBREW ACADEMY

STEVEN C. LORCH

What is the measure of educational leadership? One widely accepted criterion of a principal's effectiveness is the academic achievement of students in his school.[1] Another mark of leadership is a principal's influence on aspects of student achievement other than academic—personal and social development, for instance.[2] Excellence in educational leadership can also be thought of in terms of the learning environment, or ethos, created and then maintained by the principal in the school.[3]

Consider, for a moment, an educational leader who attains all of these standards of excellence. Students in his school are graduated with enviable academic records and are admitted to the colleges of their choice, among them the finest and most prestigious universities in the country; they have a realistic awareness of their personal strengths and weaknesses, they develop principled moral convictions and ideals, and they grow in their ability to take initiative, assume responsibility, restrain their impulses, give of themselves, and love;[4] the school itself is characterized by personal warmth, mutual trust, encouragement of critical opinion, and high expectations for personal conduct and self-fulfillment.[5] All in all, we would say that such a school points to an unusually successful record of leadership.

Dr. Steven Lorch is principal of Akiba Hebrew Academy, Merion, Pennsylvania. His professional interests include the integration of Jewish and general studies, the philosophy and practice of community Jewish education, the teaching of rabbinics, and school-climate analysis.

Now, if you will, let us go one step further, twenty years into the future. Despite the principal's absence for this period, his colleagues and successors have carried on the standards and the programs he established, and the residual effects of his leadership, one generation later, remain salutary and strong. The school continues to function as an environment well suited to the intellectual and personal growth of young people, and the students who attend the school continue to excel academically and morally. Even more remarkably, the trailblazing educational ideas which were the hallmark of the school during the principal's tenure are still fundamental to the school's curriculum and climate. We would now conclude that this educator is both an accomplished practitioner and an influential theorist, whose practice is grounded in the ideas he stands for and whose theories are refined in light of his successful experience in applying them.

The educational leader to whom I refer is, of course, Lou Newman, who served as principal of Akiba Hebrew Academy from 1951 to 1963. His highly successful stewardship during those years is, however, only part of the story of his principalship, and the lesser part, at that. In this essay, I shall attempt to set forth the three major ideas that form the nucleus of the formidable educational legacy he has left Akiba and, through Akiba, to all of American Jewish education: community, democracy, and integration.

Community

The Jewish community day school is not a unique institution, nor was it new at the time of Akiba's founding in 1946. In fact, most of the *yeshivot* and day schools on the American scene are community schools, in the sense that they are not sponsored by any one congregation or central religious body and that they are governed by independent lay boards.[6]

But the idea of a Jewish community day school as conceived by Lou Newman and developed in Akiba is different:

> It was desired that all Jewish children—Orthodox, Conservative, and Reform, and those from non-affiliated fami-

lies—should learn together their common Jewish and American heritage, while simultaneously learning to respect all other positions and the devotion and sincerity with which they are held.

It was not intended to blur differences. It was rather intended to strengthen the identification of every student with the Jewish traditions and current Jewish living—personal and social—without compelling acceptance by all of one particular interpretation of what is "the" Jewish way of life.

At Akiba we want to teach the Jewish heritage as intensively as possible. We believe that a comparison of opinions and practices will lead to a refinement of ideas and attitudes that will enable students to develop a view and practice of Judaism that will be maintained with pride and spiritual enrichment throughout their mature years.[7]

While many existing schools were communal in affiliation and in student enrollment, Akiba was to be an experiment in community living and learning. Its faculty was to be reflective of the diversity of the Jewish community, its curriculum and extracurricular program geared to the background, interests, and needs of the entire spectrum of Jewish belief and practice, its normative patterns of ritual observance broad and flexible enough to accommodate the range of its constituency, and its atmosphere imbued with respect—mere tolerance would have been inadequate—for the sincere convictions of others in the school. At the same time, no belief or practice was to be accepted uncritically, but rather all elements of Jewish life and tradition were to undergo close, though sympathetic, scrutiny. The hope implicit in this program was that students exposed to the variety of Jewish experience in all its richness would have a sound basis for choice among alternative forms of Jewish commitment and that they would, in fact, strengthen their own identity and commitment in light of the choices available to them.

In recent years, the national trend toward Jewish communal day schools, in the conventional sense of the term, has accelerated. A number of schools formerly affiliated with the educational associations of one or another of the religious denominations (e.g., Torah Umesorah, the Solomon Schechter Day School Association) have discontinued their affiliation, thereby becoming eligible for increased community funding. At the same time, their academic programs, staffing policies, and religious atmosphere have not changed substantially.

Akiba continues, in these respects, to march to the beat of its own drummer. Not only does its student body continue to span the entire range of the Jewish community; its faculty does as well. Members of the Judaic studies faculty include rabbis ordained by Reconstructionist, Conservative, and Orthodox rabbinical schools; teachers raised and trained in Israel in religious, secular, and antireligious communities and kibbutzim; and teachers whose backgrounds include training and experience in every imaginable kind of Jewish setting—Reform and ultra-Orthodox, congregational pulpits, colleges of Jewish studies, and Sunday schools. Even more significantly, one of the most important expectations of Akiba teachers is that, regardless of their personal belief system or life-style, they will succeed in creating an atmosphere of openness and mutual respect in their classrooms. While they are not expected to conceal their own point of view in class discussions, teachers are entrusted with the responsibility of presenting the range of Jewish opinion on any given issue, representing each stance fairly and sympathetically, encouraging students to express their own emerging thoughts and doubts, whether believing, heretical, or ambivalent, and dealing with students' sincere views openly and supportively.

In the curriculum of the school, too, Akiba's bias in favor of a community orientation is evident. Part of the Judaic studies core curriculum is a six-year sequence of theme courses for which texts, in the form of sourcebooks, have been compiled. These sourcebooks incorporate, for each unit of study, a broad sampling of material from a range of Jewish authorities. In each case, the antecedents of the contemporary approaches in biblical, mishnaic, talmudic, and medieval sources are traced. For example, as the culmination of their study of Shabbat in the Jewish Calendar sourcebook, students read a Conservative responsum on the issues of using electricity and riding on Shabbat, as well as a dissenting position paper; in the Jewish Life-Cycle material, they encounter Reform and Orthodox positions detailing who is qualified to officiate at weddings; the Jewish Practice sourcebook includes rationales for the performance of mitzvot from the Bible, the Talmud, Maimonides, Kaplan, Gaster, Scholem, Agnon, and Heschel, among others; and the study of women in Judaism in the Jewish Ethics course concludes with the study of two Conservative approaches to the role of women in the minyan together with accompanying position papers representing Orthodox and Reform viewpoints. The message implicit in this selection of curriculum materials is that each of the denominations within Judaism grows consistently and organically from authentic Jewish tradition.

The religious atmosphere of the school is similarly geared to accommodate the range of its constituency. As our case in point, let us examine Akiba's approach to prayer, though analyzing the school's policies regarding the wearing of *kippot* or the use of God's name (*Ado-nai* or *Hashem*) would reveal much the same spirit of understanding and accommodation. Prayer has been a subject of some ambivalence over the years at Akiba, owing in large measure to the realization that, as a public and community-based act, it forces the school to choose a particular style of practice that, of necessity, will be acceptable to some segments of the Jewish community and distasteful—or worse—to others. Such issues as the conditions under which students are required to pray, the seating of boys and girls, the participation of boys and girls in various aspects of the service, and the choice of prayer book are religiously and politically charged to a greater degree than their actual ritual significance would dictate.

In view of the significance of these issues to the community that Akiba serves, the school has developed a characteristically community-oriented approach to prayer. Services on a regular twice-weekly basis are held in the context of a broader Bet Midrash program. Bet Midrash provides opportunities for students who wish to engage in prayer to choose to join one of several minyanim, each structured to meet the needs, values, and interests of a different segment of the Akiba population, and for students who wish to study about aspects of prayer in greater depth than is devoted to them in the curriculum to join one of a number of study groups. The minyanim and the study groups meet concurrently, and students may elect—and are encouraged to try—different options during their years at Akiba. Recognizing that one function of prayer is to build up within the school a spirit of community, Akiba finds other opportunities during the school year to bring the entire school together in a single minyan. Preceding some of these occasions (notably before the annual grade-wide *Shabbatonim*), students meet to discuss and agree upon the practices and procedures that will prevail during the community-wide prayer services. Such discussions, skillfully and sensitively led by teachers whose first commitment is to provide for varying forms of Jewish practice and self-expression in school community experiences, could well serve as a model for debates on similar issues in the larger Jewish community.

Akiba's identity as a Jewish community day school was forged in the early years of its existence. Over the years, the original sense of the term "community" has been a continuing source of guidance and inspiration to Akiba: to encourage students actively to grow in their commitment to Judaism by weighing alternative approaches to Jewish belief and practice. If this means, in some cases, that it is appropriate to moderate the requirement of mandatory observances in the school, it also demands, in all cases, that the school maximize the availability and attractiveness of opportunities for Jewish identification and observance, as always, in an open, supportive, and respectful atmosphere.

Democracy

Training in democratic values and citizenship is a goal that Jewish day schools share with most other schools, public and private, in the United States. Yet, unlike many other schools, the Jewish day schools have, from their inception, been criticized for perpetuating an inherently undemocratic bias, owing to the limited population they appeal to and the lack of exposure day school students have to young people of backgrounds different from their own. This argument was first advanced by those who opposed the growth of the Jewish day school as an institution twenty, thirty, and forty years ago;[8] it continues to this day in debates in those communities that are considering founding a new Jewish day school, as well as among parents who are considering a day school education for their children.

In response to this recurring criticism, Jewish day schools have sought to establish their unequivocal commitment to democracy within the school. Thus, most day schools can be characterized as purporting "to prepare Jewish children for living in a democracy" and "to equip Jewish youth to promote the democratic way of life."[9] In like manner, Akiba Hebrew Academy, under Lou Newman's leadership, invested many of its resources in the attitudes, traits, and community participation of students as they related to the area of democratic behavior.[10] However, while most day schools discharged their duty to American democracy primarily by means of teaching American traditions and values in the American history classroom and in assemblies on patriotic themes, Akiba sought to instill a commitment to democracy in other ways as well.

As conceived by Lou Newman, educating for democratic living is more than transmitting an understanding and appreciation of the American political system and, more broadly, the American way of life. At Akiba, democratic convictions also include the commitment to embody in one's own behavior the processes and ideals implicit in American democracy. Students must be given the responsibility of keeping themselves informed about significant social, political, personal, and moral issues, of examining them closely and critically, of analyzing them and asking questions about them, and of doing all this in an atmosphere which promotes respect for the rights and opinions of others and faith in the ability to resolve disputes amicably.

. . . the school believes that tension which derives from relationships among individuals should be reduced to a minimum by facing up to the complaints of students and teachers through encouragement of critical opinion. One cannot know in advance, of course, what will prove constructive in such a case. It is our belief that strengthening the ambition to fulfill one's self in overcoming objective obstacles to friendly living, while maximizing mutual understanding, between all participants in the school's life through the service of the school to the pupil and the pupil and his family to the school, creates a climate within which learning is pursued with greater understanding of its need, and hence with greater motivation.[11]

It is no small feat to create a climate in a school which reflects the ideals of democratic living in the daily interactions among children and adults on questions of school policy and governance, personal responsibility, privilege and right, and the like. To achieve so ambitious a goal in an orderly atmosphere of mutual understanding and fairness, and to sustain so favorable a climate for learning and personal growth over the years, Akiba has developed and institutionalized a number of curricular and extracurricular structures that encourage personal interaction founded on these ideals.

Students entering Akiba's Lower School (sixth to eighth grade) are exposed to an interdisciplinary course offering, *Core,* which incorporates social studies, language arts, literature, and research and study skills in a single thematically organized course. From nine to twelve periods per week are devoted to this class in each grade. The intensiveness of this exposure accomplishes a number of ends: it eases the transition from the self-contained classroom of the elementary years to the departmentalized organization of high school; it introduces students to the integrative approach of bringing the knowledge and insight of one discipline to bear on another; and, most importantly for the democratic ideals to which the school aspires, it enables a highly skilled and sensitive teacher to evolve a set of relationships among individual students and a dynamic of the group as a whole that will make democratic living possible. In their *Core* class, children begin to learn how to think critically about issues, when to assert their point of view and when to yield it for the benefit of others, how to be sensitive to the needs and interests of others by appreciating and respecting their differences in values and personality, how to work cooperatively and assume leadership in a group setting, and, generally, how to participate in and contribute productively to the group. With some reinforcement of these skills and attitudes in other subjects and with the prospect of continued reinforcement in the Upper School, students begin to develop the capacity for democratic living and learning in their *Core* class.

When students reach the Upper School, they are exposed to a program of studies in which the skills necessary for democratic living are at a premium. In each subject, students are expected to exercise their powers of critical thinking regularly; that is, to seek evidence independently, to formulate hypotheses and interpretations on the basis of the evidence, to adjust their thinking in accordance with the evidence, and, in general, to cultivate an inquiring and skeptical spirit. In the sciences, laboratory experimentation and the inquiry method are the primary thrust of the curriculum; in history and Judaica, the reading and understanding of primary source material; in mathematics, problem solving; in English, Hebrew, and upper-level foreign languages, the tools of close literary analysis as applied to major works of literature. At the same time, group activities and projects are built in as regular, required components of the curriculum in order to facilitate the further development of mutual understanding, encouragement, and cooperation.

The single project which best exemplifies the synthesis of the critical and cooperative ideals that pervade the Akiba curriculum is the role-playing unit that all students are exposed to at least once during their study of history in the Upper School. The role-playing project focuses on a major event or period of American or modern European history and extends for six weeks: two weeks for reading and preparation of roles, three for the actual role-playing, and one for evaluating the experience. Projects have focused on such events as the American Revolution, the Reconstruction, the passage of the Social Security Act, America's entry into World War II, the English revolution of the seventeenth century, and world politics following the German surrender in 1945. In each case, the teacher emphasizes that,

> given the initial setting, the students need not feel bound to make the same decisions as the actual historical figures had made. This, in effect, meant that alternatives to what actually happened—for example, revolution or war—could be worked out, as long as these choices seemed consistent with what the pupils knew about their characters and the times in which they lived.[12]

Under these conditions, aroused by the "events" taking place around them, students are frequently suffused with the excitement of playing out the alternatives that present themselves at various points along the historical path and working together as a group to see the events through to their culmination. Aside from the impressive effects of the role-playing units on the students' understanding of historical process,[13] their importance in reinforcing the principles of democratic learning that are central to Akiba's mission cannot be emphasized enough.

Outside of the classroom as well, the life of the school is influenced by democratic processes and ideals. The policy-setting mechanisms of the school are so constituted as to invite the active involvement of all groups: students, faculty, administration, parents, and Board of Directors. Students and teachers serve as full members of Akiba's Education Committee and Board of Directors; teachers serve on the Finance Committee as well. The school administration consults with parents, teachers, and students as a matter of course, whether to invite them to express their views on revisions in school policy that are being contemplated, to request their candid evaluation and critique of programs currently in effect, or simply to ask for their thoughts and suggestions on the work of the school. The purposes of this ongoing discussion and cross-fertilization of ideas are to stimulate an awareness of the educational choices that are made on a daily basis and, no less significantly, to model for students the process of critical and hard questioning in an atmosphere of mutual interest and caring. Over the years, the school has learned to anticipate that students will not only appreciate its faith in democracy; many of them will internalize it as well.

The workings of the Student Association, the governing council of the Akiba student body, are a case in point. The officers and representatives of the Student Association are closely in touch with the concerns and interests of their constituency. They actively seek the advice of their schoolmates in creating the agenda for discussions that will take place during the year, in responding to issues that are raised, and in taking action on decisions that are made. While there is ample opportunity for such consultation to take place informally, weekly advisory classes are convened to provide for regular, continuing discussion of such matters. With the careful guidance of the advisory teachers, students come to appreciate the seriousness which the student leadership attaches to this consultative process and, in turn, learn to adapt the same process to the conduct of their own advisory meetings.

The enduring effects of the commitment to democracy which Lou Newman set in motion at Akiba more than thirty years ago can best be ascertained in the quality of the relationships among members of the Akiba community today. Perhaps most remarkable among these relationships is the unusual concern and sensitivity shown by Upper Schoolers for Lower School students. Among the many programs which reflect and contribute to the nature of these interactions are Lower School intramural sports, which are organized and coached by Upper School students; *Shabbatonim* for the lower grades, which are chaperoned and conducted by eleventh- and twelfth-grade students; and volunteer tutoring, formally organized as well as conducted on an informal basis, which is provided by older students. These activities, together with others in which all students participate on an equal footing (clubs, publications, performing arts, Student Association), provide Upper School students with a group of friends whom they can care for, in part, by teaching them democratic values by example, and, by the same token, give Lower School students a group of accessible, reliable models whom they care about and who embody, for them, the ideals of democratic living.

Integration

The integration of Jewish and general studies has been, historically, one of the underlying objectives[14] and rationales[15] of the Jewish day school. It is a term that has been used in a variety of contexts to signify a broad range of approaches to the philosophy and psychology of day school curriculum and instruction and their sociological, epistemological, and historical underpinnings.[16] As Jewish day schools have moved from the theory of integration to its practice, however, the concept has proven to be difficult to implement in any meaningful, ongoing way.[17]

Akiba under Lou Newman's leadership was committed to the integration of Jewish and general studies in practice as well as in theory. It was seen as a means of "rais[ing] to the level of conscious awareness the implications of living totally as a Jew."[18] The specific contexts in which the meaningful correlation of Jewish and general content and coursework took place included the following:

> Integration of Jewish and general studies takes place most naturally in Social Studies, History, and the Latter Prophets. It may be in an analysis of the prophetic spirit in Lincoln's second inaugural address, the influence of the Jewish community's welfare activities upon the non-Jewish community, or the vision or our prophets of a peaceful world community. Jewish and American holidays offer an excellent opportunity for integration. Thus, while reading the Haggadah at our Model Seder, we have made it a practice to interpolate our

"Annual Freedom Survey." In some dramatic form, the progress and regress of freedom and civil liberties in all their manifestations are detailed and recounted as they took place from one Passover to another, all over the world: rebellions against dictators, Supreme Court decisions, colonies which are not independent, countries under dictatorship, the population of countries under dictatorships, Ghana and South Africa, Little Rock and Louisville—all will be mentioned.

The school has also instituted what we call "bridge subjects"; they are given this name because they integrate teachings from the Jewish and general studies. Thus, our seventh grade, which has as its core social-studies theme, "Communities—How they Function," has an additional two periods per week in English with a Hebrew teacher, on the Community of Israel. The whole social-studies apparatus of research and report, trips, and audio-visual aids prove very effective in this area.[19]

More than twenty years later, some of the identical techniques for integrating Jewish and general studies are still in effect, influencing each generation of Akiba students in turn. The freedom survey is still one of the highlights of Akiba's Seder. In the study of cultures in *Core*, a unit is devoted to Israel; in eighth-grade *Core*, as part of the study of American peoples and ethnic groups, the experience of Eastern European Jewish immigrants is explored. Rather than being taught separately by members of different departments, however, these units are now presented in the same format as the rest of the course by the *Core* teacher. The model of parallel classes taught by different teachers on a theme or a period of common interest in general and Jewish studies has been adopted in the study of world history in tenth and twelfth grades.

In recent years, Akiba has instituted a number of units of study in eleventh and twelfth grades that lend themselves to interdisciplinary treatment. The units are taught separately in the general and Jewish studies classes, but are closely coordinated in the order and in the pace at which they present concepts, ideas, and institutions that address similar concerns in the Western and Jewish traditions. Coordinated among the sciences, humanities, and Judaica divisions of the school, the parallel and synchronized units that have been developed thus far deal with the following topics:

1. The nature of truth in the scientific and Jewish traditions (coordinated between Jewish Ethics and Science and Society—eleventh grade).
   Subtopics: is truth the highest value?; the truth of the printed word; distinctions between unintentional and intentional untruth.

2. Employer-employee relations (Jewish Ethics and American Social History—twelfth grade).
   Subtopics: work as routine labor vs. work as a creative act; responsibilities of workers; the rights of workers.

3. Social welfare (Jewish Ethics and American Social History—twelfth grade).
   Subtopics: is poverty deserved, undeserved, inevitable, good for society?; subsistence relief vs. a subjective criterion of need; public vs. private giving; the role of rehabilitation.

4. Slavery in ancient Israel and in nineteenth-century America (Jewish Ethics and American Social History—twelfth grade).
   Subtopics: slavery as a form of protection vs. a morally repugnant institution; slavery in an economic, social, family context; the best philanthropy is—

For each of these units, not only have the topics, subtopics, and areas of emphasis been identified, but textbooks and supplementary materials have also been adapted or developed in order to facilitate their implementation. Further correlates and applications in related fields (e.g., literature) may be added in future years. A number of other topics have also been put on the drawing board because they seem to lend themselves to similar coordinated treatment, including war and peace, the ethics of family life and sexuality, Zionism and nationalism, and medical ethics, among others.

Part of the appeal of the parallel-synchronized approach is that, aside from its accessibility to any teacher competent in his own field of study and experience, it crystallizes for students the role that Jewish and general learning can play in informing their views and their actions on issues such as those listed above, many of which are or will become matters of deep and abiding personal concern. Furthermore, by virtue of the way in which the topics are correlated, the integrative thinking that is modeled is not the finished, integrated product of a teacher; rather, it is a dynamic, integrating process, advanced in less than final form by two or more teachers, that encourages— better yet, that cries out for—the student to perceive similarities and recognize distinctions, to seek connections and structure; in a word, to do integration.[20]

Akiba has carried on its commitment to the integration of Jewish and general studies since Lou Newman first developed the idea in the school. Many of the techniques used to accomplish this goal today are similar to those that he put into practice; others have developed as a natural outgrowth of the priority the school has attached to integrative learning over the years. In any event, Akiba's continuing effectiveness in this area, as in the areas of Jewish community education and the infusion of the ideals of democratic living, is attributable in large measure to Lou Newman's lasting influence.

Conclusion

I hope I have not overstated my case. Akiba Hebrew Academy has not solved all, or even most, of the problems facing American Jewish education; during his tenure as principal, Lou Newman faced many challenges, some of which proved no less insurmountable for him than they are, day in and day out, for other Jewish educators.

Yet Akiba Hebrew Academy is an unusual and, in some ways, a unique institution on the American scene. For over thirty years, it has remained independent of the philosophical, religious, and functional patterns of other schools, defining itself instead in terms of its own vision of the future of the American Jewish community, pinpointing the knowledge, attitudes, and skills that will be needed, and evolving the means with which to train its young people to assume their positions as leaders and contributing members of the next generation of American Jews. That Akiba has been equal to the task of sustaining its vision and achieving much of what it sets out to accomplish with its students is a tribute to its remarkable educational leader, Lou Newman.

Notes

1. James Sweeney, "Research Synthesis on Effective School Leadership," *Educational Leadership* 39, no. 5 (February 1982): 346–352.

2. Ken Wilson, "An Effective School Principal," *Educational Leadership* 39, no. 5 (February 1982): 357–361.

3. Michael Rutter, Barbara Maughan, Peter Mortimore, and Janet Ouston, *Fifteen Thousand Hours: Secondary Schools and Their Effects on Children* (Cambridge: Harvard University Press, 1979); see also Gordon L. McAndrew, "The High-School Principal: Man in the Middle," *Daedalus* 110, no. 3 (Summer 1981): 105–118; and Caroline Hodges Parsell and Peter W. Cookson, Jr., "The Effective Principal in Action," *The Effective Principal* (Reston, Va.: National Association of Secondary School Principals, 1982), pp. 22–29.

4. Louis Newman. "The Akiba Hebrew Academy," *Conservative Judaism* 15, no. 2 (Winter 1961).

5. Louis Newman, ed., "Responses to NSSSE Evaluative Criteria: Philosophy" (unpublished manuscript, 1960), pp. 5–6.

6. Alvin Irwin Schiff. *The Jewish Day School in America* (New York: Jewish Education Committee Press, 1966), pp. 43, 128–129.

7. Akiba Hebrew Academy, "Philosophy," *A Manual for Parents* (1958), p. 5.

8. Schiff, *Jewish Day School*, pp. 132–135. See also Alvin I. Schiff, "From Sunday School to Day School," *Jewish Education* 50, no. 2 (Summer 1982): 6–13.

9. Schiff, *Jewish Day School*, p. 107.

10. Newman, "Akiba Hebrew Academy," p. 11.

11. Newman, "NSSSE Evaluative Criteria," p. 5.

12. Harold Gorvine, "Teaching History through Role Playing," *History Teacher* 3, no. 4 (May 1970): 8.

13. Ibid., pp. 18–19.

14. Schiff, *Jewish Day School*, pp. 121–123, 196–198.

15. Ibid., pp. 130–132.

16. Bennett Ira Solomon, "A Critical Review of the Term 'Integration' in the Literature on the Jewish Day School in America," *Jewish Education* 46, no. 4 (Winter 1978): 4–17. See also Joseph Lukinsky, "Integrating Jewish and General Studies in the Day School: Philosophy and Scope," in *Integrative Learning*, ed. Max Nadel (New York: American Association for Jewish Education, 1978), pp. 3–11.

17. Schiff, *Jewish Day School*, p. 90; Lukinsky, "Integrating Jewish and General Studies," pp. 7–8.

18. Newman, "Akiba Hebrew Academy," p. 6.

19. Ibid., pp. 9–10.

20. Lukinsky, "Integrating Jewish and General Studies," pp. 19–20.

THE IMPACT OF THE PILOT EDUCATIONAL PROJECT OF THE MELTON RESEARCH CENTER ON CONGREGATION TIFERETH ISRAEL, 1960–1966

SAUL P. WACHS

This essay is dedicated in honor of Louis and Shirley Newman, who can rightfully claim to have "raised many disciples" in the world of Jewish education. The writer and his wife, Barbara, a teacher at the Akiba Academy, a school on which the Newmans both put their stamp, acknowledge a profound debt of gratitude to this remarkable couple.

Introduction

In 1959, a grant by Samuel M. Melton of Columbus, Ohio, launched the Melton Research Center in Jewish Education at the Jewish Theological Seminary of America. A provision of the grant called for the Seminary to establish a pilot school for the Center at Congregation Tifereth Israel, the home congregation of the Melton family.

During the period from 1960 to 1970, the tenure of the writer as director of education at the congregation, many changes took place in the educational programs of the congregation and the community as a result of the project that will be described

Dr. Saul Wachs is Associate Professor of Education at Gratz College and national field consultant for the Solomon Schechter Day School Association. He is an author of the curriculum for the afternoon religious school and is currently coeditor of the national curriculum for the Solomon Schechter day schools.

here.[1] This article will chronicle and discuss some of the changes that took place within the congregation between 1959 and 1960, the last project year, and 1965 and 1966.[2]

A few sources exist for chronicling the situation prior to the onset of the project. Of these the most important is a study conducted by Rabbi Burton Cohen for the Melton Center.[3] The basis for the study was a series of interviews conducted by Rabbi Cohen with the pre-project professional staff of the congregation, parents, students, and other synagogue members who had been active in the operation of the school prior to 1960. This was supplemented by documents produced by the congregation and by the observations of the writer, who made a three-day visit to the school in the spring of 1960.[4]

The Education Program in 1959–60

The pre-project school at Tifereth Israel consisted of two departments. The largest and most important of these was the Sunday school. This department conducted sessions for two hours on Sunday mornings. In 1959–60, its enrollment was 340 students. The Hebrew school was much smaller (51 students in 1959–60), and it offered classes twice a week for three and a half hours.[5] On Sundays, students in both departments studied together in the same classes.[6] Almost all of the girls at Tifereth Israel who received any form of religious education did so at the Sunday school. It was led by an activities director, a former graduate of the program, and taught by volunteer or paraprofessional teachers. Despite serious weaknesses to be discussed below, this department was considered by the congregation to be excellent and appropriate to the needs of the students. Cohen found that the curriculum of the department was very sketchy, communicating little information to the teachers.[7] The congregation relied on suggestions made by the Union of American Hebrew Congregations, as the United Synagogue did not provide a curriculum for the one-day school above the second grade. Cohen found that many of the goal statements provided for teachers stressed the teaching of "blessings" and prayers. Since Hebrew reading was not taught to the students of the Sunday school, this meant that many students in each class were trying to learn to "read" *berakhot* and other prayers through transliteration. Given the amount of time available for the entire enterprise, it is not surprising that many students described the curriculum to Cohen as tending to be "repetitive."[8] But if the ongoing program of the Sunday school seemed to leave many students cold, its climax most definitely did not. Confirmation at Tifereth Israel was a major religious and social event in the lives of the students, their families, and the entire congregation.[9] From March to June, the students of the Confirmation class devoted two days a week to preparing for the ceremony. They mastered a cantata, prepared by the activities director–principal, and the intricacies of marching down the aisle: the "choreography of Confirmation." In addition to the ceremony, the festivities of Confirmation included a class party, open houses at the homes of the confirmands, and a supper dance at the synagogue. Cohen found a uniformly enthusiastic response to Confirmation and surmised that the excitement engendered by this ceremony might have cast a "halo effect" upon the entire Sunday school program in the eyes and minds of the congregation.[10]

The Hebrew school is described by Cohen as the "orphan" of the congregation. Its size over the years had ranged from thirteen to fifty students.[11] The teachers were often considered unqualified and the texts outmoded.[12] Periodically, the Board of Education had considered closing the department, a course favored by the rabbi, who supported the Columbus Hebrew School, the communal Talmud Torah, as a viable program of Hebrew-centered education.

On each occasion, the laity had decided to maintain the department as a service to the congregational membership. They saw the Hebrew school as a (minimalist) alternative to the Columbus Hebrew School.[13]

Faculty

In 1959–60, the faculty of the religious school consisted of the rabbi, the activities director–principal (who taught the Confir-

mation class), twenty Sunday school teachers, and four Hebrew school teachers. With the exception of the rabbi, none of
these had completed a formal program of Jewish studies at the
high school level or above. One Hebrew school teacher was a
graduate of the Columbus Hebrew School and was now engaged in Jewish studies in preparation for entry into the
Rabbinical School of the Seminary. While the Jewish background of the teachers, with the exception of this young man,
was quite weak, their level of general education was frequently
high, and they were a mature and dedicated group, serving
with little supervision but with a potential for good work.[14] The
teachers were further handicapped by a lack of good teaching
milieu and a paucity of good teaching materials. There was no
faculty library to speak of and very few audio-visual materials.
Teachers were not permitted to assign homework or to give
tests. No systematic program of in-service training existed.
Teacher morale was affected by the fact that students were
guaranteed automatic promotion whatever their attendance or
productivity.[15] The writer heard many of these complaints from
teachers during his visit to the school in the spring of 1960. He
emerged, convinced that many of the teachers wanted to
provide more effective education than was then possible, and
that they would respond favorably to the opportunity to work
in a more rigorous and professional climate.

The Board of Education

The Board of Education was the lay committee of the Board of
Trustees of Tifereth Israel charged with responsibility for over-
seeing the educational programs of the congregation. In theory, this board was to meet regularly and to review curricula,
texts, budget, programming, plant needs, and other aspects of
the program. In reality, prior to the project, the board met
infrequently[16] and, according to Cohen, limited itself, essentially, to financial decisions and the setting up of registration
procedures (at which time tuition fees were to be collected).[17] In
his interviews, Cohen was told that "There were never any
problems, everything was always fine. The reports by the

principal and rabbi always told of the excellent attendance record, beautiful assemblies, etc."[18]

Summary of Pre-Project Situation

Judged by the standards promulgated by the Conservative movement, the educational situation at Congregation Tifereth Israel in 1959–60 was far from ideal.[19] Neither structure nor curriculum nor faculty nor administration was capable of supporting a system of quality Jewish education. The school seemed isolated from current developments in the field. Its goals were overly modest; oversight was largely lacking. Yet, the faculty was dedicated and mature, and if the structure could be changed and a new set of aspirations created, it would be possible to move the school forward to a higher level of operation.[20]

The Plan

In the spring of 1960, upon returning from a visit to the school, the writer met with Mr. Louis Newman and Rabbi Seymour Fox, acting dean of the Teachers Institute of the Seminary and executive chairman of the board of the Center. Two general goals were established: First, the school would have to be brought to a reasonable level of educational productivity, one which would approximate what was being done at the time in the most effective Conservative schools. Second, the school would have to be made ready for the materials that would be created by the scholars of the center.[21] Accordingly, the following steps were taken:

1. A team of recent graduates of the Teachers Institute was assembled and brought to Columbus to serve as the core of a revitalized staff.[22] It was decided that each professional would devote up to twenty hours each week to face-to-face contact with students and another twenty hours to all forms of preparation, including faculty meetings, study sessions, lesson planning, etc. This formula, established by Mr. Newman, proved to be useful and fair.

2. Recognizing that each professional would, in all likeli-

hood, remain in Columbus for only a limited period of time,[23] it was decided to establish an apprentice-teacher program during the first year of the project so that local teachers would be retrained to assume roles within the school. Each apprentice was considered to be a strong teaching personality, lacking primarily in formal training either in Jewish content or professional education or both. The apprentices with the strongest backgrounds were paired with the professionals. They prepared for classes together, observed each other in class, and evaluated progress together. They also participated in the weekly faculty meetings of the Hebrew school and in the ongoing program of theoretical and practical planning that was carried on by the professionals. All the apprentices were asked to read appropriate books and encouraged to take courses to professionalize themselves. Such courses were offered at the synagogue[24] and at the Ohio State University, as well as out-of-town at programs sponsored by the Center and the American Association for Jewish Education (now known as Jewish Educational Services of America).

3. In order to provide for the continued education of the professionals, they too were encouraged to study at the university. In addition, the Center invited Professor Marvin Fox, a distinguished rabbi and scholar, then teaching at the university, to offer a four-hour weekly seminar in rabbinic texts to the professionals.

4. To provide for ongoing educational supervision and guidance, the Center invited Professor Bernard Mehl of the College of Education at the Ohio State University to make two visits to the school each week. There, he provided a wide variety of professional services to the faculty in general and to the writer in particular. After one year, when Professor Mehl accepted a Fulbright award, his place was taken by Professor George B. Lewis, a colleague at Ohio State University. Dr. Mehl and Dr. Lewis made important contributions to the school. For example, Dr. Lewis, as a non-Jew, questioned virtually everything that was done in the school. This led to constant reevaluation of programs and ideas that were considered "standard" and

"necessary." The results, frequently, were creative and effective.[25]

5. The administrative structure called for the previous principal (activities director) to continue as an administrative assistant to the writer, who devoted himself primarily to teaching, supervising, preparing curricular materials, and giving general guidance to the program.[26]

6. We decided it was important to involve the rabbi as closely as possible in the project. It was the policy of the Center that the rabbi be provided with information about progress and be asked to provide both religious and political guidance to the writer and his colleagues. This necessitated daily meetings resulting in a strong personal and professional bond developing between the rabbi and the writer.

Programs Introduced or Changed Through the Project

Between 1960 and 1966, a number of modifications and innovations were introduced.

1. *Arts.* A broad range of artistic activities were introduced into the school program, leading to the formation of a choir, dance group, *halil* orchestra, and dramatics group. While the particular artistic activities offered might vary from year to year, depending upon the talent of the available leaders, the principle was established that Jewish artistic creativity was to be experienced by all students within the school.

2. *Prayer.* The writer, with strong encouragement from the rabbi, introduced a daily prayer service into the curriculum. A network of class services was established so that students could gradually master the skill of acting as *shaliach tzibbur* for weekday and Shabbat services. Later, selections from the festival and High Holy Day liturgy were introduced into the *tefillah* program.

3. *Junior congregation.* The school continued the existing practice of sponsoring youth services on Friday evenings but also introduced and stressed the importance of attending services on Shabbat morning. This program was coordinated with the rabbi and *hazzanim* of the congregation and achieved a high

level of success. On Shabbat and *hagim* students would assemble for services in groupings by age and then, at prearranged times, would enter the sanctuary where the adult services were in progress, to participate in the *Musaf* service. With close coordination between the synagogue and the school, it was possible to efficiently train the youth to chant the prayers and to develop a common tradition of congregational singing as well. During the 1961–62 academic year, it was decided to dramatize achievements in this area by having students conduct the complete services for one Shabbat in the synagogue. This program was well received by the large congregation in attendance.

4. *Shabbat programming.* Starting in 1961–62, a series of Shabbat afternoon *Ongei Shabbat* programs were offered to various classes in the school. Students and parents together participated in this informal educational programming, culminating with *Havdalah* conducted by the students at the close of the day.

5. *Hebrew high school.* A major effort was made in the field of informal education. Whereas, in the past, the United Synagogue Youth chapter had tended to stress only its program of social activities, now a more even balance was struck between social, religious, and educational activities. The latter proved so successful that midway during the first year, the USY members attending these study groups requested that the leaders, in effect, convert an informal study setup into a more formal one. Thus, ahead of schedule, the Hebrew high school came into being as a new strong foundation was established for secondary education through addition of a fifth year to the elementary school. (See next item.)

6. *Hey classes.* Prior to 1960, the Hebrew school offered classes to the Daled (fourth) level. The student would spend the next year, as necessary, preparing for the Bar or Bat Mitzvah ceremony. The writer recommended for 1960–61 the establishment of a Hey (fifth-level) class that would provide six hours a week of education in addition to Bar and Bat Mitzvah training. This proposal was accepted.[27] This enabled future

classes to move smoothly from the elementary to the secondary program.

7. *Expanded informal education.* Whereas in the past, the informal educational program consisted exclusively of the United Synagogue Youth program, the professionals moved as expeditiously as possible to develop a larger and more comprehensive network of youth groups for the congregation. In 1963 a chapter of the Leadership Training Fellowship was created, and in 1964 a pre-USY group (seventh- and eighth-graders) was formed. The LTF group offered Shabbat-afternoon study sessions involving Jewish texts and leadership skills. In order to prevent any sense of competitiveness developing between the LTFers and the USYers, it was decided to limit membership in LTF to those exercising leadership roles in USY who were also students in the Hebrew high school.[28] What was somewhat unusual about the programs of these youth groups was that there was a conscious effort to integrate their activities with the formal study programs of the Hebrew and Hebrew high school departments. This was consistent with Mr. Newman's view that students were to be exposed to ideas and values in their formal study of Jewish texts and then test out those ideas in the "real world" of informal Jewish education.[29]

8. *Camp Ramah.* From the earliest stages of the project, an effort was made to send students in the school to Camp Ramah. Owing to its special status, Tifereth Israel received a large allocation of spaces at Camp Ramah in Wisconsin. Prior to the inception of the project, the number of students attending the camp had been small. Soon after the start of the 1960–61 year, an effort was mounted to interest parents and children in Ramah. Rabbi Burton Cohen, director of Ramah in Wisconsin, came to Columbus to discuss the camp and its program. The writer, Mr. Newman, and Rabbi Fox utilized several meetings of the Board of Education to explain the program of the camp and the important contribution that enrolling students at Camp Ramah would make toward the goals of the project.[30] Scholarship funds to assist students to attend Camp Ramah were raised by the congregation and its two main affiliates, the

Sisterhood and the Men's Club. Over the years, these funds
were steadily increased.[31]

9. *Board of Education.* As noted above, prior to the inception
of the project, the Board of Education had not been active in
the areas of curriculum or of educational policy-making.[32] In
fact, the Board of Education had exercised stringent control in
areas involving finance and administration and had left educational issues in the hands of the professionals of the school.[33]
Cohen had this in mind when he characterized the group as a
"rubber-stamp body." Its role now changed dramatically.
Meetings were scheduled monthly throughout the entire year.
An effort was made to create some time at each meeting for
discussion of education per se through the inclusion of one or
more of the following in the agenda:

a. The Melton Research Center, its purpose and program
b. Model classes to demonstrate content and method in the
   school
c. Reports by Dr. Mehl; later, Dr. Lewis
d. Discussions of new approaches in Jewish education, e.g.,
   B'Yad Halashon
e. Ongoing discussion of the school curriculum
f. Reports by Mr. Newman and Rabbi Fox

In 1962, a Youth Commission was established as a special
subcommittee of the Board of Education to provide oversight
for the various youth groups as well as to provide a forum in
which there would be ample time for a group of the laity to
discuss informal education in the synagogue. In 1965, subcom-
mittees were developed in the areas of adult education, confirmation, curriculum, evaluation, facilities, and secondary education. The quality of the Board of Education was reflected in
the fact that its chairman in 1965 was the president-elect of the
congregation. Its members included, at that time, two professors of the Ohio State University. This was a working committee with great prestige.[34]

10. *Adult and parent education.* Prior to 1960, there is little
evidence that adult Jewish education was considered to be an

important activity of the congregation.[35] The Sisterhood sponsored a monthly study group with the rabbi. On several Sunday mornings, the Men's Club sponsored a *minyan* and breakfast which sometimes was followed by a discussion.[36] Beginning in 1960–61, the congregation offered an expanded program of adult Jewish education. Space limitations prevent a detailed listing of courses. Many of these are similar to what is found in other congregations. One particularly successful program was launched in 1961 at parental suggestion. It took the form of a monthly seminar in the philosophy and practices of Conservative Judaism. Meeting in the homes of members, it proved to be an excellent forum for parental discussion of educational issues. By the 1963–64 year, two such groups were in existence. Led jointly by the rabbi and the writer, they resembled in format the Great Books groups. They also functioned as support groups for the writer and his colleagues. In today's terminology, they would be regarded as *havurot,* and their members exhibited steady movement toward greater participation in worship, observance of *mitzvot maasiyot,* study, and the activities of the congregation and its affiliates. Finally, it may be said that the Sisterhood and Men's Club of the congregation devoted ever more time and effort to educational programming, often utilizing the professionals and other members of the faculty as resource people for their efforts.[37]

Summary of Changes and General Situation, 1960–66

During the first six years of the project, many changes were introduced into the pre-project system of education at Tifereth Israel. At the end of that period, the congregation had a system of education that more or less resembled what was to be found in well-developed programs of other Conservative congregations. Some areas of study, notably prayer, the arts, informal education, and Bible, were particularly strong. Students were achieving at acceptable norms as measured by the expectations found in the national curriculum.[38] The school was making reasonable demands of its students. A regular program of in-service training had been established for faculty. The Board of

Education and its main subcommittee, the Youth Commission, had been developed into forums for the serious discussion of Jewish educational theory and practice. Links had been developed with Camp Ramah. A program of secondary education had been developed. A strong network of youth groups had been established. In addition, the project demonstrated that it is possible to creatively mix professional and paraprofessional teachers to their mutual advantage. As the years progressed, more and more of the local talent progressed to the point where they could be entrusted with classes in the Hebrew school department. While individual professionals might come and go, the school and the program gained a measure of stability through the ongoing service of those who were committed to the community. Thus, the congregation enjoyed the advantages of the infusion of fresh energy and talent together with reliable and stable service. Finally, adult and parent education was significantly intensified through PTA evenings, a host of study groups, and service to the affiliate organizations of the congregation which sought to intensify their own educational activities.

Responses to the Project

The achievements listed above did not come easily. While the pre-project educational program may have been of modest quality, it was generally accepted by the congregation and its leadership as satisfactory. Had the project not been proposed by Mr. Melton, a member held in unique esteem, or had there been any real costs involved in accepting it, it seems doubtful that a pilot school would have been established at Tifereth Israel Congregation in 1960.[39] This meant that any change, particularly a change that affected time, money, or the direction to be taken by the congregation, was very likely to evoke resistance on the part of some segment of its membership and leadership. Moreover, those professionally responsible for the program were outsiders, from the eastern seaboard, more Jewishly observant than the vast majority of the members, associated with an intensity of Jewish ethnic, nationalist, and religious expression that was quite different from what was experienced and accepted as "Conservative Judaism" in Columbus at that time.[40] Finally, in the aftermath of the establishment of the pilot school, there was an influx of younger families into the congregation and the school. Many of these families enthusiastically accepted the principles and practices associated with the project. This created much tension between the older leadership and the newcomers.[41] It was noted above that the Board of Education evolved into a forum for serious discussion of Jewish education. It should also be noted that its meetings, as well as those of the Ritual Committee, Youth Commission, and Board of Trustees, were also, at times, arenas for the struggle between those who welcomed the project and the intensification of Jewish education that it represented and those who resented the changes that were being made and the people who supported the changes. Whereas in the past, the founders had been almost exclusively concerned with financial issues, the "newcomers" seemed much more interested in religious, educational, and cultural areas of congregational life.[42]

A number of the "founders" saw in the changes introduced by the project a return to "Orthodoxy."[43] The following incidents are illustrative of the use of this term.

1. At the 1960 Simhat Torah celebration, one of the professionals organized Israeli folk dancing as part of the *Hakafot* (Torah processions). While the teenagers and children obviously enjoyed the dancing, some of the "founders" found it to be totally inappropriate. A few days after the celebration, the writer was visited by a representative of the "founders" and told that this behavior was a "flagrant example of *Orthodoxy* and completely unwelcome at the Temple."[44]

2. Soon after the holidays, a new and very much expanded program of adult Jewish education was launched. The first evening of classes attracted over fifty students to the Hebrew language classes alone.

The activities director "steered" a former president of the congregation past the rooms in which these classes were being held. When told by her that these people had come to study Hebrew, he was reported to have replied, "What are those ß#$% teachers trying to do, make *Orthodox* rabbis out of us?"[45]

3. A student who attended Camp Ramah during the summer of 1961 and learned of the practice of not wearing shoes on a fast-day decided to wear sneakers on Yom Kippur. While his behavior was reported to have been unobtrusive, it outraged a number of the "founders."[46]

These incidents all contributed to a growing feeling on the part of some people that the form of Conservative Judaism that they were accustomed to was being undermined by neo-Orthodox outsiders. They questioned the need for daily prayer in the school.[47] These people objected to traditional forms of prayer, particularly bowing and swaying. Meetings were held with both the rabbi and the writer and with officials of the Center to assuage these fears. Yet, a number of people continued to worry about, and in some cases to oppose, the new directions taken by the congregation.

During the period from December 1962 to May 1963, Donald Adelman collected statements made by parents and other adults that reflect these concerns:[48]

I want my child to have a good Jewish education, but I don't want him too religious.[49]

The school is forcing the kids to turn away from reality; they are filling the children's heads with all kinds of idealistic nonsense.[50]

The school is running the synagogue; it never used to be that way.[51]

The school is running our rabbi. Our rabbi has changed since the (new) school came into existence. He is not our rabbi anymore.[52]

It's not our school anymore.[53]

There's too much Hebrew in the school.[54]

There's too much emphasis on prayer. They're trying to make the children Orthodox.[55]

The school is making unreasonable demands on the children's time. We want our children to be well-rounded individuals, not ghetto Jews.[56]

Since the new school came in, the congregation is going backwards.[57]

Adelman subjected these statements to semantic analysis and showed that they were far more revealing of feeling tones than of objective fact. Statements about loss of control ignored the fact that the congregation exercised religious and administrative control over the project. Statements of curricular concern or religious concern ignored official statements in these areas by the movement. Where the program expanded into informal education, participation by the youth was voluntary.[58]

With this criticism there was an even stronger tide of support for the project. While the core of this support lay in the ranks of the "newcomers," some of the "founders," particularly those whose children became involved in the project's activities, moved to a position of neutrality and, in some cases, support for the new situation.

Moreover, there were stubborn facts that altered the general situation over these years:

1. Between 1960 and 1965, over half of the new members taken in by the congregation were young parents who, when questioned, selected the educational system as the prime reason for their affiliation.[59]
2. In 1965–66, the congregation gained more new members than all other Columbus synagogues combined.[60]
3. None of the members affiliating for the first time in 1965–

66 chose the one-day school department (over the second grade) for their children.[61]

4. Between 1960 and 1966, the complexion of Jewish education changed radically:

	1959–60	1965–66
Total hours of instruction	151½	614
Total enrollment	340	446
One-day enrollment above second grade	284	93
Hebrew school (elementary) enrollment	51	221[62]
Hebrew high school enrollment	0	37

Periodically, the issue was raised at the Board of Education as to whether the congregation should continue to offer one-day education in the face of national educational policy and the declining enrollment within this department. A number of steps preceded the ultimate resolution of this issue:

1. A four-year attendance requirement in the Hebrew school before Bar and Bat Mitzvah was adopted.[63]
2. An organized and structured three-year Hebrew high school department was established, with graduation to take place after three years of secondary education.[64]
3. Mr. Melton announced the continuation of the Melton Research Center grant to the congregation for another two years.[65]
4. An extended discussion of the meaning of Confirmation in the congregation was conducted.[66]
5. As more and more students opted for the Hebrew high school, Confirmation attracted fewer students. Further discussion was held about the future of this ceremony and the entire one-day department.[67]
6. A special committee was established to study the future of Confirmation at Tifereth Israel.[68]

7. The first Hebrew high school graduation for tenth-graders took place.[69]
8. The Confirmation-study committee recommended increasing the requirements for Confirmation, suggesting a minimum of three years of attendance prior to the ceremony and an increase of the class time to two weekly sessions.[70]
9. The writer raised the question of the elimination of the one-day program above the primary grades. A committee was established to study the matter.[71]
10. Three students who had continued their studies in the Midrashah class (eleventh and twelfth grades) participated in the Hebrew high school graduation.[72]
11. A banquet prior to the Hebrew high school graduation was attended by 148 people. Henceforth, this was to be part of the celebration of the graduation.[73]
12. The Confirmation class was made a part of the Hebrew high school department; the age of Confirmation was raised to the tenth grade; the program was extended to two weekly sessions.[74]
13. A committee was formed to consider the phasing-out of the one-day school.[75]

Thus, gradually, the congregation moved toward one system of education for all its students.

As the school grew along with the congregation, a new feeling of pride and inner directedness took over. "Our congregation has developed a great pride in itself. Other congregations have been forced to re-examine their programs, particularly in the religious and educational spheres. There is more money being spent on Jewish education today in Columbus than ever before."[76]

From the viewpoint of the writer, the crucial factor in bridging the gap between "founders" and "newcomers" was the rabbi. Given his tenure (almost thirty years at the time of the inception of the project) and his unique position in the congregation, it was possible to move deliberately and steadily toward greater and greater acceptance of the changes within the school and congregation. One of his great strengths was his almost unfailing sense of timing. This enabled him to support change that was useful and doable while acting as a braking force on the professionals' youthful tendency to move more quickly than was practical. Publicly, the rabbi used every possible opportunity to support and praise the project. The minutes of the Board of Education reveal his eloquence and tenacity in defending the project and its personnel, even when it meant "taking on" the "founders."

The rabbi's response to a letter which he received is described as follows:

> Rabbi Zelizer feels that the best answer to the letter is the response from the children themselves in their wonderful participation. As a result of this exposure, the children themselves will become better adults and better members of the community. Our methods of prayer are not "Orthodox," but our children must be taught to pray like Jews. . . . In answer to questions by members of the committee as to extreme Israeli nationalism and Orthodoxy, Rabbi Zelizer answered that it is our obligation to warm the hearts and souls of the Jewish community.[77]

The rabbi also served as a "local scorekeeper," providing, from time to time, a checklist of accomplishments:

> Rabbi Zelizer enumerated several areas in which he felt that the school had assisted in bringing about desirable outcomes. These included attendance and participation in religious services, involvement of young adults in the educational and cultural activities of the congregation. Jewishly meaningful programming by the Sisterhood and Men's Club . . . and evolution of the Board of Education to its present position as a forum for serious discussion of . . . Jewish thought and educational issues.[78]

The rabbi was very practical, but he could also speak from the heart. In one of his annual reports to the congregation he said: "I was a dead rabbi; now I am alive again."[79]

The Critical Point of Decision

Mr. Melton had provided financial support for the project at its inception and renewed this grant after two years.[80] In 1964, the grant was due to run out, and there was no indication from the benefactor that it would be renewed. The financial implications were serious. In 1959–60, the educational expenditures of the congregation had amounted to approximately 15 percent of the total congregational budget, some $15,200, of which $6,400 was recovered as income. With the inception of the project, both income and expenses were significantly affected.[81] In the late spring and early summer of 1964, there was a flurry of activity. In addition to discussion of the situation by the Board of Education and Board of Trustees, a special planning committee as well as the executive committee (officers and past presidents of the congregation) devoted time to the issue of funding the educational program. At one of these meetings, Mr. Melton presented a proposal that recommended "cutting back the curriculum provided and associated costs."[82] This plan would have allowed for the elimination of professional teachers from the Seminary, the curtailment of the Hebrew language program, and the substitution of more modest aspirations for the school. When the "dust had settled," the response was clear:

The committee passed a motion that the education system should not be reduced in any significant way; the Board is strongly urged to pass the budget as is, and the committee will work closely with the Board to help finance the current education budget.[83]

Mr. Melton presented materials from the Melton Research Center and . . . suggested the possibility that this material could be utilized by non-professional teachers. The committee . . . agreed on the following: It would be detrimental to the congregation if any severe cutback were effected lowering the standards of our educational program.[84]

The planning committee reported with a recommendation that the education budget be accepted. The Board of Education recommended that the Board of Trustees pass the education budget for 1964–65 as presented; that a high level education system be maintained; that any large cutback, in anticipation of financial difficulties, be deferred until considerable effort had been expended to raise appropriate amounts of funds. . . . The motion was approved (one against).[85]

At the end, the "founders" and the "newcomers" had united to maintain the new system of education. From a stance that viewed a balanced budget as sacrosanct,[86] they were willing to incur possibly significant deficits rather than lose the educational system they had. With no apparent help from Mr. Melton, the leaders set out to raise money. Their plan called for the establishment of an endowment fund for education together with voluntary increases in membership dues. In the months ahead, both legs of the plan saw progress. Today, the lobby of the synagogue is graced by the names of individuals who have established endowment funds for education at Tifereth Israel. The large number of names offer support for the contention that, when put to the test, the membership was committed to a serious program of Jewish education.[87]

Postscript

While many of the changes described above seem rather "conventional," it is important to remember that few of them were effected without serious effort and even struggle on the part of individuals and vested-interest groups whose separate images of the role and scope of Jewish religious education varied significantly. The gradual development of a reasonably common commitment to make education a serious enterprise in one Jewish afternoon religious school was an accomplishment that taxed the talents and energy of educational academicians, theoreticians, and practitioners working with laity who were not prepared to lightly part with their own ideas as to what properly constitutes quality Jewish education.

The full story of what happened in Columbus between 1960 and 1970 will have to be researched by someone more remote from the project than the writer. Such an effort seems eminently worthwhile. It is possible that a follow-up study on the alumni of the program will reveal that they were significantly affected by the project. Such a result would provide a contribution to a literature of success stories in Jewish education. As such a literature grows, we may hope that others will emulate Mr. Melton and provide the means to enable Jewish education to realize its full potential.

Louis Newman's Contribution to the Columbus Project

The Columbus project was blessed with the guidance of many distinguished educators from outside Columbus, such as Professor Joseph Schwab, Professor Ralph Tyler, the staff of the Melton Research Center in New York, and Dr. Seymour Fox, who played a central role throughout the conceptualization and implementation of the work of the Center, during the years described.

It was, however, Mr. Louis Newman, the director of the Melton Research Center during this period, who possibly made the most unique contribution in the following ways:

1. He established a model for the profile of a professional educator in a (supplementary) program of Jewish education:
   a. One is to limit him/herself to areas of competence.
   b. Educators must study as part of their work.
   c. Twenty hours a week were devoted to face-to-face contact with clients and an equal amount of time to study and preparations for this work.
2. He established a model for the integration of formal classes and youth education.

3. He anticipated current interest in integration within Jewish education by instructing the faculty to read public-school texts used by their students and to look for opportunities to relate Jewish knowledge and general education.
4. He stimulated the staff to constantly examine practice and justify it Jewishly and educationally. He did this at workshops, meetings, classes, and through his writings.[88]
5. He showed an ongoing concern for the personal and professional needs of the staff in Columbus. Newman never failed to notice or to validate success.
6. He continually stressed the primacy of the ethical dimension of Judaism and thus was responsible, directly or indirectly, for many of the social-action programs conducted through the project.
7. He functioned as a model educator, demanding of himself and of others high standards of personal and professional behavior.

One of the most important contributions made by Louis Newman to the members of the team was his status as an unfailing source of support and encouragement. Newman never failed to notice or to validate achievements. His reports to the congregation and the board of the Melton Research Center offered documentation of the progress of the project, carefully indicating movement from stage to stage and setting all of his goals within the larger context of Jewish education. Newman also thought well about the needs of individuals working on the project. He was on the lookout to identify the strengths and capacities of his colleagues and to point out how these could be developed and put to use in new contexts.

One always felt that as a supervisor and leader, Newman deeply cared about those with whom he worked. He was a model of the Buberian ideal of the educator. He took his colleagues seriously, worried about their problems, whether personal or professional, gloried in their achievements, and gave them the courage to raise their aspirations. This superb capacity was felt by all who worked with Louis Newman in Columbus and is typical of his approach to Jewish education and to life.

Notes

1. In this article, the establishment of the pilot school and the implementation of its programs are referred to as the "project."
2. For a fuller discussion of the topic see Saul P. Wachs, "The Impact of a Pilot Project in Religious Education Upon a Midwestern Conservative Jewish Congregation" (Master's thesis, Ohio State University, 1966) (hereafter cited as "The Impact").
3. Hereafter referred to as the "Center."
4. Burton Cohen, "Report on Operations of Tifereth Israel Religious School, Columbus, Ohio, Prior to September, 1960" (Melton Research Center, unpublished).
5. Administrative records of the religious school.
6. An unknown number of students (almost all of whom were boys) also studied in the community high school during the week and at Tifereth Israel on Sundays. Cohen, op. cit., p. 1.
7. Ibid., p. 2.
8. See Louis Ruffman, ed., Curriculum Outline for the Congregational School, rev. ed. (New York: United Synagogue Commission on Jewish Education), p. 5.
9. During the writer's tenure, it was not unusual for former confirmands and other members of the congregation to attend Confirmation and to respond warmly to the ceremony.
10. Cohen, op. cit., p. 3.
11. Ibid., p. 4. Students did not return to class after the Bar Mitzvah ceremony, so enrollment figures varied significantly between September and June each year.
12. One staple of the curriculum was the Zeman series, which had been published in the early decades of the century.
13. Cohen, op. cit., p. 4.
14. Ibid., p. 5.
15. Ibid., p. 3. In 1959, the Board of Education abolished homework in the school and prohibited students from taking schoolbooks out of the building.
16. Wachs, "The Impact," p. 83.
17. Cohen, op. cit., p. 6.
18. Ibid.
19. See, for example, United Synagogue Commission on Jewish Education. Objectives and Standards for the Congregational School, rev. ed. (New York: United Synagogue Commission on Jewish Education, 1959).

20. One very positive aspect of the congregation's history had been the special efforts taken by the rabbi with a series of individuals who eventually entered the rabbinate. Given the lack of a supportive structure, this was no mean achievement.

21. This article deals almost exclusively with the efforts taken to meet the first goal.

22. Hereafter, this core group is referred to as the "professionals."

23. Throughout the 1960–70 period, each professional devoted one to three years of service to the project. In one case (Ann Schiffman Bonowitz), a professional married a member of the congregation and remained within the community, continuing to enrich it with her expertise to this time.

24. Important contributions to this program were made by Daniel Harrison, principal of the Columbus Hebrew School, who taught a weekly four-hour *Ulpan* to some of the apprentices.

25. See Saul P. Wachs, "Supervision in a Small School," *Synagogue School* 20, no. 2.

26. While the individual in question decided to return to the business world in late 1961, this same structure was in force throughout the tenure of the writer.

27. Minutes of the Board of Education, Tifereth Israel Congregation, April 25, 1960.

28. During the period under study, the informal educational component was led by two talented professionals, Donald Adelman (1960–63) and Leon Waldman (1964–67).

29. For an extended discussion of this idea and its implementation at the pilot school, see Saul P. Wachs and Leon Waldman, "A Theory of Practice for the Conservative Congregational High School," *Educators Assembly Yearbook,* 1968.

30. Minutes of the Board of Education, Nov. 28, 1960; Dec. 4, 1960; Jan. 16, 1961; Feb. 13, 1961.

31. During the summer of 1966, ten students from the congregation attended Ramah. In following summers, this number rose significantly.

32. See above, p. 60.

33. Cohen, op. cit., p. 8. Records of the Board's activities indicated only fourteen meetings between July 1955 and April 1960.

34. This last comment is reflected in interviews conducted in 1965–66 by the writer and discussed in "The Impact," p. 132.

35. This conclusion is based, in part, on the lack of any publicity describing such a program.

36. Announcements of the prayer-breakfast program did not list any topics for discussion.

37. The Sisterhood developed an effective tour of homes for the general community designed to acquaint non-Jews with Jewish holiday observance and culture. The Men's Club conducted an annual retreat with Seminary faculty to lead intensive study sessions.

38. Louis Ruffman, ed., *Curriculum Outline for the Congregational School,* rev. ed. (New York: United Synagogue Commission on Jewish Education, 1959).

39. The grant included funds to cover any costs to the congregation over and above what would have been the educational budget had there been no project. The rabbi's approval was also necessary.

40. In 1960, one of the male professionals walked outside the synagogue during Yom Kippur for a few minutes wearing his *tallit.* He was upbraided by a former president and told that this behavior was unacceptable.

41. Henceforth, the older families will be referred to as "founders," and the newer families as "newcomers."

42. Rabbi Nathan Zelizer, interview with the writer, Dec. 7, 1965.

43. Many of the actual founders of the congregation were very observant. With few exceptions, this was not true of their children. For two somewhat different accounts of the founding of the congregation (as a break-off from an Orthodox congregation), see Marc Lee Raphael, *Jews and Judaism in a Midwestern Community* (Columbus: Ohio Historical Society, 1979), pp. 182 ff., and *Tifereth Israel Golden Jubilee Souvenir Book* (Columbus: Congregation Tifereth Israel, 1951), p. 8.

44. Wachs, "The Impact," p. 110.

45. Ibid.

46. Ibid.

47. The congregation, from its inception, had no daily minyan. Raphael, op. cit., p. 186. A daily minyan was organized in the fall of 1962 and continued thereafter.

48. Martin Donald Adelman, *A Semantic Analysis in Jewish Education* (Master's thesis, Ohio State University, 1965).

49. Parent-teacher meeting, Jan. 20, 1963, cited in ibid., p. 37.

50. Men's Club meeting, Feb. 17, 1963, ibid.

51. Youth Commission meeting, Feb. 4, 1963, ibid.

52. Youth Commission, March 6, 1963, ibid.

53. Board of Education, Feb. 11, 1963.

54. Youth Commission, May 1, 1963.

55. Ritual Committee, Jan. 14, 1963.

56. Youth Commission, Dec. 3, 1963.

57. Board of Education, Oct. 10, 1962.

58. Adelman, op. cit., pp. 39 ff.

59. Interview with Sheldon Lessem, executive director of Congregation Tifereth Israel, Nov. 22, 1965.

60. Ibid.

61. As of the 1964–65 academic year, this program was transferred to Shabbat. This change exposed the students to the Shabbat service. It also solved a problem of space engendered by the growth in the size of the other departments.

62. In 1959–60, there were no minimum residence rules required for Bar or

Bat Mitzvah. In 1960–61, a Hey class was established in this department. In 1963–64, a Hebrew program for seven-year-olds (meeting twice a week for four hours) was added to the department.

63. Board of Education, Mar. 27, 1961.

64. Board of Education, Aug. 21, 1961.

65. Board of Education, Dec. 10, 1963

66. Board of Education, June 3, 1963.

67. Board of Education, June 9, 1964.

68. Board of Education, Feb. 2, 1965.

69. June 1965.

70. Board of Education, Aug. 2, 1965.

71. Board of Education, Mar. 1, 1966.

72. June 1966.

73. Reported at Board of Education, June 7, 1966.

74. Board of Education, Aug. 9, 1966.

75. Ibid. A program for the phasing out of one-day-a-week education above the primary grades was approved by the Board of Education in February 1968. Confirmation was merged with the high school graduation.

76. Based on interviews conducted by the writer in 1965–66. See Saul Wachs, "The Impact," pp. 131 ff.

77. Board of Education, May 1, 1961.

78. Board of Education, Jan. 7, 1963.

79. Address by Rabbi Nathan Zelizer at the annual congregational dinner, May 3, 1964.

80. See above, p. 57.

81. In 1965–66, educational expenditures were 36 percent of the total budget, and with "hidden expenses" added, e.g., janitorial time, etc., were judged by the executive director to be 57 percent of the total budget. Interview, Nov. 22, 1965. The subsidy was for $28,000 a year provided by the Center. In 1965, income had risen to $43,487 and expenses to $58,998. The total congregational budget had risen almost 75 percent during that period. For fuller discussion of statistics, see Wachs, "The Impact," pp. 134 ff.

82. Board of Trustees, May 19, 1964.

83. Executive Committee, June 15, 1964.

84. Special Planning Committee, June 16, 1964.

85. Board of Trustees, June 16, 1964.

86. See Wachs, "The Impact," p. 133.

87. The Melton family has continued to offer generous support for the school and the congregation. One can only wonder as to whether Mr. Melton's proposals (see above) were a kind of "test" of the congregation's commitment to the project. If so, the answer was clear.

88. See, for example, *Memorandum for Hebrew and Sunday School Teachers* (New York: Melton Research Center, 1961).

Bibliography

Adelman, Martin Donald. "A Semantic Analysis in Jewish Education." Master's Thesis, Ohio State University, Columbus, 1962.

Cohen, Burton. "Report on Operation of the Tifereth Israel Religious School, Prior to 1960." Melton Research Center (unpublished).

Congregation Tifereth Israel. *Golden Jubilee Souvenir Book*, 1951.

————. Minutes of the Board of Education.

————. Minutes of the Board of Trustees.

————. Minutes of the Youth Commission.

Fox, Seymour. "Education for the Twentieth Century Jews: A Pilot Program." *Hadassah Magazine* 48, no. 1 (1966).

Newman, Louis. *Memorandum for Hebrew and Sunday School Teachers*. New York: Melton Research Center, 1961.

Raphael, Marc Lee. *Jews and Judaism in a Midwestern Community: Columbus, Ohio, 1840–1975*. Columbus: Ohio Historical Society, 1979.

Ruffman, Louis. *Curriculum Outline for the Congregational School*. Rev. ed. New York: United Synagogue Commission on Jewish Education, 1959.

United Synagogue of America. *Objectives and Standards for the Congregational School*. Rev. ed. New York: United Synagogue Commission on Jewish Education, 1958.

Wachs, Saul P. "A Kallah for Columbus." *The Torch*, Spring 1965.

————. "Report to the Board of Directors of the Melton Research Center." June 1963 (unpublished).

————. "The Achievements of the Pilot Education Program for 1961–62: Report to the Academic Board of the Melton Research Center" (unpublished).

————. "The Congregational Hebrew High School." *Synagogue School* 27, nos. 1–2 (Fall 1968).

————. "The Impact of a Pilot Project in Religious Education Upon a Midwestern Conservative Jewish Congregation." Master's thesis, Ohio State University, Columbus, 1966.

————. "Supervision in a Small School." *Synagogue School* 20, no. 2 (1962).

———— and Waldman, Leon. "A Theory of Practice for the Conservative Congregational High School." *Educators Assembly Yearbook*, 1968.

THE EVOLUTION AND UNIQUENESS OF THE JEWISH EDUCATIONAL STRUCTURE OF GREATER BOSTON

DANIEL J. MARGOLIS

The ten-year period of Lou Newman's direction of the Bureau of Jewish Education of Greater Boston was marked by a phenomenal set of changes and new programs. In the sixty-two years the Boston BJE has functioned, Lou became only the agency's third executive director. He brought to the position and to the Boston Jewish community ideas to meet the "new realities," as he called them. These conditions are still changing, a dynamic to which the BJE is still responding with evolving formulations for new programs, services, and plans. Though Lou might claim not to have a "sense of history," the essay below and some of the ideas and plans discussed reflect not only Lou's interpretation of the present and future needs of Jewish education in Boston (and elsewhere) but also his respect for the past accomplishments of his predecessors—Louis Hurwich and Dr. Benjamin Shevach, zt"l. In addition, even now it is clear that Lou's contributions, in and of themselves, will leave their indelible mark in the annals of the Boston BJE and American Jewish education.

In a very real sense, Lou Newman and Shirley have been my teachers, since the time we first met at the Seminary and later at Camp Ramah. Knowing them and their entire extended family and working with them has been a privilege.

Dr. Daniel Margolis is a product of the Brookline, Massachusetts, public school system and the Boston Hebrew School structure, including Kehillath Israel Hebrew School and Boston's Hebrew (Teachers) College, and has a doctorate from Teachers College at Columbia University. He has taught, directed Ramah camps, been Assistant Director of the Institute for Jewish Life, coordinated the Middle Division at Boston's Schechter Day School and the Graduate Program in Jewish Education at Brandeis University, and is now executive director of Boston's BJE and on the faculty at Brandeis and Hebrew College.

Today it would be called a systems approach. Certainly, when he began to formulate his design for the organizational structure of Jewish education in Greater Boston, Louis Hurwich did not call it a systems approach. However, the all-encompassing model for educational structure and change which characterized the Jewish school network in Greater Boston was indeed a system.

It was a system based on a rational understanding that schools and institutions do not exist in a vacuum, that there are various constituent groups (and their ideological positions) involved in the establishment, maintenance, and evaluation of a school, let alone a school system, and that nothing can happen educationally or structurally if even one of the component pieces is either missing or ignored. Louis Hurwich developed a system—one piece at a time—which grew to include all of the necessary institutional and human support structures.

The Boston structure was coherent, cohesive, and consistent. It was true to its philosophical principles, and, therefore, it withstood the pressures of fads and other changes not carefully thought out. The system persisted in time despite significant and rather radical social changes. In fact, if there were to be any major criticisms of form of the "Boston system," they would have to focus on the lack of an internal set of mechanisms to provide for a process of rational "program review" and structural change to respond to "new realities."

In this essay, I shall review somewhat analytically the Jewish educational system which Louis Hurwich established, comment on its potential as a model for analyzing individual schools involved in a change process, and suggest ways of building in the necessary dimensions to ensure reflexive institutional continuity and evolution in an era of rapid social change.

The accident of a cash surplus in the 1917 campaign of the Federated Jewish Charities resulted in the first community-wide decision to provide financial support for Jewish/Hebrew education in Boston. Though this was a milestone in the development of the Boston system, and a required ingredient in the establishment of any coherent entity—namely, the availability of sufficient and broad-based community financial support—it was predated by two other necessary pieces. In several major neighborhoods with Jewish populations, there were already some schools in existence, all with their own particular ideological stances and lay and professional supporters committed to those positions. Chelsea, the North End, and the West End, for example, each had several "central" supplemental schools subscribing to their own set of methods and content in addition to many private *hadarim*. Sunday schools also drew large numbers of students, and they, too, functioned with teaching staffs (albeit volunteers in these instances) and support from *baalebatim*. The stimulus for the decision to provide direct funding for the Hebrew and Sunday schools came from a report commissioned by the "Federated" and written by Louis Hurwich, who was brought in from Indianapolis to make a study of the Boston Jewish schools. He represented the third ingredient—a personality, a central figure around whom those committed to the primacy of Jewish education could rally.

By the beginning of 1918, then, three major elements for a coherent Jewish educational system existed in Greater Boston: a central figure, sufficient funding from a credible, broadly-based community agency, and working schools, reasonably sound politically, professionally, and pedagogically. However, more was needed.

Today it would be called a support system or network. Against the common "enemy"—the "assimilationist" Federation—the larger existing schools decided to join together to provide a common direction for themselves. Two associations of related schools were started in response to the Hurwich survey and in order to implement its recommendations. The Associated Boston Hebrew Schools (representing twelve Hebrew schools) and the Bureau of Jewish Religious Schools (representing the synagogue Sunday schools) were both essentially "grass-roots" groups initiated and supported by the respective institutions. They functioned in parallel for over two years until they merged into the Bureau of Jewish Education, with Louis Hurwich as its first superintendent. Element number four was in place as "Boston thus became the first community in the United States to organize Jewish education on a community-wide basis, and as a community responsibility."[1] Thus began the first professionalized central agency for Jewish education. Its mandate was derived from both the schools and the community: serve, improve, and coordinate Jewish education in Greater Boston.

How the Bureau of Jewish Education interpreted its mandate and translated it into a practical program comprises the fifth element in the "system"—the raising of standards. By standards, Hurwich referred to both physical and educational criteria. While urging the erection of new and attractive school buildings on one hand, Hurwich recognized on the other that the key to improved *educational* standards lay first and foremost with the capacities and preparation of the teachers. In 1918, Hurwich responded to this need by opening the Hebrew Teachers Training School— בית מדרש למורים —which only three years later became the Hebrew Teachers College. At the same time, the Sunday school teachers attended a training program organized by the Bureau of Jewish Religious Schools. In short, the systematic training of Jewish teachers was the fifth major element in the "grand design" for Boston's Jewish educational system under the aegis of the BJE.

> There was a two-pronged task: to maintain conditions which will keep away outside interference, thereby allowing the College free and orderly development; and to keep the College as an integrated function within the warp and woof of the entire web of Hebrew schools. A continued flow of Hebrew school graduates to the Hebrew High School *(Prozdor)* had to be maintained at the College intake end, and, at the other end, the best use had to be made of the new groups of teachers produced annually by the College.[2]

There is no better indication of Hurwich's view of the Boston system as an integrated "web," each thread, no matter its starting point or its own particular "task" in the fabric, being woven into an intricate yet coherent design.

But there was yet another component to the element of raising standards, namely, the area of educational content. At a time when the need was for unification, Hurwich and Dr. Nissan Touroff (then dean of the Hebrew Teachers College) developed a uniform six-year course of study for all the Hebrew schools which wanted to adopt it. It was a demanding and comprehensive curriculum outline, which underwent constant revisions over the years. (It is interesting to note that the curriculum itself was subject to change more readily than the total system of which it was so vital a part. My hypothesis for this is that the BJE תכנית למודים—a curriculum which became both famous and infamous throughout the country—had its own internal support structure somewhat more realistically comprising the annual achievement tests and their attendant degree of pupil, teacher, and school accountability, teacher in-service training, and principals' workshops whose charge was to review the curriculum and its demands on a regular basis. Frankly, one key element to the continuing susceptibility of the curriculum to change was its high degree of visibility and objectivity or measurability. Some of the other aspects of the BJE program, even today, are much less visible and objectifiable, and, therefore, much less amenable to scrutiny and change.)

Still, with all of its revisions, the Bureau curriculum and its tests (and the publishing of their results with school and teachers' names attached) provided the basic standardization of content on which the centralized community system thrived for over forty years. It was a true "safety net" below which no committed Jewish educator or proponent of Jewish education was willing or dared to fall, if (and it became a very big "if") he felt committed to the principles of pedagogy and Yiddishkeit embedded in it and promulgated by the system as a whole.

The uniformity of content had to be maintained and sustained in practice, however. The Bureau undertook not only to develop and measure the curriculum and its efficacy, but also to guard the quality of its instructors and instruction. Supervision, evaluation, placement, and in-service training became the sixth aspect of the "Boston system." As Hurwich put it, "By itself, water will not rise above its source. Similarly, instruction will not be better than the instructors who render it."[3] BJE staff visited schools and classrooms on admittedly "inspectorial" missions; teachers were evaluated both in-service on their teaching practice and, prior to their placement in "affiliated" schools, on the basis of their credentials as to their suitability for meeting the rigorous demands of the curriculum. Teachers and principals were recommended for advancement and *salary increases* according to their performance and their active participation in in-service training programs organized by the BJE. While this process was begun during Hurwich's twenty-five years as superintendent of the Bureau, it was fine-tuned by his successor, Dr. Benjamin J. Shevach.

Shevach, not only an accomplished Hebraist and Jewish educator but also an outstanding educational psychologist, described the need for a thorough program of teacher supervision and training thus:

> If the teacher's graph of mental progress is going down year by year, while that of his students is rising rapidly, the teacher can hardly understand his students, however good his intentions may be. The purpose of the in-service courses is, thus, *to keep the teacher mentally alive.*[4]

The Jewish educators—teachers and principals—were seen as more than mere conduits or vehicles for the "system" and its content. While a Hebrew Teachers Organization started in 1912, Touroff and Hurwich later supported it as a means for ascribing status and dignity to the individual teachers and to the profession as a whole. A *ḥevrah* of Hebrew teachers formed, followed ten years later by a separate group for principals started by Touroff. Under Shevach the two organizations merged into the Hebrew Teachers and Principals Association of Greater Boston (אגודת המורים והמנהלים דבוסטון וסביבותיה), fostered by the BJE and nurtured as neither a union nor a fraternity but a curious mixture of both. The HTPA was intended to be a "support group" meeting both professional concerns and social needs. "The teachers and principals never limited their organization to their own material needs only. The welfare of the schools and maintenance of educational standards have always ranked high among their interests. Without their continued cooperation, neither the Bureau nor the Hebrew College could have achieved what they did."[5]

The sense of cooperation and mutuality of interest among the parties in the "system" led to another component in the structure—the Code of Practice. A hybrid document, intended to serve several masters, the Code outlines proper procedures for the treatment of personnel while also delineating the criteria for becoming and *remaining* a fully accredited affiliated school. The Code never tilts in favor of one party over another. Instead, it serves primarily as a "preserver" of the "system" as a whole. However, it is an important ingredient in the systemic structure because of the guidelines it establishes for both professional and "lay" behavior.

Of the seven major elements in the system described so far, most are directed to the schools and their professionals. Lay school supporters (School Committee members and parent representatives) were not formally represented in the system until 1945. At that time the United Hebrew Schools came into being as a counterpart to the HTPA. The UHS was organized as an autonomous member of the "trinitarian arrangement" to speak and act "for the lay directors of its affiliated schools." Though Hurwich had built in a professional and lay interlock between the UHS and the BJE (the director of the BJE served as the educational consultant to the United Hebrew Schools, and some directors of each group served on the other group's board), Shevach turned the entire arrangement into a very effective structure for the preservation of the system and its principles. He did so out of necessity.

The fact is that, without the cooperation of these two organizations [UHS and HTPA], the Bureau would remain absolutely impotent. . . . It would take us far afield to describe how this whole-hearted cooperation has been achieved without any real authority on the part of the Bureau. For real authority in most other Bureaus derives from the fact that the affiliated schools are all subvented up to 50%–60% of their budgets. The usual approach is that of "Crime and Punishment," viz., no submission to the dictates of the Bureau—no subventions!

We in Boston possess no such weapon; frankly, we wouldn't want it. If the Bureau preaches subventions for needy schools [the BJE had long since lost its role as a conduit for Federation funds to individual schools; most of the allocations had been eliminated during the twenty-five years since the Depression, anyway], it is for the purpose of helping them to carry on their work in the light of *educational requirements advocated by the Bureau—which they have been more than willing to follow without subventions* [emphasis added]. . . .

However, the mechanism that has been evolved is highly delicate and sensitive, and it is needless to state that utmost effort must be exerted in order to maintain its smooth functioning.[6]

And the "system" developed— and it was good. In addition to the aspects already mentioned, Boston's Jewish educational system had as good a grounding in the theory of education and Jewish education as that of any city. (The education faculty at the Boston Hebrew College today includes the names Eli Grad, Michael Libenson, Rose Bronstein, Sol Schimmel, and Louis Newman.) There has been continuous access to the communal decision-making and opinion-forming processes, through the Federation, the Jewish press, the synagogues and their regional and national movements, along with reasonably cooperative relationships with other community agencies in planning and programming where mutual interests have coincided. Vacations and summers were built into the system with the establishment of Camp Yavneh, the Hebrew-speaking summer school and camp of the Hebrew Teachers College (1944), and the BJE's Hebrew school and day-camp at an essentially Jewish seaside resort area (1948).

It was, and continues to be, a total system. Louis Newman, who succeeded Shevach in 1973 as the BJE's third executive director, recognizing both the flaws in the structure (derived from some built-in structural inflexibility) and the potential for good Jewish education in the structure, reestablished working relationships with Hebrew College and Brandeis University; expanded the staff and its service to the entire community of schools and educational agencies; and created several central-ized educational services while promoting and working to enhance the individualistic natures and "philosophies" of the independent schools.

Yet, there were problems, and they persist. As a central agency in a historically centralized Jewish educational commu-nity, the BJE today, like the system it serves and plans for, is faced with the same dilemma described by Shevach in 1959. It is that dilemma which raises the essential criticism of the "Boston system"—its historic inability to change methodically and thoughtfully in the face of "new realities." It is the di-lemma of an agency with specified and articulated values, a system reflective of those values which it and its sister institu-tions helped to create, existing in a world where values are not well articulated and, when they are, are so diverse and diffused as to reflect no coherent whole.

Shevach put it:

All the activities of the Bureau bear the stamp of given values. We hope that these values reflect somewhat the spirit of the Jewish school in Babylon, Spain, Germany, and yes, we confess "the unpardonable sin," the spirit of the East-European ḥeder. Moreover, we honestly and sincerely be-lieve that these values are still potent. . . .

[The Bureau head today] is expected to be a quasi-center-director, a semi-Rabbi, an impromptu arbiter of controversies between teachers and principals, and principals and Bale-batim, an educational philosopher, a curriculum maker, a

bookkeeper, a business manager, a supervisor, a psychologist, a teacher, a publicity agent, a roving ambassador of
good will. . . . He is expected to support *diversity in unity*,
and is blamed if he fails to produce the desired *unity in
diversity*. He is expected to act like a chameleon and to take
on the colors of the particular locus wherein he perchance
finds himself. He is to support zealously the Sunday School,
and he is to be an ardent protagonist of the All-Day School.
He is expected to coordinate activities which are mutually
contradictory. He is to be the authority, without being autho-
rized; he is held responsible, without being given commen-
surate authority.[7]

It is not only the Bureau director Shevach is describing, but
also the Bureau itself and the educational system for which it
supposedly is responsible. In the face of the breakdown of the
community and its surrounding society, which forms the context for the "new realities" in Jewish education, the "system"
has only two choices: retreat to the comfortable world of
known principles and behaviors and thus ignore the increasing
and expanding "unfriendly" world out there, or retool and
restructure itself. A system with such longevity and dedication
to its mission and mandate as Boston's system was (and is)
cannot easily turn around nor be turned around by others.
Adding to the dilemma is the omnipresent and ongoing reality
which prohibits and inhibits the needed reflection upon the
proper restructuring process—namely, there are schools out
there and people—students, teachers, families, educators—
who need help. These are the "fires" Lou Newman has described that need to be put out even before the system can face
itself and think about change.

In Shevach's time and in his view, the Talmud Torah represented the most important aspect of the system to preserve.
Shevach recognized that

Stressing the importance of the Talmud Torahs had become
unpopular within recent years. The Bureau had been criti-

cized severely for its faithful adherence to the outmoded, East European Talmud Torah tradition. We admit that the Talmud Torah today is suffering from a disease, but certainly not the incurable illness its enemies suggest. . . . It has not made its peace with the unfavorable conditions, and it refuses to be pushed into a corner. It rejects the substitutes forced upon the Jewish school by external conditions, and continues stubbornly to teach in the original the traditional books which for many generations formed the substance of Jewish education. Aiding the Talmud Torahs, guiding them, encouraging them, and, what is of equal importance, inculcating the spirit and substance of the Talmud Torah tradition into the newly-established schools in suburbia, have constituted (and we hope will continue so in future years) the primary task of the Bureau.[8]

It is understandable for any system and its proponents to support their own view of "the world." When they do so without building in a way to look at their activities and ideals carefully, openly, reflexively, it is then that dangerous rigidity sets in. Every system must be evaluated periodically, but regularly and thoughtfully. Every agency or organization and its personnel must be prepared to engage in this self-scrutiny, in the form either of long-range planning or of some routine program review. The historical dimension in any human organizational endeavor is a critical analytic tool often ignored by educational practitioners. The ימים נוראים should provide the Jewish metaphor or analogue for institutionalizing this kind of process in our educational systems, a time set aside regularly to perform חשבון הנפש.

The "system" and all the good it stands for cannot survive if it adheres monolithically to the ideals of the past and the structures which were appropriate for another time and another reality. On the other hand, the system will not survive without adhering to some set of thoughtful principles of education and Judaism, especially in the context of today's *klal Yisrael*, as diverse as we are.

Like Shevach before him, Lou Newman has guided the "Boston system" by choosing to do some of the task, by deliberately choosing to concentrate on pieces of the total structure, while trying to preserve at least the entity, all the while attempting to articulate a new set of stances for the future. In preserving the entity, one preserves not only its individual pieces but also the connections among them, their interrelationships. One new principle may be substituted for an old one; one new program or support group may replace one that no longer is effective; but all the pieces must fit if it is to remain a *system* of Jewish education—a statement by the Jewish community that Jewish education is important or, better, *its most important enterprise.*

We have described, albeit inadequately, the genius of the Jewish educational structure in Greater Boston as a system. As a model it can inform us of the need for a necessary and sufficient interrelationship in any educational entity among all of its parts, each one of which is critical to the success and viability of the system as a whole. We have seen the elements to be: articulated ideals and theory, adequate physical and financial support from the entire community, access to decision-making and opinion-forming, "working" schools and people dedicated to them, standards of curricular content and uniformity of content (even if many options are provided for within the structure), objectifiable accountability, supervision and evaluation, intensive preparation and continued training of educators, support groups for and of laypeople and professionals, and the central figure(s) both of the present and the past, those who are מסורים ומשוגעים לדבר, along with a real profession for them to enter and through which they can advance. We have also seen the need for a central agency charged with the key planning and coordinating tasks for the entire community.

Schools, too, under their lay and professional leaders, can benefit from using the system analog as an analytic tool as it was applied here to Boston's Jewish education and its historical development. A school looked at as a system can reveal deficiencies in such diverse areas as physical environment or home/family support programming, subject-matter depth, and personnel practices. If many deficiencies emerge (as they invariably do), the system as analytic device allows the educational leader to be able to justify "breaking into" the whole entity at *any* point, using a variety of approaches, and working on any aspect of the system, with the realization that each aspect affects every other, and, ultimately, changing one piece will effect change on the whole.

The human constituencies must interrelate with each other and with the structural or institutional elements. There must be a sufficient structural backup for planning and evaluation to end up in an "implementable" and practical reality. As Hurwich, Shevach, and Newman have understood, a community's program of Jewish education is as strong as its parts and as viable as the system is whole—ideationally and practically. And, by omission, the "Boston system" informs us of the need to build in periodic reviews and self-evaluations with the practical end-in-view of significant change, not as *reaction* to new conditions, but in order to be an effective, *active*, and educative change agent upon and within the Jewish community.

Notes

1. Louis Hurwich, "Jewish Education in Boston (1843–1955)," *Jewish Education* 26, no. 3 (Spring 1956): 24.
2. Ibid., p. 26.
3. Ibid.
4. Benjamin J. Shevach, "How the Jewish Community in Metropolitan Boston Is Organized for Jewish Education," mimeographed (Boston: Bureau of Jewish Education, 1959), p. 11.
5. Hurwich, op. cit., p. 32.
6. Shevach, op. cit., p. 14.
7. Ibid., p. 9.
8. Ibid., p. 10.

A NEW DIRECTION FOR JEWISH EDUCATION IN AMERICA

SHELDON A. DORPH

Encouraging Developments

As concern with Jewish identity and Israel-consciousness has grown, the past twenty years have seen the burgeoning of new approaches, curricula, and styles in American Jewish education. To fill attractive Hebrew school buildings, one finds new Jewish textbooks—attractively and expensively prepared by Jewish publishers, new audio-visual aids, learning centers, open-classroom techniques, and individualized instruction. The growth of overnight Jewish camping has been supplemented with summer teen programs to Israel, synagogue summer day camps, the introduction of Israeli music, arts and crafts, and dance into the Jewish school curriculum. Teacher-training has received increased emphasis—spearheaded by the work of the Melton Research Center.[1] The growth of teachers' centers on the model of the Kohl Teachers' Center in Chicago, and the immediate grass-roots success of the Conference on Alternatives in Jewish Education are examples of encouraging developments which have struck a responsive chord in the

Dr. Sheldon Dorph is educational director of the Jewish Academy of Los Angeles and directs the New Jewish High School and Los Angeles Hebrew High School. As a Ramah director and principal of afternoon and day high schools, he has sought to translate the theoretical knowledge gained from mentors Dr. Philip Phenix of Teachers College and Dr. Seymour Fox of Hebrew University into Jewish educational settings. Dr. Dorph is the series editor of the Shalav Hebrew Series published by Behrman House.

Jewish educational community.[2] All of the above, when added to the ongoing work of schools, seminaries, and bureaus of Jewish education, represent a rather significant outlay of Jewish communal funds over many years.

The Chronic Problem

At the same time, concrete research evidence has emerged within the last few years documenting:

- the *secularization* of Jewish community structure[3]
- the emergence of the synagogue as a *child-centered* institution, without serious education and commitment required of its adult members[4]
- the *decline* in synagogue and federation affiliation by American Jews, any consistent pattern of Jewish ritual observance, and enrollment of Jewish children in Jewish educational programs[5]
- the long-range ineffectiveness of any form of Jewish education (afternoon or day school) which terminates *below* high-school age[6]
- the fall in Jewish fertility to a bare replacement level[7]
- the quick rise in assimilation, intermarriage, and loss of Jewish identity, which predict a drastic decline in the U.S. Jewish population over the next one hundred years[8]
- the continued transfer of responsibility for Jewish education and identity-formation from family and synagogue-community to synagogue school, and the inability and inappropriateness of schooling to educate for identity[9]

The above gestalt of data and research documents and confirms the warnings of Jewish communal leaders over the past two decades. At this point in time, there ought to remain no one who doubts the problem we face or who does not admit that our educational and communal efforts to date have been inadequate, ineffective, and perhaps largely misdirected—in spite of the hopeful developments mentioned earlier. Surely the newest Federation studies will set off a cacophony of "geshries" and a rush to spend more Jewish community dollars. It is, therefore, appropriate and perhaps even important to take a fresh look at the problem of Jewish education and identity formation—for no other reason than to prevent the pouring of community dollars down the same old educational and social welfare drains.

Toward an Authentic Theory of Jewish Education

There is little in the theory and method of modern Jewish education that is not derivative, and while that may be one of the causes of the failure of Jewish schooling, the fact is that until Jews succeed in developing a powerful and generative theory of education which is drawn from our tradition and responsive to our needs and purposes, we shall be dependent on the work of others.[10]

The purpose of this paper is to explicate such a theory of Jewish education and commitment, drawn from Jewish tradition. Such a theory will (1) point out in what ways most of our recent educational efforts have been misdirected and show a basic misunderstanding of the crisis facing American Jewish community life, and (2) indicate a new direction and format for educational intervention which may make a significant impact upon the chronic problem of Jewish identity in America.[11]

And since it is not the power of explication (of Torah)—*midrash*—which is essential, but rather the deed—*maaseh*—it is the duty of all teachers to teach the students the upright path upon which they are to walk . . . and to educate them in fulfilling the commandments.[12]

Based upon a rabbinic statement in Mishnah *Abot*, [13] the above medieval source highlights the fact that in Judaism, the idea, the explanation, the concept, the professed principle, the verbalized value, have limited importance without a mode of implementation and actualization in the life-style and day-to-day living of the Jew. This basic tenet of Jewish tradition has been stated and restated throughout the long history of Jewish religious thought. Thus Martin Buber:

> . . . in our case teaching is inseparably bound up with do-
> ing. . . . it is impossible to teach or to learn without living.
> . . . Either the teachings live in the life of a responsible hu-
> man being, or they are not alive at all. . . . Among all the
> peoples of the world, Israel is probably the only one in which
> wisdom that does not lead directly to the unity of knowledge
> and deed is meaningless.[14]

Within Judaism there is a similar attitude concerning the relationship of a man's deeds to the intentions of his heart and
spirit. Abraham Heschel has noted this most insightfully:

> It is not only important what a person does; it is equally and
> even more important what a person *is*. Spiritually speaking,
> what he does is a minimum of what he is. Deeds are
> outpourings, they are not the essence of the self. . . . On the
> other hand, we must never forget that in Judaism we answer
> God's will in deeds. God asks for the heart, but the heart is
> often a lonely voice in the marketplace of living. . . . God
> asks for faith and the heart is not sure of its faith. It is good,
> therefore, that there is a dawn of decision for the night of the
> heart, deeds to objectify faith, definite forms to verify belief.
> . . . The problem of the soul is how to live nobly in an animal
> environment, how to . . . train the tongue and senses to
> behave in agreement with the insight of the ages. It is to this
> problem that Jewish observance is meant to be an answer.
> But do we still teach Judaism as an answer to the questions of
> the inner life?[15]

Thus we have noted that in Judaism, it is the system of deeds—
of rituals, ceremonies, holidays, and cultural acts—which both
concretizes the great ideals and events in Judaism *and* forms a
mode of expression for the inner religious spirit of a man.
Thus, one and the same action system unites the realms of
intellect and emotion to create the Jewish system of valuing.

None of the foregoing is a new insight into the essence of Judaism—it is well known. Nor is Judaism the only religion whose ritual and observance system seeks to incorporate the main ideas, values, or events of the religion. Likewise, other religions have used a system of behavior and ritual to channel the inner religious spirit of individuals. If there is a difference between Judaism and other religions in this regard, it is one of degree rather than one of kind.

But when it comes to the question of *how* a religion, in each generation, seeks to renew the connection between event or idea and ritual, Judaism has developed a rather unique approach. For Judaism has incorporated into the core of its observance, ritual, and celebration an *educational* process. It is this educational process which has the power to renew the meaning, the value, the concept embodied in the ritual itself. At the same time, this educational process injects a new appreciation for the ritual into the spirit of the practicing individual.

Close study of the biblical sources on the observance of Passover yields two principles essential to the Jewish educational process.[16]

Principle I: The Integration of Individual and Communal Institutions in Ritual Observance

Ex. 12:11–13, 14–20, and 43–50 emphasize, in different ways, the involvement of individual, family, and community in the Passover. This integration of the individual with communal institutions *around ritual* was to become an essential characteristic of the Jewish educational process which made possible renewal of meaning and commitment in each generation.

Principle II: Rededication Through Ritual

Ex. 13:1–16 preserves the commandment of how Passover is to be observed when the Israelites reach the land of Canaan. Ex. 13:11–16 notes that upon arrival in Canaan, the Jew is to set aside the firstborn of animal and human life for the Lord. Both of these passages, each commemorating an event or value in Jewish history, have used a ritual as the method of embodying the event. Each has anticipated that experiencing the ritual would stimulate the next generation to ask its meaning or significance. This questioning becomes the occasion for expounding the idea or value behind the ritual and thus renewing its meaning. It is in this way that succeeding generations become rededicated to both values and ritual observance in Judaism.[17]

This process is made even more explicit and general in Deut. 6:17–25, where Moses addresses the people of Israel as they are about to enter the Promised Land. In this passage, Moses exhorts the people to keep the laws of God. Indeed, he claims such observance is the key to their well-being and to God's keeping His promise (covenant) to their forefathers (Deut. 6:17–19). Moses then anticipates that a man's son will ask the meaning of the laws enjoined upon the Israelites (Deut. 6:20), and suggests an answer to the son in terms of freedom from Egyptian slavery and the inheritance of the Promised Land (Deut. 6:21–23). The text adds that the observance is for the good and survival of the people (Deut. 6:24–25).

This same linking of idea or value with observance and education can be found in the *Sh'ma* (Deut. 6:4–9). Thus, commitment to the words of God can be expressed in one's own discourse and deeds, in how one educates his children, in how one marks his home and his community. This last passage in the Torah has brought us back to the concept of the integration of individual and communal institutions in Jewish ritual. For the *Sh'ma* makes it clear that the rituals which actualize the idea of love of God are to be carried out by the individual, in his home, and by the community. We can now turn to a summary of the fascinating educational process which we have gleaned from these biblical sources.

Summary: A Jewish Educational Process

We have tried to state an educational process which we believe to be authentically Jewish and essential to Judaism.[18] Five essentials characterize this process of education:

1. Events, ideas, and values are embodied in ritual observ-

ances. The experience of ritual observance in an integrated communal environment gives rise to a curiosity, a questioning which becomes the occasion for the adult to educate, to explain to the next generation.

2. This educative process at one and the same time increases understanding of the ritual itself and exposes the value or idea behind the ritual—leading to rededication of the coming generation to Judaism. The nature of this "educational process" is crucial to the viability of Judaism, where each generation must be rededicated (reeducated) to the enactment of deeds, which are central in Judaism.

3. *Education cannot be reduced to schooling.* As a process, education goes beyond the classroom and teacher and becomes a function of the adult religious community and its expressed values.

4. The educational process assumes and requires a *committed adult life-style* which embodies the values and behaviors it seeks to impart to the young. It is out of contact with, and exposure to, a viable Jewish *adult* life-style that the young come to ask concerning its significance.

5. The educational process described requires *specific adult models* who are accessible to the young, who personally live committed Jewish lives, and who can answer the questions of the young regarding the significance and meaning of their Jewish behaviors and values.

We began this study with a consideration of the concepts of deed *(maaseh)* and explication *(midrash)* in Jewish tradition. It should be clear that the educational system in Judaism as outlined above is essentially an amalgam of deed and explication, and that these two concepts parallel the two structures noted in our biblical investigation, as well as the two possible breakdown points in the system.[19]

Two Points of Process Breakdown and Jewish Education Today

It should be noted that within this system, there are two points of possible breakdown:

1. The inability of individuals, family, and community institutions to display a pattern of ritual behavior that will *stimulate* the next generation to ask questions.
2. The inability to explain meaningfully to the next generation when it does ask "What is the meaning of this law, ritual, norm?"

These possible breakdown points parallel the two structures which we noted in our study of biblical sources: (1) integration of individual and institution in Jewish ritual, and (2) rededication through explication of ritual.

It should be clear that most of our educational effort is concentrated around the assumption that our problem in American Jewish identity and education lies in breakdown no. 2. For the most part, American Jewish educators assume that if we write a better textbook about Jewish values, or train a teacher in how to teach Jewish holidays, or learn to decorate schools for holidays, or if we outline a new curriculum in subject matter, then we are attacking the issue of creating Jewish commitment and interest in Jewish identity among our children.

I would like to suggest that most of these efforts are directed toward the *wrong* breakdown point in the process of Jewish education. Heinemann puts the problem of Jewish education and dedication in the modern world most succinctly:

> In view of the fact that the great majority of those praying in synagogues and of those parents sending their children to Hebrew school desecrate the Sabbath, it became possible for teachers of Judaism to emphasize and vigorously teach the value of the ritual commandments without wondering whether impossible demands would lead only to alienating . . . the students. . . . The educators were thereby forced to implant in their listeners a warped picture of Judaism . . . as if its requirements were merely legal and not practical, functional demands. This was an image which radically contradicted the true image of Judaism from the days of the prophets on.[20]

Thus, we have come full circle. For the above quotation from Heinemann indicates that the *underpinnings* of the process of education we have been describing had begun to break down as the modern world came into being. The breakdown of the integration of institution and individual had rendered explanation and rationale sterile. The loss of integration and an adult Jewish life-style meant that answers were being given to questions which were no longer being asked; that the meaning of the commandments was an academic question—for the commandments, by and large, no longer functioned in the life of the individual, his family, or his Jewish community. This disintegration represents the core problem, largely unrecognized, in American Jewish education.

Again: Our Chronic Problem

Place the child in a world of his own and you take from him the most powerful incentives to growth and achievement. Perhaps one of the greatest tragedies of contemporary society lies in the fact that the child is becoming increasingly isolated from the serious activities of adults.[21]

If our chronic problem lies in breakdown no. 1, the disintegration of Jewish adult communal institutions of observance and life-style, then one must ask of Counts's 1932 statement: What does one do if there are *no* "serious activities of [Jewish] adults"? What does one do if there is not only isolation of children from the adult Jewish community but also a crisis in purpose and life-style among the mature bearers of Jewish culture? If one can document the problematic quality of Jewish life indicated by the research quoted earlier in this paper, then what meaning has the phrase "serious activities of adults" in the Jewish framework?

The problem of our youth is not youth. The problem is the spirit of our age; denial of transcendence, the vapidity of values. . . . The problem will not be solved by implanting in

the youth a sense of belonging. Belonging to a society that
fails in offering to satisfy authentic human needs will not
soothe . . . frustration and rebellion. . . . What youth needs
is a sense . . . of reverence for the society to which we all
belong.[22]

. . . drug abuse, particularly among teenagers, is usually
the result of an overdose of adolescence in a society whose
institutions have generally failed the adolescent; a society in
which family structure is in disarray, values are in confusion
and the "rites of passage" from adolescence to adulthood are
generally absent; a society in which the pleasure of "now" is
ascendent, change is a truism, and adolescents have only an
insignificant role and few places to go—except to a school.[23]

Both the Jewish theory of education suggested in this paper
and the ancient Greek concept of *paideia* held that it is the
community and the culture that educate.[24] The crisis in American Jewish education consists in this very loss of an educating
adult Jewish community and life-style. This is the factor which
makes the education (rededication) of the young so problematic, for we present no distinct, positive Jewish adult model in
our society. Without such an image of cultural and communal
Jewish adulthood, the direction, purposes, and methods of
education—schooling or otherwise—become unclear.

Some Guidelines for Redirecting Educational Energies

1. *Judaism is not for children.* It is clear that our first task is to
stop focusing our Jewish educational efforts on our children. It is not
insignificant to note that the first school institution in the
rabbinic period was the Bet Midrash. Placed next to the synagogue, it was a house of study for *adults* (teens and older).
Only upon the establishment of an adult community of learning and education did the rabbis turn to the question of
primary education.[25] Education for Jewish adult living requires
primary associational groups of committed adults living according to that life-style, so that those being educated (old or
young) may (a) participate with the adult community in that

life-style; and (b) view it as a *satisfying, viable, serious* mode of adult life for modern man. Thus, the culture must be embodied not only in larger communal structures and family groupings, but also in identifiable, face-to-face adult groups, which display the desired values and behaviors in their ongoing group life-style and provide participative experience in that culture for the young. If a life-style cannot be lived by the adult members of a culture, it certainly cannot have much value as an option for the new generation.

2. *Accessible adult models.* Education for adult Jewish living requires that there be specific *accessible* adult models of committed Jewish living, who not only model behavior, but are able to answer the questions of searching youth—regarding the significance, values, meaning, and energizing myth of that life-style. The lack of accessible, positive adult models in the Jewish community constitutes a serious problem for Jewish education. Research on behaviors, values, and cognitive structures of socializing adults, as the living *bearers* of culture and mediators of culture to the young, confirms the importance of such models in a theory of education as rededication.[26] While Mead noted the general problem of adult male identification for American boys,[27] we emphasize the special discontinuity between the Jewish life of the male child up to Bar Mitzvah and the widespread lack of committed adult Jewish male models for boys.[28]

3. *Building Jewish community and learning environments.* Understanding that the crisis in Jewish education and in American Jewish life lies in the breakdown of Jewish community and arenas of Jewish living, points to a radical reformulation of how Jewish learning takes place and what its purposes are.

Education for Jewish adulthood means that education *cannot be reduced to an isolated school context.* Since it must be relevant and functional in an adult world, *education should take place in broad, rich living contexts, rather than in narrow, specialized classrooms and isolated contexts.* Such contexts must be highly participative in nature and create bonds of *continuity* in numerous sense.

3a. *Continuity in time.* There must be a *year-round* pursuit and expression of cultural values and behaviors within the activities of the community. Secondly, the time structure of modern life has largely limited religious education to the *leisure time block* (as opposed to work and work-related time blocks).[29] Some way must be found to penetrate the world of school-work time, so that religious life-style becomes a part of that major time block in a person's life. In yet a third way, the community must reestablish time continuity and participation in the life of its members. This has to do with the great moments of the life-cycle and the calendar cycle. Moments of birth, marriage, sickness, aging, death, celebration of the cycle of the year must be reconstituted as participative moments for both community and family—as religious time.

3b. *Continuity in arenas of life.* On an individual and small-group level, this means that, to the greatest degree possible, the various arenas of living—home life, work time, leisure time, synagogue and community life, social contacts, and formal schooling—must "hang together" Jewishly, or at least not contradict or undermine the values and behaviors of a Jewish life-style. On a broader communal scale, it implies a necessity to articulate the behavior and structure of adult communal institutions with the Jewish cultural values expected of the young.

3c. *Continuity among age populations.* The various age groupings within an educative community must be bridged. There must be numerous opportunities for *joint* participation in Jewish living among youngsters, teenagers, and adults. Only through such joint participation in ritual, problem-solving, and celebration is each member of the community able to perceive the next stage of his life as offering a meaningful, attractive, and accessible Jewish life-style.

All of the tendencies in American education are antithetical to these forms of continuity. American education is highly specialized and isolated from community. It is almost synonymous with schooling and segregates youth from the world of work, the world of adult labor. It places a strong emphasis on training for the corporate system of work, and the aggregate value system of the great society. This model of American education and life has deeply affected the American Jewish notion of education and youth. The same emphasis on schooling, independent of family and synagogue, is evident. The separate treatment of childhood and youth, their isolation from adult Jewish activity in prayer, education, communal issues and problems were documented. *All of the evidence* points to a radical discontinuity and fragmentation in Jewish life—in time, in arenas of living, and in age population.[30]

While societies with a single cultural norm (such as Manus in Mead's study) may be able to afford such radical discontinuities in the life of their members, a minority culture in a world of normative pluralism *cannot* afford such discontinuities between the world of the young and the world of adult values and behaviors. *Unless the adults* of a culture are willing to live by the values and behaviors of the culture and share their lives and community in participative modes with the young, there is *no reason* for the young to opt for inclusion in that particular culture, its values, or its ethnic identity.

A Final Word

We have tried to demonstrate that most recent educational effort and energy has been misdirected and has failed to address the central problems of Jewish education and rededication today: the need for reconstruction of Jewish community around adult Jewish life-style—as a basis for further Jewish socialization, identity, and existence. We are aware of the enormous human energy, commitment, patience, and determination required to deal with this aspect of Jewish education and community. The thought that meaningful educational change involves *adult* social and communal change is an enervating one. In response to the enormity of the task and the resultant debilitating sense of despair—two comments:

The next step lies not in a more concrete plan, but in a *search for a group of people,* some "missing community," with the courage and energy to re-examine how education, most broadly conceived as the interaction between reflection and action, can invigorate the lives of all its citizens.[31]

The second is drawn from the text of the Bible:

> Balak, son of Zippor, who was king of Moab at that time, sent messengers to Balaam, son of Beor . . . saying, "There is a people that came out of Egypt; it hides the earth from view and it is settled next to me. Come then, put a curse upon this people."[32]

In spite of Balak's desire to curse Israel, the story concludes:

> As Balaam looked up and saw Israel encamped tribe by tribe, the spirit of God came upon him. Taking up his theme, he said . . . "How fair are your tents, O Jacob, your dwellings, O Israel!"[33]

This has been the abiding, eternal covenant of the Lord of Israel with the people of Israel, that the spirit of God dwells among the community of Israel; that within that community there is a power which can turn every curse into a blessing.

And if both Newmann and Oliver, in their search for the courageous "missing community," and this writer, in his affirmation that the community of Israel is that courageous "missing community," have waxed somewhat rhetorical and sermonic rather than dispassionate and objective, so be it. For education and religious communal living are both arts—not sciences. And without passion, there can be neither art nor religious community.

Notes

1. It is my opinion that the most significant, lasting work of the Jewish Theological Seminary of America's Melton Research Center has been in the field of teacher-training and enrichment rather than in the more publicized, yet less effective, materials it has published. This aspect of Melton's contribution to Jewish education deserves greater attention and emphasis.

2. More recent conferences have been held at the University of California, Santa Barbara (1980), Oberlin College (1981), and Brandeis University (1982).

3. Eli Ginzberg, "Jews in the Changing Urban Environment," *Conservative Judaism* 27, no. 4 (Summer 1973).

4. Herbert Gans, "The Origin and Growth of a Jewish Community," in *The Jews: Social Patterns of an American Group*, ed. Marshall Sklare (Chicago: Free Press, 1958 and Westport, Conn.: Greenwood Press, 1977), pp. 205-248.

5. Based upon data found in *The National Jewish Population Study* (Council of Jewish Federations and Welfare Funds, 1974) and *The 1975 Demographic Study* (Combined Jewish Philanthropies of Greater Boston).

6. Harold S. Himmelfarb, *Jewish Education for Naught: Educating the Culturally Deprived Jewish Child* (Analysis no. 57, Institute of Jewish Policy Planning and Research of the Synagogue Council of America, 1975).

7. Harold S. Himmelfarb, *Fertility Trends and Their Effects on Jewish Education* (Analysis no. 60, Institute for Jewish Policy Planning and Research of the Synagogue Council of America, November–December 1976).

8. Fred Massarik, "Intermarriage: Facts for Planning," *National Jewish Population Study* (New York: Council of Jewish Federations and Welfare Funds, 1974), and Elihu Bergman, "The American Jewish Population Explosion," *Midstream* 23, no. 8 (October 1977): 9–19.

9. Lloyd Gartner, ed., *Jewish Education in the United States: A Documentary History* (New York: Teachers College Press, 1969), see Introduction. Also see Marshall Sklare, *America's Jews*, as well as a host of American educators on the difficulties in teaching values and commitments through the agency of the school. Especially: Charles E. Silverman, *Crisis in the Classroom* (1970), and Richard H. Delone, "The Ups and Downs of Drug Abuse Education," *Saturday Review*, September 11, 1972.

10. Walter Ackermann, "The Present Moment in Jewish Education," *Midstream* 28, no. 10 (December 1972): 8.

11. This paper is a condensation of the first chapter of an unpublished doctoral thesis: Sheldon Dorph, *A Model for Jewish Education in America: Guidelines for the Restructuring of Conservative Congregational Education* (Ann Arbor, Mich.: University Microfilms, 1976).

12. Simcha Asaph, ed., *Sources in the History of Education in Israel* (Tel Aviv: Dvir Publishers, 1954), vol, II. pp. 140–141. Quoted from "The Book of Memories" of unknown authorship and date. Its authorship is attributed to

Rabbi Samuel Abuhav of Venice (d. 1694). This work appeared in print in approximately 1650. Translated from the Hebrew by S. Dorph.

13. Mishnah *Abot* 1:17.

14. Martin Buber, "Hebrew Humanism," in *The Writings of Martin Buber*, ed. Will Herberg (New York: World Publishing Co., 1956), p. 319.

15. Abraham J. Heschel, "Jewish Education," in a volume by the same author, *The Insecurity of Freedom* (Philadelphia: Jewish Publication Society, 1966), pp. 232–233.

16. The choice of the Passover ritual as a model requires some explanation. The Passover ritual is the most systematically described of the holiday rituals in the Bible (excluding the sacrificial ritual in the Book of Leviticus).

The Passover experience is a seminal one. It is used as an explanation and justification for many of the laws and rituals of the Israelites—both ethical and ceremonial.

The clearly familial and communal nature of the Passover ritual made it easily adaptable to a Judaism without the Temple cult. Indeed, early rabbinic sources record the Seder ritual in great detail.

One might speculate as to the fact that the Passover ritual might have served as a model for the development of the observance pattern of other Jewish holidays. This would require major research into Jewish sources.

For a close study of the Passover ritual, see Dorph, *Model for Jewish Education*, chap. 1.

17. The use of the words "education" and "rededication" as near synonyms require a word of explanation. In Hebrew, the root of חנך yields both "education" (חנוך) and "rededication" (חנוכה). The implication of this paper is that education is a process of rededication of succeeding generations to the value and behavior systems of Judaism.

18. For a detailed account of how these two principles of Jewish education as rededication to Judaism functioned during various periods of Jewish history, see Dorph, *Model for Jewish Education*, chap. 1.

19. The concepts of deed (*maaseh*), explication or explanation (*midrash*), and study itself (*talmud torah*), stand in a relationship of tension.

The statement of Mishnah *Abot* 1:17 ("It is not the explication of Torah which is essential, but rather the deed") establishes the decisive importance of practice in Judaism. Yet Mishnah *Peah* 1:1 states, regarding those deeds whose fruits one enjoys in this world while the principal remains to all eternity, that the deed of the study of Torah equals all others.

This tension become explicit in the Gemara, where we read, "R. Tarfon and The Elders were once reclining in the upper storey [*sic*] of Nithza's house, in Lydda, when this question was raised before them: Is study greater or practice? R. Tarfon answered: Practice is greater. R. Akiba answered, saying: Study is greater. Then they all answered and said: Study is greater, for it leads to action" (Babylonian Talmud *Kiddushin* 40b).

Throughout Jewish tradition, this tension and balance between knowledge and deed has been preserved and become a tradition of Judaism (see also

Baba Kama 17a; *Tosafot* to *Kiddushin* 40b; Joseph Hertz to Mishnah *Abot* 1:17, Behrman House, N.Y.).

20. Isaac Heinemann, *Taame Hamitzvot B'Safrut Yisrael*, vol. 2 (Israel: Jewish Agency Department of Youth, 1942), p. 183 (trans. S. Dorph).

21. George S. Counts, *Do the Schools Build a New Social Order?* (New York: Teachers College, 1932), p. 5.

22. Abraham Joshua Heschel, "Children and Youth," in *The Insecurity of Freedom*, p. 39.

23. Richard H. DeLone, op. cit., p. 30.

24. Charles E. Silberman, op. cit., p. 5. Also see G. D. Cohen, "Translating Jewish History into Curriculum: From Scholarship to Paideia—A Case Study" in *From the Scholar to the Classroom* (New York: Melton Research Center, 1977), pp. 33–58.

25. See George Foote Moore, *Judaism: In the First Centuries of the Christian Era*, (Cambridge: Harvard University Press, 1959), vol. 1, p. 213, and Louis Ginzberg, "The Jewish Primary School" in his collection *Students, Scholars and Saints* (Philadelphia: Jewish Publication Society, 1938), pp. 2–3.

26. See S. Dorph, op. cit., chap. IV; also, Robert A. LeVine, *Culture, Behavior and Personality* (Chicago: Aldine Publishing Co., 1973), pp. 61–68, and Melville J. Herskovits, *Cultural Anthropology* (New York: Knopf, 1955), especially pp. 336–338.

27. Margaret Mead, *Growing Up in New Guinea* (New York: Mentor Books, 1930), pp. 140–141.

28. The great majority of synagogue attendees, volunteer workers, enrollees in adult Jewish education, promoters of Jewish education for children are women—the mother of each family. While boys form the majority of religious school students up to age 13, girls are the majority of Hebrew High School and confirmation students past bar/bat mitzvah. See Ackermann, "The Jewish School System in the United States" in *The Future of the Jewish Community in America*, David Sidorsky, ed. (New York: Basic Books, 1973), pp. 196–210.

29. See Thomas G. Goman and Ronald S. Laura, "A Conceptual Analysis of Time Blocks and the Scope of Religious Education," in *Religious Education*, 55, no. 1 (January–February 1970): 22–29. They present an interesting and important thesis: That the effectiveness of religious education will be severely limited unless it is able to penetrate all the time blocks (including school, work, and work-preparation time). Relegating religion to another "leisure-time" activity, like football games and mowing lawns, has serious consequences for its effectiveness and relevance to life.

30. See Dorph, *Model for Jewish Education*, chap. 3.

31. Fred M. Newmann and Donald W. Oliver, "Education and Community, " *Harvard Educational Review* 37, no. 1 (Winter 1967): 104.

32. Numbers 22:4–6.

33. Numbers 24:2–4.

SPORTS AND JEWISH EDUCATION:
A Personal and Curricular Note

JOSEPH LUKINSKY

For Lou and Shirley

In the summer of 1951 I was a counselor and teacher during Lou Newman's first year as director of Camp Ramah in Wisconsin and very much involved in sports, becoming sports head (we each had many jobs in those pioneering days) in '52 and '53. I had done some work in Chicago with young baseball players, trying to relate sportsmanship and competition in an uneasy way, but the idea that Newman taught us that summer, that everything we did was potentially Jewish and educationally relevant, was a challenge and an eye opener.

Partly, I think, we were scared stiff of Newman as he walked everywhere and observed what we were doing, so serious, so rigorous, so comprehensive. None of us had met anyone like him before. Would he think that we were living up to his intense expectations? Each event of every day was a test, to show that we were part of the "in" group, the *real* educators, the idealists.

In this context I was asked to conduct a series of workshops for counselors on play and sports, including how to lead sports activities, how to teach games, how to play with kids.

I was reading at that time the work of Maurice Samuel and

Joseph Lukinsky tries not to separate his work as Associate Professor of Education at the Jewish Theological Seminary and Teachers College, Columbia University, from his fascination with the reality and metaphor of baseball. He recently served for the fourth time on the faculty of the School of Education at the Hebrew University.

especially his great neglected work, *The Gentleman and the Jew*,[1] in which Samuel portrays two opposing world-views: the ethical, peaceful, noncompetitive Jewish (or Judeo-Christian) perspective versus the ethic of the "gentleman," the ethic of the "playing fields of Eton" where the Battle of Waterloo was "won."

For Samuel, sports are pagan, as far removed as they possibly can be from the Eastern European Jewish ethic of his parents and grandparents. Growing up in England, he had been seduced by this paganism in his early years as he sought to be a real Englishman, ashamed of his greenhorn parents who knew nothing of football and rugby, standings and scores. But now, felt Samuel, sports, instead of sublimating the aggressive instincts, as claimed by those who see athletics as character-building, really exacerbate them; instead of channeling the warlike drives into peaceful pursuits, sports keep them alive until they can erupt in the greatest "sport" of all, war itself. A powerful argument was being offered by Samuel that aroused the concern of an American lover of sports, even as it penetrated to levels of consciousness of which I was just becoming dimly aware.

All around me was evidence of Samuel's argument, even in those days before the advent of Super Bowls, television, and million-dollar salaries—the violence, the commercialism, the gambling and fixing, the desire to win at any cost, the "nice guys finish last" mentality of Leo Durocher and (a bit later) the philosophy of Green Bay Packers coach Vince Lombardi's Lombardi-ism: "Winning isn't everything; it's the *only* thing." Yet, I loved what was good in sports, the physical effort, the adventure, the joy of stretching oneself beyond what seemed to be limits, the images of the great baseball heros of my boyhood—these I wasn't ready to give up so easily. I tried to present this tension at those camp training workshops back then and, somehow, over the last thirty-two years have kept coming back to the topic, over and over again, collecting mounds of material, thinking and speaking about it, conducting workshops and discussions, haunted by the possibilities and using it as a metaphor for deeper things.

In the Sixties, when I taught at Brandeis University, I tried to get at the topic again in two ways. First, I tried to work up material on the variety of themes listed in the outline included at the end of this article, which we developed at that time, along with supporting bibliographical materials. Unfortunately we never published our results, which could have been a useful crystallization, for purposes of education, of materials, including fiction, that were then beginning to appear in profusion. This was the time when the *New York Sunday Times* Sports Section started its now well-known "page two," which tries to dig deeper than the scores and the standings, for example.

At this time I was a member of the Moral Education subgroup of the TTT project (Training Teacher Trainers) at Harvard Graduate School of Education, working with my friend and colleague Stephen I. Brown (now of SUNY Buffalo) on the issue of what we called "Math and Morality" (M & M). Here the sports idea was transferred to mathematics. If we are really serious about education and values, then any field is potentially a resource, even mathematics. We were not claiming that math alone, no matter how it was taught, would make a person more ethical; that was not the point. But we thought that the way it *is* taught should not be contradictory or counterproductive, that it should be seen as potentially supportive, and, at best, even a stimulus and challenge, a resource for getting at some of the great issues of religion and morality, such as the tension between intuition and reason, empathy, awe, wonder, and paradox in the context of other resources for moral education. There was to be no attempt to distort mathematics to serve dogmatic ideological ends. It just seemed to us that looking at math from the perspective of moral education generated ideas in both that we had not realized before. The same was true about education and sports.[2]

Morris Raphael Cohen, the great philosopher of City College of New York, and a student of William James, once proposed that baseball be considered as "the American Religion," and a candidate for James's "moral equivalent to war."[3] He was speaking partly with tongue in cheek, but there was, I thought, something in what he had said. When I came to JTS in 1973, the first advanced seminar that I taught had a sports and education component. I liked very much the ideas of Johan Huizinga in *Homo Ludens*[4] (Man, the "Player") and Peter Berger in *A Rumor of Angels*,[5] who see play as enabling us to enter a different mode of time and regain the "deathlessness of childhood." These ideas seemed to me to bring us closer to the realms of religious and moral experience that we always claim to deal with in the field of Jewish education. I could not see how these resources could be overlooked in America, where sports play such a commanding role. (I write these lines on "Super Sunday," when the salaries, the brutality, and the commercialism vie with the aesthetic, the mastery, and the pursuit of excellence for a commanding position. Like it or not, it has become the great American communal event, replacing isomorphically for many the experience of going to church.)

As I continued to work on this topic, it was never far from my other professional interests. I took up the issue of the Jewish day school, where the "secular" and the "religious" strive with one another, and the talk of professionals relates to the integration of the two as well as the integration of the "total Jewish personality" (i.e., no "split thinking," wholeness, "truth is one," and all the disciplines of knowledge as a kind of "Torah in potential"). I contributed to the discourse on this topic with an address at the American Association for Jewish Education Conference on Integration in the Day School in May 1978,[6] but all along, I think, I had the image of Lou Newman prowling the camp grounds in 1951 looking for ways to make everything count.

In more recent times I have been influenced greatly by the work of Philip Phenix, especially his *Education and the Worship of God*.[7] which has become one of the best resources for the broader topic of which sports and math are subsets. His search for the "sacred-secular" is for that dimension of the everyday world and the knowledge thereof seen from the perspective of ultimate meaning.

I left Ramah after 1953 for over ten years before returning in 1964 to serve for several more summers in different capacities, so I missed the period of influence of Joseph Schwab upon the "curricularization of informal activities" in which the activities of camp life were to be approached with rigorous curricular deliberation in the same way as were formal classes. This approach was applied at that time to sports as well as other activities.[7a]

Besides the resources I have already mentioned, I also like and use those writings on specific sports which treat them in a humanistic, ethical, and aesthetic frame. The writings of Roger Angell on baseball in the *New Yorker* are especially enlightening, absolutely the best of the genre.[8] For Angell, baseball is an opportunity for transcendence, for stepping into a realm of eternal time where the game goes on forever in the "Ballpark of the Mind." I also am very moved by great sports novels, such as Mark Harris's *Bang the Drum Slowly*, which use the sports context as the setting for human drama, bordering on the domain of religious myth. I find the genre of exposé books, starting with Jim Bouton's *Ball Four*, useful in some respects, but for many reasons ultimately disappointing.

Last year (1982) I was privileged to be sent by the National Humanities Faculty to give a two-day presentation at the Akiba Academy in Philadelphia, another of the places where Lou Newman's influence has been felt by so many people. At one of the sessions we came back to the notion of sports and religious education, this time in the context of rules, rule following, rule breaking, and rule generating, comparing Leonard Koppett's amazing article on the proposed use of the zone defense in the National Basketball Association[9] with the Rambam's discussion of the rule-making process in *Hilkhot Mamrim* in *Mishne Torah*.[10] At the end of the three-hour session, which brought together teachers and students in a common inquiry, I asked a teacher who was from England and had known Maurice Samuel to take his role in a sociodrama. A student took the role of Morris Cohen, and so, in the dialogue between them and with the group, we had come full cycle.

Sports have a massive and negative impact upon American life today. Agreed. But there is still potential for meaning and significance. I thought so in 1951, and I think so now. The task seems especially relevant to those educational "places" which struggle to avoid isolationism and to bring Judaism into the world, places where it is remembered that the seal of the *Kadosh Barukh Hu* is *emet*. In this reflection I have tried to recall the curricular path that I have followed in one area in response to Lou Newman's challenge in 1951. We haven't scratched the surface yet.

Judaism and Sports
   I. Jewish view of life as contrasted with the ethos of sport
  II. The claim of sports as character builder and as "education for character"
   A. Physical fitness
     I. Noncompetitive sense
     2. As dimension of competitive sports
   B. Drugs in sports
     1. Medicine, hormones, steroids, vitamins, diet, medical treatment
     2. Hypochondria—stoicism continuum, injury, courage, "game must go on," pressure to play even with injury
   Ç. Competition
     1. Pros–cons; search for balance, winning vs. respect for person's growth, education, long-term values
     2. Effect of professionals on amateur sports, on young people, sportsmanship—losing, "nice guys finish last"; "Winning isn't everything. It's the only thing"
     3. Materialism, commercialism, models for kids, effect on kids in terms of commercialism, cynicism, violence, sportsmanship
   D. The aesthetic/religious/humanistic dimension of sport: literature of sport; awe–wonder; the loneliness of the long-distance runner
   E. New self-awareness of athletes
     1. The debunkers (Meggysey, Bouton, etc.)

F. Racism, ethnicity ("Jews in Sports")
   1. Women
   2. The promise and the reality
   3. The myth of sports
   4. Sports in *Israel*
G. Authority/democracy—the role of the coach
H. The "culture" of sports
   1. Sports as civilization
   The accompanying experiences—parasitic activities (TV, radio talk shows) gambling/politics/family (little league)
   2. Vicarious sport—spectatoritis vs. participation
   3. The aggressive/violent fan syndrome—outlet or stimulus to aggression?
III. The role of the athlete
   A. In school (identity; the nonathlete)
   B. Life as anticlimax
   C. Dead ends
   D. Narrowness, "jock" mentality
   E. Self-image
IV. The Maurice Samuel "Gentleman and the Jew" argument
   A. Two contrasting *ethics*?
   B. Life is like a game?
   C. The "rehearsal for war"

Notes

I would like to recognize the contributions of Sherry Werb Leffert, who was my research assistant at Brandeis University, and the students in my advanced education seminar at the Jewish Theological Seminary of America during the 1973–74 academic year.

1. Maurice Samuel, *The Gentleman and the Jew* (New York: Alfred A. Knopf, 1950).

2. Stephen Ira Brown and Joseph Lukinsky, "Integration of Religious Studies and Mathematics in the Day School," *Jewish Education* 47, no. 3, Fall 1979.

3. Morris Raphael Cohen, "Baseball," *City College Alumnus*, December 1980, originally written for the *Dial* in the wake of the Black Sox scandal of 1919.

4. Johan Huizinga, *Homo Ludens* (Boston: Beacon Press, 1950).

5. Peter L. Berger, *A Rumor of Angels: Modern Society and the Rediscovery of the Supernatural* (Garden City: Doubleday, 1969).

6. Joseph Lukinsky, "Integrating Jewish and General Studies in the Day School: Philosophy and Scope," in *Integrative Learning: The Search for Unity in Jewish Day School Programs*, ed. Max Nadel (New York: American Association for Jewish Education, 1980).

7. Philip Phenix, *Education and the Worship of God*, (Philadelphia: Westminster Press, 1966). See also Phillip Phenix, "Promoting Personal Development through Teaching," *Teachers College Record* 84, no. 2 (Winter 1982).

7a. Joseph Schwab, "Learning Community," in *The Center Magazine*, 8, no. 3 (May-June 1975): 30–44.

8. Roger Angell, *The Summer Game* (New York: Popular Library, 1975) and *Five Seasons* (New York: Popular Library, 1978).

9. Leonard Koppett, "Should the NBA Adopt the Zone Defense?" *New York Times*, April 4, 1978, p. 38.

10. Maimonides, *Mishne Torah, Hilkhot Mamrim*, chap. 2.

BUILDING A JEWISH COMMUNITY

ARTHUR S. ELSTEIN

The summer of 1981 marked thirty years since I first met Lou Newman at Camp Ramah in Wisconsin. It was also the year my wife and I sent our elder son, the second of three children, to Ramah in Canada for the first time. I had the distinct feeling of participating in a tradition that was itself a link in the larger chain of Jewish tradition.

Lou had come to Camp Ramah in 1951 as the new director and promptly began to revolutionize it. We spoke all summer of השיטה המתקדמית, our Hebrew equivalent for "progressive education." I do not have the literary power to describe the recollected ambiance of those glorious years without becoming maudlin and overly sentimental. Let it suffice to say that through his ability to recruit outstanding and dedicated *madrichim* and through his personal example, Lou encouraged and nurtured an environment that has had beneficial and lasting effects on many people and has contributed significantly to changing the shape of Jewish education in America for the better. These effects are still being felt and may yet change the structure of Jewish religious life and organization in America. The roots of the *Jewish Catalogs* in the Ramah experience point to what I refer to, although those books are the fruit of the work of *chanichim* some years after my generation.

Arthur S. Elstein, Ph.D., is Professor of Medical Education at Michigan State University. The coauthor of three books and numerous articles, his major professional interests are the psychology of clinical reasoning and decision making under risk and uncertainty. He is a founding member of Congregation Kehillat Israel and past president of the Society for Medical Decision Making.

I do not work professionally in the Jewish field, but it has been the major avocational commitment of my life. My vision of the potential of Jewish education has been shaped in large measure by the methods and philosophy of Lou and Shirley Newman and the people they attracted to Ramah. To have been a camper and then on the staff of the Wisconsin Ramah in the fifties, as I was, is to have participated actively in a shining educational experience, still vividly recalled. During the summer of 1982, I had the opportunity to review some of the new materials developed by the Melton Research Center, and they called to mind again the stimulation of my years at Ramah and the many links between the two organizations.

The purpose of this brief essay, however, is not to celebrate the past but to tell a story of nonprofessional Jewish life and institution building out of the mainstream of the fifteen or so urban areas where 85 percent of American Jews live. I hope to indicate the part played by Lou Newman's work in enabling a stronger Jewish community to grow in a small midwestern university town that he has, to my knowledge, never even seen.

In 1968, my wife and I moved to East Lansing, Michigan, from Boston with our then three-year old daughter. I had accepted a position on the faculty of the newly organized College of Human Medicine at Michigan State University. Except for two leaves of one year each, we have lived in East Lansing since and are raising three children. We found Jewish education to be far from what we hoped for and joined other young faculty, some of whom had also been to Ramah camps, in forming an alternative. The effort began with a Friday night cultural group and a school for young children. By 1970, it had evolved into a new synagogue with a school, and we were embarked on a long program of development. Our family has been deeply involved in these activities ever since. The synagogue has grown from twenty-five families to one hundred, with approximately ninety children now enrolled in the school. Having rented space for many years, we marked a major milestone in 1982 by purchasing our own building—an unused school building in Lansing—which we are now remodeling into a synagogue and school.

Through all these years, we have operated without full-time paid Jewish professionals. Our teachers are Jewish students at the university, from both Israel and the United States, supplemented by a few efforts from members of the congregation. The school board coordinates curriculum and works in teacher development to the extent possible, given that we all have other full-time jobs. Our *chazanim, ba'alei k'riah*, and *gabba'im* are members of the congregation, all unpaid. Rabbis visit regularly to lecture and to teach, but they do not conduct *tfillot*, we do. We have learned and are continuing to learn how to pray, learn, and live together as a small, voluntary, participatory Jewish community. In the past two years, we have organized a *chevra kadisha* which studied the laws and customs of burial and mourning, and we have introduced a level of traditional Jewish observance hitherto unknown in this community. Late in 1981, we grieved together as we buried, in shrouds and a plain pine box, a young woman who had coordinated our adult education program and had died of cancer tragically much before her time.

Yet we are not, strictly speaking, a traditional community. We counted women in our minyan and gave them aliyot as part of our organizational policy before (but not much before) the Conservative movement approved these practices. In our *divrei-torah* on Shabbat and holidays, speakers have offered historical-critical and modern literary or psychological interpretations of the text as much as they have drawn on the traditional homiletical-exegetical approach. We clearly have much in common with the writers of the *Jewish Catalogs* in the effort to find an alternative to mainstream American Judaism in the last quarter of this century.

Where do the resources and commitments for this level of Jewish activity come from? If we were a Young Israel congregation, it might not seem so atypical, but where do non-Orthodox American Jews, mostly college-educated professionals and including many university professors whose fields of expertise are not Jewish history or Jewish texts, learn to do this? The Ramah movement cannot claim all the credit, but it certainly has been a major influence, as demonstrated by the fact that a significant number of the dominant people in this institution are either former Ramah campers or are parents who are sending their children to Ramah.

In reviewing our experience in building a Jewish community, I have tried to identify what was communicated at Ramah that was so important in starting and sustaining our efforts. I can identify four elements: first, *ahavat Yisrael*, a love of the Jewish people and our civilization that makes the effort worthwhile. Second, basic Jewish skills, so that one knows how to live a Jewish life and how to create Jewish culture where it does not exist. Regrettably too few of us have these skills, and that is a problem for us. Third, a love of Jewish learning and some skill at going about it, independently if need be, with guidance when it can be had. Fourth, the consciousness that Jewish life is what we make it for ourselves and that without paid professionals, we can still live Jewishly. As our congregation grows— may it be so—we hope that we can avoid entrapment in what we perceive to be a major social and psychological problem in the large Conservative congregations characteristic of the major urban concentrations of Jewish population: by their very size, these institutions facilitate passivity and vicarious Jewish living where active involvement is needed. Such involvement is more easily attained in a smaller community, as the *havurah* movement has made eminently clear.

Of course, some members of our community are more deeply involved and others are more peripheral. Like other synagogues, our attendance peaks on the High Holy Days and falls off on Shabbat and festivals. But we do call upon each person to contribute what he or she can in skills and commitment—teaching, davening, remodeling, painting, planning, baking—and these calls are heeded more because we all know that what we do not succeed in doing will probably not be done. There are weaknesses in this approach: We are fortunate in having access to a continual stream of Jewish college students who teach in our school, but that is a mixed blessing, for we are forever replacing teachers who graduate and move on to other communities. We lack teachers who have made Jewish education a lifelong commitment, and that is a grave problem. Surely our educational program would be improved if we had such people. Yet on balance, I am struck by how much has been accomplished and the extent to which we have built a warm, meaningful Jewish environment for adults as well as children. If we ever become large enough to be able to afford full-time professional staff, we hope they will help what is good to grow and will not inadvertently diminish our involvements.

The growth of this community owes much to the legacy of the Ramah camps and to Lou Newman's contributions to Jewish education. As we try to transmit our values to our children and to increase our own understanding of our place in the Jewish tradition, his dedication to education and his faith in the human potential for good continue to inspire our work. *Ad me'ah v'esrim!*

RELIGION AND ETHICS

DAVID L. LIEBER

In his delightful spoof, *Green Pastures*,[1] Marc Connally has God observe: "All things nailed down are coming loose!" I suppose every generation has felt that way, yet this is probably more true in our time than it has been in many decades. The cynical behavior of the so-called leaders of industry and government, the selfish pressures of single-interest groups, the devil-take-the-hindmost attitude of the people who are "making it"—all have conspired to undermine the social compact which is America. Everywhere we are witnessing a drift away from genuine dialogue, from an attempt at communication between people and groups even within the same society, in favor of what is euphemistically known as "confrontation," the exercise of raw power—violent or nonviolent—to achieve one's ends. The prevalent mood seems to be expressed in the emotion-packed words of William Butler Yeats:

> Things fall apart; the centre cannot hold;
> Mere anarchy is loosed upon the world,
> . . . .
> The best lack all conviction, while the
> worst
> Are full of passionate intensity.[2]

It is no wonder, then, that many have given up on the future, that a sense of impotence, and even impending doom, is widespread in educated circles.

David L. Lieber is president of the University of Judaism, Los Angeles, California.

What we are witnessing is really the bankruptcy of techno-logical values and visions. Just as the rise of fascism and nazism brought an end to the naive faith of the nineteenth century in inevitable progress, so thoughtful people are begin-ning to realize today that there is no necessary compatability between the mounting achievements of science and technology and the basic needs of the human being. On the contrary, the former have created all kinds of problems with which we are no longer able to cope, and no satisfactory social policy has emerged to harmonize the conflicting interests which have been released.

The older ties have been completely destroyed. The Western World no longer has a stable, tradition-bound society, which for all of its faults did have a pattern of loyalties, commitments, and values. The rapidly expanding urban society requires new skills, new bodies of knowledge, high mobility, a good deal of individualism—all of which are antithetical to the traditions of the past and to the organic growth of community, which they helped mediate. In consequence, most men find themselves uprooted, alone in time, bereft of the support, assurance, and direction of a tested style of life. Without common values and symbols to unite him with his fellows, contemporary man is also alone in space. Finally, he is alone in spirit too, since he lacks a sense of continuity with the past and of moving in a desired and meaningful direction.

In premodern times, the churches and synagogues provided the cement, the integrating principle, for the developing civili-zations. This no longer seems to be the case, since they have not been able to keep up with the changing moral and spiritual needs of our society. One does not have to recall the warfare between science and religion or to review the woeful story of the church's unholy alliance with the forces of reaction in the nineteenth and early twentieth century to make the point. The fact is that even today, in spite of all the ferment taking place within them, the churches are all too often followers, rather than leaders, in facing up to the genuine moral issues of the times. Moreover, the programs they have adopted are not

qualitatively different from those advocated by secularist re-
formers, some of them avowedly Marxist in orientation. And
even those groups religiously motivated in origin, such as the
Southern Christian Leadership Conference of the late Martin
Luther King, have also been infected by the tensions and
pressures of the streets, lending themselves all too easily to
demagogic efforts in order to broaden their appeal to the
apathetic masses. Under the circumstances, one can well
understand Nietzsche's cry at the end of the nineteenth century: "God is dead."[3] "We have killed him." What Nietzsche
realized long before others was that God had died in the soul of
his contemporaries, that He had ceased to function as a significant factor in the life of Western man.

For a while it seemed that the traditional religions might be
displaced by the newer ideologies, such as racism, chauvinistic
nationalism, and communism. Each of them had a very wide
and deep appeal, providing their devotees, as they did, with a
unified world view and a program of action. They developed
all of the earmarks of the traditional religions: a body of
literature which suggested a new way of viewing human
history and its development, a class of official interpreters of
that literature and guides to the implementation of its programs, a call to action, to a fight to the death against the forces
of evil, in order to usher in the promised millennium. These
ideologies generated passionate commitment on the part of
millions and ultimately were responsible for the destruction of
the old order. They still are very much alive today, but at least
in the West, no longer seem as appealing as they once were.
Many now see them for what they are—a reversion to the
myths of primitive paganism, with their worship of crude
power and lack of respect for the human personality. Anyone
who has witnessed them in operation in the societies in which
they are dominant cannot help but be convinced that they are
incapable of developing a new, more adequate moral code for
our times. In short, none of them is a genuine response to
Nietzsche's call for a "transvaluation of values." Each leads to
the destruction of the traditional value system and its replace-

ment with the *Blut und Eisen*, the racist doctrines of the Nazis, or the "dictatorship of the proletariat" of the totalitarian Communist state.

As the fundamental values of the so-called Judeo-Christian civilization became virtually inoperative, the barbarism which in most cases had been kept in check only by a thin overlay of custom and tradition was given free rein. Man was no longer viewed as a creature of God, created in His image, whose murder brought a curse upon the earth. Rather, man was no different from any other part of nature, to be controlled and manipulated at will. His being was of no transcendent or even intrinsic value. He had only the worth that his society was willing to ascribe to him. Hence, he could be considered superfluous, even noxious, to be dispatched as efficiently and quickly as possible. Auschwitz was one result. Another was a radical form of pessimism, a total loss of faith in the possibilities of human life. Still a third was French existentialism, which attempted to overcome the nihilism generated by the collapsing world order. Essentially it accepted the absurdity of man's condition, the moral pathos of his existence as a creature adrift in a purposeless world. At the same time, it taught that man makes himself, that it is through his free choices that his values are established. Furthermore, each man is responsible not alone for himself, but for all men, because in choosing the self he wants to be, he also chooses for all of them. In other words, to choose is to affirm the value of what one is choosing, involving the affirmation of it for all men.

It was a bold effort, and in the heady days following the victory over Hitler, the existentialism of Sartre and Camus, heroes of the resistance, received wide attention. It soon became apparent, however, that it did not suffice either to provide solace for the individual who sought a transcendent meaning to his existence or, more importantly for our discussion, to offer a firm foundation for morality. It was well and good to speak of each individual as freely choosing his own moral code and willing it for others, but what, in the final analysis, distinguished that from total subjectivism? If, in fact, there were no objective standards by which these choices could be judged, assuming that none had been made in "bad faith," in what sense could one life be judged to be "better" than another, or one culture than another? How could one defend the view, for example, that Hitler was an evil genius or a madman and not the prophet of a higher form of civilization? On what grounds could one maintain that loyalty to the state did not take precedence to the promptings of one's conscience or sense of compassion?

The failure of existentialism highlights the dilemma of the modernist. From the cultural anthropologist, he has learned that moral, as well as legal, rules are the product of a given society, and though they may have validity in a particular cultural setting, they ought not to be applied to all peoples in all societies. Yet, he recognizes that unless one can appeal to some transcendent referent or "ground" of moral value, there is no way to claim that a particular course of action is morally superior to another. On the one hand, he has been infected by the cultural relativism which has grown out of his studies of history and anthropology. On the other, he yearns to anchor his values in a moral universe which transcends individual cultures and times.

This dilemma is reflected in modern moral theory, as well. Thus, in recent years, a number of moral philosophers have begun to move away from the extreme subjectivism of logical positivism and emotivism. There still are many who continue to argue that moral judgments like "It is wrong to kill" are the equivalent to the statement, "I don't like killing. Don't do it!" More and more thinkers, however, recognize that if a judgment is to be genuinely moral, it must be characterized by universality and objectivity. If I say, for example, that it is wrong to kill, I mean, first, that no one ought to kill unless there are justifiable reasons why he may do so, and second, that I am prepared to defend my judgment with relevant and valid reasons. In other words, there is such a thing as a "moral point of view" which is a necessary condition for the existence of a moral society. Unless it is taken seriously, no human society can survive, let alone provide for the satisfaction of the needs of its members. Morality, then, arises from the minimum conditions of human existence. Man's needs, his powers, his rationality, his interdependence in a world of precarious and limited goods—all require a moral code which will enable him to pursue his wants and evade the evils which everywhere are about him. He *must* be responsible if he is to survive, for without responsibility—responsiveness to the claims of others—he simply cannot live on a human plane.

Ethical theorists then go on to analyze the various components which must go into the making of a moral code. Starting with human needs and drives, they call attention to the importance of existing social forces and institutions. The latter may have to be modified or replaced, but no moral order can exist without them. Similarly, they point to the intricate relations that exist between means and ends, motives and consequences, between that which is right and that which is good. At the same time, they treat ethics as an independent discipline, maintaining, and I believe successfully, that there is *no* necessary logical connection between religion and ethics, as has so often been assumed in Western tradition.[4] And it is good that they have been able to do so, since morality is indispensible for human existence and its foundations must be secured *with or without* religion.

Yet, it is clear that morality does have to pay a price when it is sundered from a religious world-view based on Hebrew scripture. For as Henry Sidgwick concluded more than a century ago, "On empirical grounds alone, it is impossible for anyone to convince himself in the cool of his study that it is rational to sacrifice his own ultimate good for that of another." In other words, the egocentric predicament is such that both conscience and sympathy alone are not sufficient to provide a logical base for the reconciliation of one's duty with one's self-interest, when one's very life is at stake.[5] The alternative, then, at the very best, is that of an enlightened type of selfishness or the positing of a special kind of intuition concerning the good. The former will not do so, since there are times when there is a conflict between satisfying one's own deepest needs and purposes and those of society. The latter, the method of intuition, is too idiosyncratic, too much conditioned by our upbringing, to lead to the establishment of principles which will be universally acceptable. The third possibility is that of basing everything on a subjective, existential kind of personal decision, which, in the final analysis, we have already seen to be both anarchic and irrational. Whichever of the three alternatives one selects, the felt moral imperative itself comes to underline the tragedy of human existence—the wide cleavage between man, who is a valuing, aspiring creature, and the blind universe, which grinds on endlessly without any concern for him or his values. For both of these reasons, then—the desire to ground morality on what appears to be ultimate considerations and the deeply felt need to view it as an expression of a cosmic order which governs all things—thinkers have for centuries looked for a conceptual tie between religion and ethics. At the same time, those who, like Sidgwick, felt compelled to give up the theistic faith of their fathers were unable to free themselves from the conviction that at bottom ethics could not be rationalized without it.

Despite these considerations, the dominant view in moral theory today is that from a logical point of view, morality is and must remain autonomous. That is to say, contemporary philosophers maintain that moral conclusions cannot be deduced from premises which are entirely nonmoral. Even so sympathetic a critic as William Frankena, who is prepared to allow for a very broad definition of justification when it comes to justifying ethical conclusions, one which is not strictly bound by the canons of logic, argues that nonreligious considerations may suffice to do so.[6]

It seems important, then, to determine not whether ethics can do without religion, for it appears that it can, but what dimension, if any, the religious life can add to the ethical, at a point in history when moral nihilism has become so rampant. It will not do, then, to identify the two, as religious modernists are so fond of doing,[7] for if there is no significant difference between the two, the secular humanists are right; we have no need for the extra baggage of religion! The important point is that religion adds another dimension to life, the dimension of faith—faith that the universe is constituted in such a way that it is not futile to pursue moral ideals, that events will not frustrate our moral strivings.[8] That faith is derived from seeing *"what* and *how* man is in the world,"[9] in a way other than the arts and sciences enable us to see him. It sensitizes us to the qualities that are possible in human life and culture, in a way that no other mode of perceiving existence can do. It does so when it provides us, who are conditioned by time and space, with a mode of judging ourselves and our world as we reach out to the sacred, to that which transcends time and space, through the use of the various arts and symbolic forms, moral reflection and action.

It is precisely because the ancient Israelites had such a way of looking at the world and relating to it that they were the first to develop a sense of the sacred—of the awesome majesty and power of the divine—as the source of the moral law and its ground. This is what Buber meant, it seems to me, when he argued that to understand the relationship between religion and ethics one must not simply compare their teachings, but rather must seek to "penetrate into that area within each sphere where they become solidified in a concrete personal situation,"[10] for the two are interrelated not alone in their fruits, but in their roots.

This is again illustrated by what happened in ancient Israel to transform one of the numerous Near Eastern peoples into God's "peculiar possession." From what we can gather, their ancestral ways, their mores, were not significantly different from those of their neighbors, until they were transformed by a flaming vision, by the faith that they had been elected by the God of history to serve His own special purposes, and by the covenant which they subsequently entered into to be obedient to Him and His Torah. This faith then released a powerful propulsion, which led to the radical revision of their Near Eastern heritage and the ultimate development of the Judaism that we know. Responding to the call to become "a kingdom of priests and a holy nation," their descendants fashioned a community in which the lofty values of the prophets were translated into a daily regimen in which morality occupied a central position, in which mundane activities were transformed into an outreach for the divine. A similar process can be demonstrated to have taken place in other societies as well, when at different periods of history religious regeneration enabled their members to transcend the moral ideals which had failed them, in favor of higher moral standards and goals.

Unique and complex situations often challenge the highest socially approved norms and ideals, and it is precisely at a time such as that when the moral resolve must be strengthened, even as its limited vision is transcended. Otherwise, one is faced with a grim choice between the twin evils of reaction and anarchy, a blind refusal to recognize new realities, and an equally blind lashing out at all that the human race has achieved. The moral community is shattered and the rule of the jungle established. One then speaks of "power" rather than "rights," of "interests" and "desires" rather than "responsibilities."

This is clearly the situation we are beginning to find ourselves in today, and there is no telling where and when it will end. A long time ago, we were warned that a civilization based on the growth of material power alone must break down, as ours has, for want of a coherent core of values that unites its members. If it is to be restored, the values it promotes cannot merely be translated into a set of abstract moral principles. A man may know his duty cerebrally, but unless his passions are enlisted on the side of his knowledge, he will remain selfish and mean in his behavior. What we need is not only *understanding* of the good, but *devotion* to it. Without this devotion, a man's attitude will remain egocentric or his efforts will be only half-hearted. Only when he acquires a profound emotional conviction about his ideals will he be lifted out of his routinized existence and his entire life be transformed and integrated.

This, in part, is what religion is all about; namely, finding a vision deep and realistic enough to guide us safely in this age of monstrous tensions, and persuasive enough to help us make the arts of life prevail over the prodigious techniques of death. But how do we "get" this kind of religion in our cold, abstract, and impersonal society? One answer, surely, lies in the development of religious communities in which warm, intimate human relations are able to live. It was in such communities that human beings first learned the ways of fellowship. It was in them that they developed the capacity for personal communion, which is, I believe, the main psychological source of religion. Here, men of genius created the great religious symbols and myths of the human race. Here, too, they learned to commune with that which was deep and mysterious and beyond, to call it God and to think of it in human terms.

It is no accident, then, that religion uses the language of face-to-face community; that it speaks of love, brotherhood, and the fatherhood of God. It is no accident, also, that the higher religions seek to project these concepts to the widest possible scope; to take the love cultivated in the most intimate groups and extend it to the widest circles the human imagination can trace in the hope that the day will come when all of mankind will be united in one community in the service of God. Only in such a community will genuine unity prevail, for the longings of the individual will be fulfilled in an open and free mutuality with his fellow man.

Religion at its best, then, enables man to break out of the bonds of his egocentricity, to transcend the narrowness of his parochial ideas, committing himself to a force, or a being, or a process that men call God, to enable him to attain to the highest possible good. As such, it keeps him from absolute commitment to any limited good and releases him from bondage to any relative value. It establishes a demand for righteousness far beyond the socially accepted standards of any time and place, breaking down human arrogance and opening the gates of forgiveness to all. It establishes a bond between men vastly deeper than personal affection or kinship, mutual interest or shared ideal, as they view themselves as active participants in the moral order of the universe. It does not ignore the depths of the evil that exists in the world, but, at the same time, it keeps men and women from being demoralized by it, holding before them the possibility of a creative transformation which they can neither foresee nor bring about exclusively through their own efforts.

To be sure, pragmatic usefulness is no argument for the truth of religion. Nor can the fact that ethics cannot be fully rationalized without it establish its claims.[11] Still, as this paper suggests, there is more to religion than a few outworn dogmas or rituals. On the contrary, its perennial appeal is due to the fact that it strikes a responsive chord in the human heart. Many centuries ago, a prophet of Israel exclaimed, "The righteous shall live by his faith,"[12]—not by his father's faith, but by *his* faith—a faith which transfigures his difficulties and gives him the courage to meet them. It is this kind of faith that we require today, and to its cultivation we must devote ourselves.

Notes

1. Marc Connally, *Green Pastures* (New York: Farrar, Straus & Giroux, 1929).

2. In "The Second Coming," quoted by Archibald MacLeish, *Poetry and Experience* (Boston: Houghton Mifflin, 1961), p. 140.

3. *Di Fröhliche Wissenschaft*, bk. 3, 125, in *Werke* II (Salzburg: Das Bergland Buch, n.d.), p. 599.

4. Cf. W. K. Frankena, "Is Morality Logically Dependent on Religion," in *Religion and Morality*, ed. G. Outka and J. P. Reeder (New York: Doubleday, 1973), pp. 295–317.

5. Cf. his so-called dualism of practical reason in *The Methods of Ethics* (London: Macmillan, 1907).

6. Frankena, op. cit., p. 316.

7. For a history of this trend in modern Jewish thought, cf. N. Rotenstreich, *Jewish Philosophy in Modern Times* (New York: Holt, Rinehart & Winston, 1968).

8. Cf. R. M. Hare, "The Simple Believer," in *Religion and Morality*, ed. G. Outka and J. P. Reeder (New York: Doubleday, 1973), pp. 393–427.

9. W. A. Avnett, *Religion and Judgment* (New York: Appleton-Century-Crofts, 1966), p. 141 et passim.

10. "Religion and Ethics," in *The Eclipse of God* (New York: Harper & Bros., 1952), p. 128.

11. For the contrary view, cf. R. M. Green, *Religious Reason* (New York: Oxford University Press, 1978).

12. Habakkuk 2:4.

THE RAVISHING OF DINAH:
A Commentary on Genesis, Chapter 34*

NAHUM M. SARNA

Having returned, at last, to his native land after a prolonged absence filled with trials and tribulations, the aged patriarch no doubt looks forward to spending his remaining years in relative calm and comfort. But his serenity is shattered by a fresh series of misfortunes, the first of which is the ravishing of his only daughter, Dinah, by the infatuated son of the ruler of the neighboring city-state of Shechem. The affair results in an assault on its population by Jacob's sons. The survival of the clan is thereby imperiled.

This narrative exemplifies, once again, a major theme of the patriarchal stories, namely, the sexual depravity of the inhabitants of the land. This has been illustrated by the accounts of Lot and the men of Sodom, and by the repeated threats to the matriarchs Sarah and Rebekah. The "Helen of Troy" motif, discussed in the Comment to 12:11, is here vividly represented.

The juxtaposition of the present narrative to the previous one creates an impression of rapid chronological sequence, although no time indication is given in the text. However, it is clear that Jacob must have spent several years in the neighborhood of Shechem prior to the incident now related, otherwise

*This is a chapter from the forthcoming *Commentary to the Torah* to be published by the Jewish Publication Society of America. Nahum M. Sarna is the General Editor and Chaim Potok is the Literary Editor of the Series. The copyright is held by the JPSA, and no part of this chapter may be reprinted in whole or in part without the written permission of the Society.
Nahum M. Sarna is the Golding Professor of Biblical Studies at Brandeis University.

Dinah and her two brothers would have been far too young to have played the roles here assigned to them.

Vv. 1–7 *The Violation of Dinah*

1. Dinah] The information about her parentage is already
    known from 30:21. It is repeated to clarify the singular
role of Simeon and Levi (v.25). They were her full brothers.
went out] Girls within the nubile age group would not nor-
    mally leave a rural encampment to go unchaperoned
into an alien city. By implication, the text draws critical attention to Dinah's unconventional behavior through use of the
verbal stem y-ṣ-ᶜ, "to go out." Like its Akkadian and Aramaic
equivalents, it can connote coquettish or promiscuous conduct.
the daughters of the land] This phrase too carries undertones
    of disapproval, as is clear from 24:3, 37 and other pas-
sages.
Shechem son of Hamor] In 33:19, Josh. 24:32, there is reference
    to "the sons of Hamor." Judg. 9:28 indicates that in the
period of the Judges, the Hamorites were regarded as pure-
blooded aristocrats, the remnant of the ancient Shechemite
nobility. The term *ḥamor* means "ass." As was noted in the
Comment to 15:9, "to kill a donkey foal" means "to conclude a
covenant" in the Mari texts. Hence, "sons of Hamor" may be a
term for "those bound together by treaty," "sons of a confederacy." The city-state of Shechem appears to have had a mixed
population. It may well have originated through a confederacy
of several ethnic groups.
the Hivite] See Comment to 10:17.
chief of the country] —not "the city," because the city-state of
    Shechem in pre-Israelite times extended its control over
a vast area that at one time included the central hill country as
far as the borders of Jerusalem and Gezer to the south and
Megiddo to the north, a domain of about 1000 sq. miles.
Egyptian and Akkadian texts reflect this situation. Thus, the
inscription of Khu-Sebek about the Asiatic campaign of Sen-
Usert III (Sesostris III, ca. 1880–1840 B.C.E.) reports, "His majesty reached a foreign country of which the name was Shechem

(Sekmem)." An Amarna letter similarly refers to "the Land of Shechem."

Hamor's title "chief"(*nasi'*) is unique. The head of a Canaanite city-state is otherwise generally termed "king." The peculiarity reflects political and historical reality. The ruler of Shechem has dominion over both rural, that is, tribal, territory, as well as the urban center, in this case a confederacy of various ethnic elements. Such a complex situation does not permit absolute power. Indeed, Hamor does not act like a king. He has to call a town meeting to lay his plans before the citizens, and he obtains their approval by means of persuasive argument, not by coercion or fiat.

2. took . . . lay . . . force] Three Hebrew verbs of increasing severity underscore the brutality of Shechem's assault on Dinah.

3. drawn . . . love . . . spoke] Three expressions of affection correspondingly describe his feelings after the deed. Unlike the case of Amnon, whose spent passion quickly turns into intense hatred of his victim (2 Sam. 13:15), Shechem is hopelessly enamored of Dinah.

4. to his father] Marriage arrangements were customarily negotiated by a parent on behalf of the son.

"Get me"] Lit., "take for me," the same Heb. stem *l-k-ḥ* as is used in v. 2 for the abduction. This "taking" is to make amends for the other.

5. that he had defiled] The subject is Shechem of v. 4. The dastardly act is now defined in religio-moral terms, a judgment reiterated in vv. 13, 27. Even more than the terrible offense against the person and dignity of the girl, and the assault upon the honor of the family, is the pollution of the moral environment. The entire community becomes infected by such wanton deeds.

Jacob kept silent] The need to exercise restraint, pending the arrival of his sons, is understandable, but his passivity throughout the entire incident is remarkable.

6. Apparently, Hamor arrives before the brothers and is left cooling his heels until they come home. Shechem has accompa-

nied his father, but judiciously remains in the background until it is opportune for him to enter the picture.

came out] —the same verbal stem used for Dinah's action in v. 1. This second "going out" is intended to ameliorate the disastrous consequences of the first.

to speak to him] —to enter into negotiations leading up to marriage.

7. having heard the news] Apparently, Jacob urgently summoned his sons.

an outrage] Heb. *nebalah* is a powerful term overwhelmingly used of abhorrent offenses of such enormity that they seriously threaten to tear apart the fabric of Israelite society. For society's own self-protection, such atrocities can in no circumstances be tolerated, and cannot be perpetrated with impunity.

Israel] Strictly speaking, this is an anachronism. The idea is that those sacred, inviolable norms that constituted the moral underpinnings of the later people of Israel were already operative at this time.

a thing not to be done] —not in Israel, nor in any civilized society.

Vv. 8–12 *The Speeches of Hamor and Shechem*

The legal situation is quite unclear, and the ancient Near Eastern law collections offer little help. Only the Middle Assyrian laws (A. § 55) treat of the rape of an unbetrothed virgin. The offender must compensate her father a fixed amount in silver over and above the bride-price for virgins, and the father can decide whether or not to let his daughter marry her violator. This is practically identical with the law of Exod. 22:15–16, which prescribes that the ravisher must take his unbetrothed victim to wife unless her father decides otherwise. Either way, he must pay the bride-price for virgins. In the present instance, the question arises whether Jacob, an alien semi-nomad, could claim redress against the ruler of the city. Hamor deals with the family only on account of his son's amorous and matrimonial interests. He completely omits any mention of the crime, as though nothing has happened! Actually, the terms offered by Hamor are quite unrelated to the immediate and stated purposes of his visit. They are clearly a cunning appeal to avarice as a means of placating Jacob and his sons, purchasing their docility and inducing them to let bygones be bygones. The presumed effectiveness of the strategy is reinforced by the intimidating reality that Dinah is still being held in Hamor's house within the city (vv. 17, 26). When Hamor is through, the aggrieved family is considered to be sufficiently mollified for Shechem to present himself. He too ignores his crime, and offers neither apology nor regrets. He does, however, intimate a willingness to pay generous compensation.

10.   move about] This seems to be the basic meaning of the stem s-ḥ-r. It would imply unlimited grazing rights. But the term could just as well be used in its developed sense of "to trade, barter," which is how the ancient versions render it.

acquire holdings] This last is the most valuable of the privileges offered, even as it is also a subtle and pointed reminder to Jacob of his present alien and disadvantaged position.

12.   bride-price . . . gifts] Heb. mohar, mattan, From Exod. 22:16 and 1 Sam. 18:25, it is clear that mohar can only be a technical term for the payment made by the prospective husband in return for the bride. It would correspond to the Akk. tirḫatum, discussed in the Comment to 24:53. The amount is usually fixed by custom. Shechem's indicated readiness to pay far beyond that constitutes a tacit recognition of the need to make reparations.

The second term would appear to correspond to the Akk. biblum, the ceremonial gifts made to the bride's family, called migdanoth in 24:53. An Akkadian marriage document from Alalakh records: "In accordance with the custom of the city of Aleppo, he [the groom] brought him [the bride's father] a betrothal gift (nidnu)." Heb. mattan is the cognate of nidnu, and probably here refers to the same thing.

Vv. 13–17 *The Brothers' Response*

Outwardly polite, Hamor, in effect, has besmirched the characters of Jacob and his sons. He has, by inference, attributed to them a sordid, mercenary, concern that outweighs all other considerations. He has thus added insult to injury. Accordingly, in their reply the brothers first address themselves to the business at hand, Shechem's desire to marry Dinah. They make clear that the prerequisite of circumcision is more important to them than all material allurements.

13–14.   The brothers' response is introduced by three expressions of speech as a counterpoint to the three terms used for Shechem's assault on Dinah and the three terms of affection (vv. 2–3).

with guile] The narrator informs us at once that the brothers' seeming acceptance of intermarriage with the Shechemites is merely a ruse. No moral judgment is intended. It would, in fact, be gratuitous. The victim of the assault is still being held by the perpetrator (vv. 17, 26), who has not even admitted to a crime, let alone expressed regret. There is no way that Dinah can be liberated by a tiny minority in the face of overwhelming odds except by the exercise of cunning.

he had defiled] We are reminded of the enormity of the offense in order to place the "guile" in proper perspective.

their sister] —so again in v. 27, in contrast to vv. 1, 5, which describe Dinah as Jacob's daughter. The phrase functions both to dissociate Jacob from their plans and to stress the special obligation that devolves upon brothers in this type of society.

14.   uncircumcised] Although the institution of circumcision is here used as a device by which to immobilize the males, there can be no doubt that the stipulation reflects normative practice among the tribes of Israel. Gen. 17:9–14 makes circumcision the indispensable precondition for admittance into the community of Israel, and Exod. 12:43–49 logically forbids an uncircumcised male to participate in the passover sacrifice.

It should be noted that the speech of the brothers is heavy with irony. The offending member through which the violence of Shechem's carnal passion found expression is itself to become the rod of his own punishment!

17. we will take our daughter] —once again the stem *l-k-ḥ*, as in vv. 2, 6. Its use has an ominous ring about it.

Vv. 18–24 *The Response of the Shechemites*

For his son's personal gratification, Hamor has unilaterally agreed to conditions that make grueling demands upon his fellow citizens. He must therefore win their approval, and he does so by insisting that his proposals are only meant to advance the material well-being of the city. Of course, Hamor and Shechem do not disclose their private, selfish, interest in the matter.

19. lost no time] The text is anticipating developments in order to indicate Shechem's furious ardor. He could hardly have appeared at the public assembly had he just been circumcised.

the most respected] He served as a role-model for the others, who were soon influenced by his initiative.

20. public place] Lit., "the gate," which served as the civic center. See the Comment to 19:1; 23:10.

their fellow townsmen] Lit., "the men of their city," the popular assembly of free citizens who must rule on major items of public business, such as the granting of special privileges to an alien group. Similar urban political institutions with the same name are well documented in the Amarna texts for several city-states in the Syro-Canaanite area.

21. our friends] The reference may well be to some existing treaty arrangement between the city of Shechem and the clan of Jacob. City-states that dominated a wide area usually regulated their relationships with the nomadic groups within their domain by formal treaties.

23. Conveniently forgotten by Hamor is the promise of landed property rights for the newcomers; perfidiously inserted is the assurance of dispossessing them of their belongings. Seeing that the occasion is a formal, public ratification of

the agreement, it is clear that Hamor has been guilty of double-dealing and is acting dishonorably.

24.   The citizens who comply with the terms are described as "All who went out of the gate of his town." In the case of Abraham's negotiations with the Hebronites, reported in 23:10, 18, the involved citizenry is designated "all who entered the gate of his town." The distinction, if any, is unclear. Each phrase may be an ellipsis for, "All who go out and enter . . . ," i.e., all free citizens. Another, more probable, suggestion is that "go out" is short for "go out to war." The verb *y-ṣ-ᶜ* is used in such a context in 2 Kings 5:2; Amos 5:3. This would encompass the males of military age, the group available for intermarriage with Jacob's clan. Support for this interpretation may be found in vv. 25, 29, which show that only adult males were slain. Incidentally, the use of *y-ṣ-ᶜ* forms an associative link with vv. 1, 6, extending the chain of events that issued from Dinah's original "going out."

Vv. 25–29 *The Punitive Action*

The ruse works. The able-bodied males are incapacitated. Two of Dinah's brothers slaughter them and rescue their sister. The other brothers plunder the city.

25.   On the third day] By now, all the males have been
          circumcised.

Simeon and Levi] These were Dinah's full brothers, who would
          feel her molestation and humiliation all the more keenly.

took each his sword] —to avenge the violence of Shechem,
          who "took" Dinah (v. 2).

unmolested] Heb. *betaḥ* may connect with the verb to mean
          "meeting no resistance" or "confidently," or it may refer
to the state of the city, "unsuspecting, caught off guard."

26.   took Dinah . . . went away] The entire affair began with
          Dinah "going out" and being "taken" (v. 1, 2). It concludes with the same two verbs, but in reverse order. As far as Simeon and Levi are concerned, the account is settled. These two take no part in the plunder of the city.

27.   The other brothers desisted from carnage but now seize

the opportunity to pillage. The city itself is not destroyed.

because] The narrator is at pains to stress that the brothers
were stirred to action because of the defilement of their
sister, not simply for the love of loot.

28–29.   The passage balances v. 23. Instead of the Hivites
appropriating the possessions of the sons of Jacob, their possessions pass into the hands of their intended victims.

Vv. 30–31 *Jacob's Reaction*

Jacob now intervenes for the first time to berate Simeon and
Levi for recklessly jeopardizing by their actions the very survival of the entire clan. No indication is given here as to how he
relates to the larger moral issue that innocent people are
punished for the crimes of a few. On his deathbed Jacob
strongly censures Simeon and Levi for acts of violence and
cruelty:

> Simeon and Levi are a pair;
> Their weapons are tools of lawlessness.
> Let not my person be included in their council,
> Let not my being be counted in their assembly.
> For when angry they slay men,
> And when pleased they maim oxen.
> Cursed be their anger so fierce,
> And their wrath so relentless.
> I will divide them in Jacob,
> Scatter them in Israel.
>
> (Gen. 49:5–7)

While there is no certainty that the reference is to the assault on
the city of Shechem, it seems probable, although the text
would then suggest excesses on the part of the two brothers
not recorded or hinted at in the present narrative.

30.   brought trouble] The Hebrew phrase is literally an ellipsis
for "muddy the waters," figuratively used for "disturb
the peace, cause trouble."

making me odious] —ellipsis for "making my breath to stink."
the Perizzites] See Comment to 13:7. According to Josh. 11:3;
     17:15, this people occupied the central hill country, that
is, the region of Shechem.
31.   The two brothers have the last word. As with the Book of
Jonah, the closing rhetorical question provides an irresistible
argument. The women of Israel are not to be objects of abuse.
They cannot be dishonored with impunity.

Notes

Introduction

The details of the chronological problem are as follows: Jacob
found himself married to Leah at the end of the seventh year of
a twenty-year term of service with Laban (29:20–23; 31:41).
Since Dinah was Leah's seventh child (30:21), she must have
been born, at the earliest, six years before Jacob headed home,
although 29:35 suggests she was very likely not more than five
years old at the time. If we allow for a two-year interval until
Jacob arrived at Shechem, Dinah would have been seven or
eight. Simeon and Levi, Leah's second and third sons, who
slaughter all the males in the city, would have been respectively fourteen and thirteen. It should be noted that Jacob
refers to the tender age of his children when he meets with
Esau (33:13). All this makes it hardly likely that the events of
this chapter occurred soon after the arrival at Shechem.
     According to 30:22, Joseph and Dinah were about the same
age. When Joseph was sold into slavery, he was seventeen
years old (37:2), by which time the family had moved away
from Shechem. This allows for a ten-year interim between
Jacob's arrival at and latest possible departure from Shechem,
sufficient time for Dinah to have become a mature, nubile
young lady and her two brothers grown men.

1. Dinah] So Naḥm.
went out] Cf. postbiblical *yoṣ'eth ha-ḥuṣ, yᵒlaṣ'anith*, "a wanton

woman, a gadabout," Akk. *waṣû*, "to exhibit promiscuous behavior"; Aram. *nafqa'/h*, "a prostitute"; cf. Rashi, "She
was a gadabout."
daughters of the land] So 27:46; 28:1, 6, 8.
2. chief of the country] For Khu-sebek, see ANET, p. 230; for
    Amarna, EA 289:22–24, ANET p. 489 (*māt šakmi*). The
usual title is "king"—Gen. 14:2, 18; 20:2; 26:1; Num. 20:14; 21:1,
21, 26, 33; 22:9; esp. Josh. 12 *passim*. For *nasi'* as tribal chief, cf.
Gen. 17:20; 25:16; Num. 1:16; 7:2; 25:18; Josh. 13:21. The frequent use of *nasi'* in Ezekiel (12:10; 19:1; 21:17; 27:21; 32:29, etc.)
is a special case resulting from contemporary geopolitical realities and his own ideology.
force] Heb. *va-ye'anneha*. The stem denotes maltreatment, hu-
    miliation, as is clear from Gen. 15:13; 16:6; 31:50; Exod.
1:11–13; 22:21–22. It is especially used in connection with
sexual offenses; cf. Deut. 21:14; 22:24, 29; Judg. 20:5; 2 Sam.
13:12; 14, 22; A rabbinic tradition in Yoma 77ᵇ, Gen. R. 80:4
interprets the present usage as implying unnatural intercourse.
Note that the order of the second two verbs is the reverse of
that in 2 Sam. 13:14.
4. to his father] Cf. Gen. 21:21; 24:1–4; 28:8 f.; 38:6; Josh. 15:16
    f.; Judg. 4:2; 1 Sam. 18:17, 19, 21, 27; 25:44.
"Get me"] For *l-k-ḥ*, "to take a wife," cf. 19:14; 24:3, 4, 7, 37, 38,
    40, 67; 25:1; 27:46; 28:2, 6, 9; 38:1.
to speak to him] Cf. Judg. 14:7; 1 Sam. 25:39; Cant. 8:8.
7. having heard the news] So Josh. Ant. 1:xxi: 1, p. 163. Gen. R.
    80:5 raises the possibility of connecting the phrase with
the following clause, thus interpreting the text to mean that the
brothers only heard about the affair when they happened to
return home.
outrage] Cf. Deut. 22:21; Josh. 7:15; Judg. 19:23–24; 20:6, 10;
    2 Sam. 13:12; Jer. 29:23.
not to be done] So Gen. R. 80:5, Rashi.
10. move about] Targs., LXX, Vulg. "trade."
17. We will take our daughter] Cf. Targ. J., "We shall take by
    force."
25. On the third day] So Joseph Kara, Hizk.
unmolested] The first possibility is supported by LXX, Gen. R.

80:9, Rashi, Radak, the second by Targ. O. and Targ. J.,
Rashb., Bekh. Sh., Shadal; cf. Judg. 8:11; 18:27; Ezek. 30:9.
30. brought trouble] Cf. Gen. R. 80:10. For the verb, cf. Josh.
6:18; 7:25; 1 Sam. 14:29; 1 Chron. 2:7.
odious] So Rashb.; cf. Exod. 5:21.

Excursus to Chapter 34

The narrative, for which there exist no extrabiblical sources,
features several unusual items that suggest traditions of great
antiquity. The first is that it contrasts with the general picture
of peaceful relationships between the patriarchs and the local
peoples. Then, Levi is a secular, warrior figure in contradistinc-
tion to the later image of the tribe bearing that name as being
dedicated to priestly and religious duties, and playing no
military role in the wars of conquest. The martial image of
Simeon is also out of accord with later developments. This tribe
early lost its independence, was swallowed up by Judah, and
became insignificant (Josh. 19:1, 9; Judg. 1:3). The Song of
Deborah ignores it (Judg. 5). The alliance of Simeon and Levi is
unparalleled. Strangely, Reuben and Judah, also full brothers
to Dinah, are not mentioned by name as being specially concerned with vindicating their sister's honor.

These singular, anomalous, aspects of our story militate
against a late fictional account. For this, a late author would
surely have drawn upon the conventional, familiar data in
order to impart it an air of verisimilitude. The conclusion
suggests itself that Gen. 34 records an incident that belongs to
the prehistory of the Israelite tribes, the period prior to Joshua's
wars of conquest. This is strengthened by the reference to
Shechem as a "country," a designation that makes sense only
in terms of conditions prevailing in that era, as the Comment to
v. 2 demonstrates. Similarly, the ruler's not being accorded the
title "king," usually given to the heads of the Canaanite city-
states in the Torah and in Joshua-Judges, is another indication
of authenticity. The narrator was obviously familiar with a
special political reality.

It is to be noted that the narrative speaks only of the fortunes of a family, of individuals within it, not of tribes. But it is difficult to understand the terms of the agreement with the Hivites unless one is dealing with a much larger unit than Jacob and his sons. Given the ages of the latter, how meaningful is the pledge to give their daughters in marriage to the men of the city (vv. 9, 16, 21)? The possibility exists that the characters of the story are really personifications, corporate personalities, much as John Bull and Uncle Sam respectively represent the English and American peoples. The actual presence of this phenomenon in the Torah is abundantly illustrated by the Testament of Jacob in Gen. 49, in which the individual and the tribe imperceptibly merge. Seen in this light, Gen. 34 would be an account of an assault upon Shechem by Israelite tribes in a very early period. Such an interpretation is of special interest because, as a matter of fact, the history of that city in relation to Israel is shrouded in mystery.

The Hebrew sources have preserved no traditions about the Israelite occupation of this city by force. The silence is wholly surprising in view of Shechem's strategic importance as the natural capital of the central hill country, lying at the intersection of major arteries of communication. Its unusually large size and its historic role, as evidenced by Egyptian and Amarna texts, not to mention the fact that it was the first Canaanite city at which Abraham stopped over when he arrived in the country, the site where he built his first altar, the place where he first received the divine promises of nationhood and territory, make it inconceivable that a successful campaign against this city by Joshua would not have been recorded, had it occurred. Further to confound matters is the absence of Shechem from among the several notices about still-unconquered Canaanite enclaves (Josh. 13:13, 15:63, 16:10, 17:11–13; Judg. 1:21, 27–33). As a matter of fact, archaeology does not support any devastation of Shechem in the Late Bronze period or early Iron Age when so many Canaanite cities mentioned in Joshua show signs of violent destruction.

Despite all this, we find reports that Joshua built an altar and conducted a solemn national ceremony in the environs of

Shechem, and that he assembled all the tribes of Israel at that city for a rite of covenant renewal (Josh. 8:30–35, cf. Deut. 11:26–32, ch. 27; Josh. 24). In other words, Shechem is found to be in Israelite hands in Joshua's day, but how it came to be so is an enigma.

It is not possible to claim that Gen. 34 represents the story of its capture, for the clan of Jacob fled the place immediately after the assault. Nor can it be argued that Joshua occupied and rebuilt a city that had all the while been in ruins. This is contradicted by both archaeological research and by our own story, which says nothing about the devastation of Shechem itself. The only feasible solution is that Shechem was taken over gradually by peaceful infiltration. Indeed, the story of Judg. 9 supports a theory of symbiotic relationship between the Canaanites and Israelites until the city was destroyed by Abimelech in the period of the Judges. Indeed, the archaeological remains testify to the violent destruction of Shechem during the second half of the twelfth centruy B.C.E. (cf. Judg. 9:45), after which it lay in ruins for about two hundred years.

In sum, the narrative of Gen. 34 has preserved authentic historical traditions deriving from preconquest times, and cannot be used to sustain a theory of the retrojection of later events back into the patriarchal period.

TRADITION AND EXPERIENCE IN THE BOOK OF JOB

NAHUM M. WALDMAN

Introduction

The number of different interpretations of the Book of Job is legion. Understanding the interchange of views in the book is complicated by literary problems; arguments for unity of authorship must compete with evidence of multiple authorship and a complex editorial process.[1] In this paper we shall view the question of unity or diversity of authorship as of less importance than the fact that the book before us is a collection of views, a kind of symposium on human suffering and the justice of God.

I would like to suggest that the philosophical concerns of the Book of Job are inseparable from the educational ones. One cannot divorce the contents of a world-view from the process by which it is acquired and then maintained when challenged by other hypotheses. Education involves the effort to construct a realistic and integrative view of the world, based upon what is learned (drawing upon the experiences of others) and upon what is personally experienced. When these clash we must find a new integration of what is valid in the thesis and in the antithesis. Tradition must not squelch discovery, but a personal

Dr. Nahum M. Waldman is Professor of Bible and Hebrew Literature at Gratz College, Philadelphia. He is the author of numerous articles on Hebrew literature and on parallels and affinities between Hebrew and Akkadian.

truth must not become so egocentric as to obliterate the results of accumulated culture or new experience.

The Book of Job contains world-views which have emerged as a result of challenges to earlier ones. We shall compare the view of the friends on divine justice with views which were current in pagan Mesopotamia. Job challenges his friends on the basis of his personal experience. Traditional certitude must give way before personal discovery. However, the implications of Job's discovery threaten the integrative function of the monotheistic faith. New experience is necessary to correct this excess; this is the revelation of God in the whirlwind.

The building of hypotheses for the integration of knowledge and their continual testing against experience is one of the main tasks of the educational process. I offer this attempt to see the Book of Job in educational terms in tribute to Louis Newman, a distinguished educator who has devoted his career to a probing search of world outlook, moral values, and the course of action that must result from this process of discovery.

Job and Earlier Literary Models

An investigation into the Book of Job necessarily involves a study of earlier writings in similar genres and a measure of the distance the biblical book has traveled from its possible models. We will examine some of the earlier compositions.

The Sumerian composition that Kramer entitled "Man and His God" is the earliest Job-type lament. A young man complains bitterly that he is looked upon with hostility by the king and rejected by his companions. He wants to present his case before his god, who is neglecting him: "you have doled out to me suffering ever anew." There is a complaint against the injustice of men and the god: "My companion says not a true word to me . . . (and) you my god do not thwart him." The sufferer, however, does not maintain that he is totally innocent: "My god, now that you have shown me my sins . . . I, the young man would confess my sins before you." The poem is framed by the pious exhortation at the beginning, "Let a man utter constantly the exaltedness of his god," and final reporting that the god heard his plea and swept away the demon of sickness afflicting him.[2]

A more expanded composition in Akkadian is the well-known *Ludlul bēl nemeqi*, "I will praise the lord of wisdom," the title being taken from the colophon. This composition presents the plaint of one Shubshi-meshre-shakkan, whose protecting god and goddess have abandoned him, leaving him prey to illness and evil omens, while his former friends gleefully anticipate his death. He is sick, mocked, and rejected: "My intimate friend has brought my life into danger, my slave has publicly cursed me in the assembly." The sufferer protests his piety: "For myself, I gave attention to supplication and prayer; to me prayer was discretion, sacrifice my rule; the day of reverencing the god was a joy to the heart . . . . I instructed my land to keep the god's rites and taught my people to value the goddess's name."

Despite his bitter suffering, the author retains faith that the day will come "when, among my friends, their Sun-god will have mercy." He is then visited in his dreams by a young man of superlative physique, by another young man who purifies him ritually, and by a divine-appearing young woman. Again, in a dream, an incantation priest comes in the name of Marduk and promises him prosperity and healing. The final tablet of the composition praises Marduk, who restores to life, and describes the stages of recovery and praise of the gods before the various gates of Babylon.[3]

Lambert points out that, with the discovery of more tablets, the original characterization of *Ludlul* as the "Babylonian Job" is seen to be incorrect. The problem of the suffering of the righteous is only a small part of the composition, and the role of Marduk the restorer is more prominent. However, with the tension between these two aspects, the problem remains unsolved.[4]

From Ugarit, whose alphabetic mythical texts have proven such a rich store of comparative material for the study of biblical poetic diction and structure, comes a brief Akkadian composition, numbered RS 25.460, which resembles the Akkadian *Ludlul* in its depiction of pain and suffering and in its lavish praise of the god Marduk. The sufferer tells how the diviners were unable to enlighten him about the nature and prognosis of his suffering. His wives prepared him for the grave by anointing him with oil. He could not sleep at night, and he consumed his suffering as if it were food. Marduk ultimately saves him, and he utters this praise: "I praise, I praise (the work) of my lord, (the work) of Marduk I praise, (the work) of my angry god I praise." Marduk has broken, crushed, and abandoned him, but he has also raised him up.[5] The protestation of righteousness is not prominent here, as it is in Job, but the inscrutability of a god who tortures and equally mysteriously restores remains a problem.

Another relevant piece of comparative literature is the Babylonian acrostic poem called the *Theodicy*. It is in the form of a dialogue between a sufferer and a friend who responds to his bitter complaint about divine injustice. The friend, while observing the external forms of politeness, actually insults the intelligence of the sufferer, for example: "You make your fine discretion like an imbecile's" (line 14), "your thoughts are perverse; you have forsaken right and blaspheme against your god's designs" (line 79). The sufferer points out the unresponsiveness of the gods to morality: "Those who neglect the god go the way of prosperity; while those who pray to the goddess are impoverished and dispossessed" (lines 70–71). The friend falls back on the idea that the divine mind is inscrutable and admits that mankind has been created by the gods with an evil nature: "(the creator gods) gave perverse speech to the human race; with lies and not truth, they endowed them forever" (lines 279–80). The intensity of the moral protest is ultimately abandoned, and, at the conclusion, the sufferer asks his friend for pity, begging, "May the god who has thrown me off give help; may the goddess who has abandoned me show mercy" (line 296).[6]

Thus, Babylonian literature presents two views: one which sees a direct relationship between good deeds and reward, and another which sees the very same deeds ignored by the gods.

A Babylonian proverb collection states: "Every day worship your god / sacrifice and benediction are the proper accompaniment of incense / present your free-will offering to your god, / for this is proper toward the gods / prayer, supplication and prostration / offer him daily."[7] However, *Ludlul* laments: "I wish I knew that these things were pleasing to one's god."[8]

The Uniqueness of the Book of Job

It cannot be denied that the biblical Book of Job is indebted to earlier models of its genre for some of its general themes and phraseology, but there is also a marked difference. This consists in the stubborn persistence of Job in maintaining his innocence against all that his friends accuse him of. It also relates to his demand that God appear to him directly and, without using His power to bully him, allow him to plead his case. While it is true that once God appears, Job is silenced and humbled, this resembling the capitulation of man before the gods in the Mesopotamian literary pieces, what is unique in the Bible is that the summons to debate is accepted by God. God must at least address some of the issues. Whether the imposition of the suffering was arbitrary, as in the earlier literature, or is related to the testing theme, depends on literary analysis: whether the story and the poem are separate or connected. The fact, however, that God speaks to Job means that He is less than totally arbitrary.

The biblical and Mesopotamian conceptions agree in that they assume an organized, moral world order. Sumerian and Akkadian hymns address various gods as world rulers whose decrees are inviolable. Moreover, the concept of an assembly of the gods whose decisions are binding upon all gods is often attested.[9] A few examples will suffice: The god Enlil is addressed in a Sumerian hymn as "lord, god, king, who are the judge (and) decision maker of the universe."[10] Elsewhere he is called "Father Enlil, lord of the rightful command."[11] Ishtar, in an Akkadian hymn, is called the queen of the gods before whom the other gods bow down, and "in the assembly her word is powerful; it is dominating."[12] Shamash, the sun god, is considered to be the guardian of right and justice, as he daily traverses the heavens and sees all that transpires below.[13]

The personal suffering of an individual set against this belief occasioned the problem of theodicy and stimulated many attempts to solve the contradiction. One answer was that the distance of the gods made their actions inscrutable: "Who knows the will of the gods in heaven?" With a god, the expected morality can be inverted, e.g., "What is proper to oneself is an offense to one's god." Another solution is that the gods made men evil by nature, giving "perverse speech to the human race." That idea, however, contradicts the assumption that suffering is only temporary and that the gods will restore the sufferer to his former state.[14]

For the Mesopotamians, however, an element of unpredictability existed in the cosmic structure, and certain gods were believed to be violent and not amenable to moral restraints. Speiser noted: "Nothing was settled for all time, nothing could be taken for granted; hence the anxiety and the insecurity of the mortals, who must be forever intent on propitiating the gods in order to obtain a favorable decision."[15]

Enlil, who governs an orderly cosmos, is also arbitrary and violent. A Sumerian hymn laments: "What has he planned against me in his holy mind? A net he spread, the net of an enemy."[16] In the Babylonian flood story, Enlil is condemned for his violent anger and his unwillingness to distinguish between the righteous and the wicked: "How could you, unreasoning, bring on the deluge? On the sinner impose his sin, on the transgressor impose his transgression."[17]

The Assyrian *Erra* poem describes a struggle between mindless violence, as practiced by the god of the scorched earth, Erra, against mankind, and a moral protest by the god of fire, Ishum. The Seven, gods of battle, urge Erra on to destruction, and he, concurring, states: "I shall cut off (the life) of the righteous man who acts as intercessor; the evil man, who cuts throats, him shall I put in the highest(?) places(?)." Against this inversion of values the god Ishum protests, saying: "Hero Erra, you killed the righteous man, you killed the unrighteous man;

you killed him who sinned against you, you killed him who did not sin against you." At the conclusion of the poem, Erra admits that his wrath exceeded all bounds: "Like one who ravages a country I made no distinction between good and bad." Then, in an equally arbitrary manner, he restores the world to order and peace.[18]

In the light of these different Mesopotamian traditions we can evaluate the positions of Job and his friends. This does not mean, necessarily, that the author of Job had direct familiarity with the earlier literature, although it is not inconceivable that traces of it, in translation, may have reached him. This is a matter for speculation. What we may state is that the options presented by the Babylonian material were not unknown to him.

The Mesopotamians, while affirming a world order, also expected a violation of that order. The same god whom they praised as world ruler could also unleash blind fury. The starting point for Job and his friends, on the other hand, is the integrated monotheistic faith. There is only one God, only one divine will, and this God is just and morally predictable.The biblical book begins with the expectation of moral intelligibility and divine accessibility, not inscrutability and distance. The friends hold this view, while Job's bitterness is due to the disappointment he feels at the failure of his expectation. The challenge of Abraham, "shall not the judge of all the earth do justice?" (Gen. 18:25), underlies the entire dialogue. With fine insight did the rabbis note the connection of Job's position with that of Abraham, as well as the anger that separates them: "What Abraham said was the same as what Job said, but Job consumed it as an unripe fruit (he spoke rashly), while Abraham consumed it as a ripe fruit" (*Midrash Tanhuma, Vayera* 5). The verses upon which these comments are based are Gen. 18:23 and Job 9:22.

Tradition and Experience

The friends represent an integrated religious point of view. While differences in style and emphasis have been noted,[19] they are united in their faith in the moral integrity of God and the predictability of His retribution. God's justice cannot be impugned, and a mortal who arrogantly maintains that he is just, even when divine beings are found wanting (4:17–18; 15:15–16; 25:4–6) must have sinned if he is suffering so. His protests are no more than a rationalization of his own sin (15:5).

This world-view is based upon several sources of information: personal experience (4:7–8; 5:3; 20:4), the experience of earlier generations (8:8; 15:7, 17 ff.) and divine revelation (4:12 ff.; 11:5; 15:8). The faith of the friends not only derives from these different kinds of experience, but it shapes their world, organizing it into a coherent and reassuring pattern. The value of their faith is that it has overcome completely the sense of cosmic disunity that disturbed the Mesopotamians.

Job's position is that his personal experience and his knowledge of himself are as valid a source of information as the experience, tradition, and revelations, of the friends (12:3; 13:2). So certain is he of his position and his moral integrity that he is prepared to defy the full force of the experiential and traditional verification of the friends' position and risk being called arrogant for claiming, against all common experience, that he is blameless.

A significant part of Job's utterances are a lament over his miserable physical condition and an appeal to God's sympathy, for is He not the one, after all, who created him (7:8; 10:8 ff., 20)? Job's stressing of his imminent death has been explained by Glatzer as showing the influence of the Garden of Eden story upon the writer of Job. When man attains a knowledge that God does not want him to have, the penalty is the taste of death.[20] Job fears God's power, for, while he demands an opportunity to debate with Him, he wants a guarantee that God's inordinate power will not be directed against him (9:33–35; 13:18 ff.). On the other hand, imminent death makes Job bolder. He has nothing more to lose, but he will not give up his integrity (13:13–15).

Gordis has written that Job, in rebelling against tradition, has actually enriched it.[21] This interpretation, true as far as it goes, is not enough. When Job insists on his personal truth, his moral integrity, God, of necessity, becomes a brutal and destructive bully (6:4; 7:14; 9:11–13, 22; 10:17; 16:12). Job's new truth threatens to break up the unity of the monotheistic faith, with its affirmation of the coexistence and harmony of God's power, benevolence, and concern. This is exactly what Eliphaz and God accuse him of (15:4; 40:8). Job's descriptions of God make Him very similar to the violent Mesopotamian gods Enlil, Nergal, and Erra, whose destructiveness is not governed by moral considerations. The image of God the warrior in the Book of Job differs from this image in other biblical books in that elsewhere God is using His power to establish and maintain an orderly, moral universe. God destroys the sea-serpent, Leviathan or Rahab (Isa. 27:1; 51:9; Ps. 74:13–15; in a negative sense: Job 7:12; 9:13; 26:13). God uses arrows (Deut. 32:23, 42; Ps. 7:14; 18:15; 58:8; 144:6; in a negative sense: Job 6:14).

The answer of God in the whirlwind is not the only attempt to bridge the gap between tradition and experience. Elihu claims that God seeks to turn man from evil through visions and dreams. When this fails, illness and pain are used to reach man's consciousness. When man is at the brink of death, his virtues save him, and man then realizes that the suffering was a chastening discipline. While some see the poem on wisdom in chapter 28 as totally misplaced and irrelevant to the context,[22] it may be suggested that it is yet another solution to the dilemma of the book. The search to know is futile, for all that one can and should know is that fear of the Lord is wisdom; God is inscrutable but piety has value.

God's answer to Job has meaning because, despite his rebellion, Job is a believer. He accuses the friends of falsifying the truth of God's ways merely to curry favor. God will appear and in His majesty will overawe the friends, who attempt to show favoritism on His behalf. The puns on *tiśśā'ûn* "show favor" (13:8, 10) and *śe'ētô* "His majesty" (13:11) are significant in tying the thoughts together. Rabbi Joshua ben Korchah understood the complexity of faith and denial struggling with each other when he said that Job served God out of love (Mish. *Sotah* 5:5). Job knows that his witness is in heaven (16:19) and that his redeemer lives (19:25).

While some authors have claimed that God gives no real answer and begs the question, others see a positive content in the message from the whirlwind.[23] Job will not know, in cognitive terms, why the innocent suffer, but God affirms that there is a world order which provides for the needs of the various species and which curbs all excesses of power, such as the encroachment of the aggressive sea (42:13, 15). The shining of the dawn includes the denial of light to the wicked (42:13, 15). The wondrousness, independence, and survival of the various creatures are evidence of a divine plan. The content of the message of God to Job is only partly cognitive, partially informative. The rest is cognitively a blank, but the experience of the mystery has a positive aspect. Just as God limits all the forces in the universe, so that each will play its proper role, the experience of the mystery controls the excess in Job's reliance upon his limited personal experience. It stops him from crossing the line to nihilism or dualism. The experience of the mystery reassures him that there is a moral order and reaffirms the integrative view of the world.[24]

The idea that the *mysterium tremendum* conveys a sense of ultimate unity, while the cognitive, intellectual problems remain unsolved, is the outgrowth of mystical experience and is not subject to analysis. Nicholas of Cusa, of the fifteenth century, wrote: "Hence I observed how needful it is for me to enter into the darkness, and to admit the coincidence of opposites, beyond all the grasp of reason, and there to seek the truth where impossibility meeteth me."[25]

Notes

1. Otto Eisfeldt, *The Old Testament: An Introduction* (New York and Evanston, 1965), pp. 454–470; Robert Gordis, *The Book of God and Man* (University of Chicago, 1965); Nahum N. Glatzer, ed., *The Dimensions of Job* (New York: Schocken Books, 1969); idem, "The Book of Job and Its Interpreters," in *Biblical Motifs: Origins and Transformations*, ed. Alexander Altmann (Cambridge: Harvard University Press, 1966), pp. 197–220.

2. S. N. Kramer, in *Ancient Near Eastern Texts Relating to the Old Testament*, ed. James B. Pritchard 3d. ed. (Princeton, 1969), pp. 589–591; idem, Supplement to *Vetus Testamentum* 3 (1960): 172–182; Marvin Pope, *The Anchor Bible: Job* (New York, 1965), Introduction, pp. l–lxvi.

3. W. G. Lambert, *Babylonian Wisdom Literature* (London: Oxford University Press, 1960), pp. 32–62; Pritchard, *Ancient Near Eastern Texts*, pp. 596–600, trans. Robert D. Biggs.

4. Lambert, *Babylonian Wisdom Literature*, p. 27.

5. J. Nougayrol, E. Laroche, C. Virolleaud, and C. F. A. Schaeffer, *Ugaritica* V (Paris, 1968), pp. 267–269.

6. Lambert, *Babylonian Wisdom Literature*, pp. 63–89; Pritchard, *Ancient Near Eastern Texts*, pp. 601–604.

7. Lambert, *Babylonian Wisdom Literature*, 105:135–140.

8. Ibid., 41:33. Complaints about suffering and injustice from Egypt include a dispute over suicide (see H. Goedicke, *The Report About the Dispute of a Man With His Ba* [Baltimore: John Hopkins Press, 1970]), *The Admonitions of an Egyptian Sage* and the *Lamentations of Khakheperre-Sonbe*; see W. K. Simpson, ed., *The Literature of Ancient Egypt* (New Haven and London: Yale University Press, 1972), pp. 201–233.

9. Thorkild Jacobsen, "Primitive Democracy in Ancient Mesopotamia," *Journal of Near Eastern Studies* 2 (1943): 159–172; idem, *The Treasures of Darkness* (New Haven and London: Yale University Press, 1976), pp. 86–91.

10. Translated in Pritchard, *Ancient Near Eastern Texts*, 575:138–140.

11. Ibid., 576:4.

12. Ibid., 383.

13. Jacobsen, *Treasures of Darkness*, pp. 86, 134 (The sun god in Sumerian is called Utu); Lambert, *Babylonian Wisdom Literature*, pp. 121–138 (*The Shamash Hymn*).

14. Lambert, *Babylonian Wisdom Literature*, pp. 14–20, 64–65.

15. E. A. Speiser, "Ancient Mesopotamia," in *The Idea of History in the Ancient Near East*, ed. R. C. Dentan (New Haven, 1967), pp. 43–44.

16. Jacobsen, *Treasures of Darkness*, p. 102.

17. *Gilgamesh*, tablet XI, 179–180; Pritchard, *Ancient Near Eastern Texts*, p. 95.

18. Luigi Cagni, *The Poem of Erra, Sources from the Ancient Near East*, vol. 1, fasc. 3 (Malibu: Udena Publications, 1977).

19. Gordis, *Book of God and Man*, pp. 76–103.

20. Nahum Glatzer, "Introduction: A Study of Job," in Glatzer, *Dimensions of Job*, pp. 8–9.

21. Robert Gordis, "The Temptation of Job—Tradition versus Experience in Religion," in Glatzer, *Dimensions of Job*, p. 84.

22. Eissfeldt, *Old Testament*, p. 463; Pope, *Job*, p. xviii; Gordis, *Book of God and Man*, pp. 100–103.

23. Eissfeldt, *Old Testament*, pp. 467; Gordis, *Book of God and Man*, pp. 121–134, 154–156.

24. Another example of God's appearance, which reassures man that there is a moral order which remains, however, incomprehensible, is Exodus 33:12–23. See the writer's article "God's Ways—A Comparative Note," *Jewish Quarterly Review* 70 (1979): 67–72. Relevant here is the rabbinic interpretation of Job 9:24, "The earth is given into the hands of the wicked." Raba said, "Job sought to overturn the vessel," that is, to blaspheme God. Abayye said, "Job was merely speaking of the Satan," but giving Satan so much power approaches dualism. This controversy duplicates an earlier one between the tannaim Rabbi Eliezer and Rabbi Joshua. Again Raba states: "Job sought to excuse the world from judgment," by claiming that the evil inclination was placed in man by God. This resembles the view expressed in the *Babylonian Theodicy* (see above, note 6). God's response is that He also gave man the Torah with which to heal the evil inclination, that is, man's freedom is asserted together with the moral integrity of creation (*Baba Batra* 16a).

25. Quoted in F. C. Happold, *Mysticism: A Study and an Anthology* (Baltimore: Penguin Books, 1963), p. 305.

THE IMAGE OF GOD AND THE FLOOD:
Some New Developments

JEFFREY H. TIGAY

Those who were privileged to spend some of their formative years in association with Lou Newman came to understand what the rabbis sought in *shimmush talmidei chachamim:* not only to learn the master's teachings, but to observe his personal qualities in the hope of emulating him, not only as an educator, but as a human being. Few of us may be so bold as to claim success in emulating Lou, but I think we would all gladly admit that we have tried.

One of the constants of Lou Newman's career as an educator has been the way he approaches important texts. If Moses stormed heaven and captured the Torah, as the *paytan* puts it, Lou would lay siege to the text and methodically force it to surrender its meaning and implications. Few skills are of equal importance in Jewish education. Judaism has been described as "a religion which expects each adherent to develop judicial qualities."[1] This definition explains why the study of legal texts has always been at the core of Jewish education: To make informed behavioral decisions, the Jew must know the law and how it has been applied in concrete situations. As a prerequisite to disciplined decision-making, one had to study classical Jewish texts and extract their implications.

In the sixties, much of Lou's effort was devoted to just such

Jeffrey H. Tigay is Ellis Associate Professor of Hebrew and Semitic Languages and Literatures at the University of Pennsylvania. He is author of *The Evolution of the Gilgamesh Epic* and is currently preparing a commentary on Deuteronomy to be published by the Jewish Publication Society.

study of Genesis and Exodus as part of the Melton Research Center's project on the teaching of the Torah. It was my privilege to be part of the first experimental groups that assembled at Camp Ramah in the Poconos under Lou's direction in the summers of 1963 and 1964, and to work closely with him for the next several years. In the years since, I have come to realize that few experiences did as much to prepare me for a career in biblical studies as the experience of reading these texts with Lou.

The intervening years have also brought some new discoveries concerning some of the texts which demanded most of our attention. I would like to discuss two of these discoveries here as my expression of gratitude to a teacher who did so much to help me understand Genesis and learn how to read a text.

The Image of God

The passages in Genesis (1:26, 27; 5:1 [cf. 3]; 9:6) which state that man was created in God's image and likeness have been subject to as great a variety of interpretations as any in the Bible. That the Hebrew words in question (*ṣelem* and *d'mut*) normally refer to statues and physical appearances is clear from their usage throughout the Bible[2] and has been underscored by a recently discovered Aramaic inscription on a statue which refers to the statue itself in these very terms (*d'muta'*, *ṣ'lem*).[3] As late as the time of Maimonides there were Jews who interpreted the image of God as referring to man's (and God's) bodily form, as Maimonides indicates in the opening statement of the *Guide of the Perplexed* I, 1.[4] Rabbinic texts reflect such an interpretation by some (but not all) sages of the talmudic period, such as the famous tale about Hillel, who considers bathing a commandment since man was created in the image of God and even statues of human kings are washed.[5] Such a literal interpretation of the terms in Genesis seemed compatible with the fact that the Bible does indeed consider God corporeal and visible (Ex. 33:20–23; Num. 12:8).[6] It is true that since Hellenistic times there have also been writers, such as

Philo, who interpreted the image of God as a metaphor referring to man's mind or other incorporeal qualities,[7] but such
interpretations could be dismissed as reflecting the philosophic
allegorization typical of the Hellenistic period rather than the
original meaning of the phrase.

Recently, however, the metaphoric interpretation of the image of God has been enhanced by evidence that even in the
pagan cultures of the ancient Near East the phrase was sometimes applied to humans in a metaphoric sense. Certainly the
phrase usually referred to statues of gods, but there were
writers who went beyond the normal usage. Adad-shum-uṣur,
an exorcist-priest in the service of the Assyrian royal court
(seventh century B.C.E.), often compared the kings he served to
gods. The contexts of these comparisons, expressed in memoranda he wrote to one of the kings, make it clear that he is not
referring to their appearance or bodily form. In one of these
memoranda he responds to a letter in which the king had told
him, "I heard from my father that you are a loyal family, but
now I know it from my own experience." Adad-shum-uṣur
replies: "The father of the king, my lord, was the very image of
the god Bel, and the king my lord is likewise the very image of
the god Bel. This has fallen to me from the mouth of my two
masters! Who will ever (be able to) repeat (it), who will match
(it)?" In another memorandum, Adad-shum-uṣur urges the
king not to engage in certain mourning or apotropaic rites for
more than half a day, since "the king, the lord of the world, is
the very image of the sun god." In both of these notes, Adad-
shum-uṣur uses the Akkadian cognate of ṣelem, ṣalmu. In a
third letter he uses muššulu (related to Hebrew mashal), a
synonym of Hebrew d'mut; after quoting a proverb stating that
"man is a shadow of a god," Adad-shum-uṣur observes that
"the king [in contrast] is a likeness of a god." In a fourth note
Adad-shum-uṣur expresses the same idea without using any of
the nouns meaning "image." After agreeing with a suggestion
of the king's, he concludes: "What am I to say, an old man who
has got no reason? (But) what the king, my lord, has said is as
perfect as (the word) of a god." Finally, there is a memorandum

from another writer, Asharidu, apparently from Babylon, who uses the metaphor in the course of describing the royal officials' dependence on the king's favor: "The king of the world is the very image (ṣalmu) of Marduk: when you have been angry with your servants we have suffered the anger of the king, our lord, but we have also experienced the king's favor."[8] Comparison of the king's favor to that of a god can also be expressed without reference to image, as in "His lord, the king, looked favorably upon him, with a shining face, like a god." Clearly the point of all these comparisons is to say that the king is godlike in his qualities (cf. II Sam. 14:20), not his appearance, a conclusion which is underscored by the fact that some of the same compliments can be expressed by means of the simile "like a god" in place of the metaphor "image of god." Though the precise divine qualities the writers have in mind are not always specified, the contexts suggest that the king's authority, status, majesty, wisdom, anger, and favor are being described.

Something similar is suggested in an epic poem about an earlier Assyrian king named Tukulti-Ninurta (thirteenth century B.C.E.). There the king is described as one who:

By the fate (assigned by) Nudimmud (i.e., the god Ea) his form is reckoned as the flesh of the gods,
By the decree of the lord of the lands he was successfully cast into/poured through the womb of the gods.
He is the eternal image of (the god) Enlil, attentive to the voice of the people, to the mood of the land.[9]

Here, though the text had previously been describing Tukulti-Ninurta's physical form, the line describing him as the image (ṣalmu) of Enlil goes on to describe an intellectual quality, attentiveness to his subjects. Finally, a behavioral comparison is implied by a passage applying the phrase to an exorcist-priest: "the spell (recited) is the spell of Marduk, the exorcist-priest is the image (ṣalmu) of Marduk."[10] In this passage the exorcist lends strength to his spell by asserting that he represents, or is identified with, Marduk, the preeminent exorcist among the gods.[11]

The image of god is used metaphorically in Egyptian literature, too, in a passage strikingly reminiscent of Jewish philosophic usage. In an Egyptian wisdom text presenting a debate
between a scribe and his son, the son tries to convince the
father not to ignore what he, the son, is saying:

> Do not be so overpowering in your severity; I am done
> violence by your intentions. Should it not happen to a man
> that he drops his arm and listens to an answer instead? Men
> are in the image of the god in their custom of hearing a man
> in regard to his reply. It is not the wise alone who is in his
> image, while the multitude are every kind of cattle. It is not
> the wise alone who is his pupil, having alone become intelli-
> gent, while all the mob is stupid.[12]

Here, as in the *Tukulti-Ninurta Epic*, the metaphor refers to
attentiveness, understanding.

If the concept of the image of the god has such an extensive
history as a metaphor in the pagan cultures of the ancient Near
East, one can hardly deny the possibility that it could have
been used in this way in Genesis as well. Many of the over-
tones noted in the Assyrian and Egyptian texts would fit the
contexts of Genesis 1 and 9 well. It is true that a physical
resemblance between God and man cannot be excluded from
the picture. The Bible not only entertains a view of God as
visible, but once uses "the image of God" in a context where it
could refer to man's appearance: The statement in Gen. 5:1 that
God made man "in the likeness (*d'mut*) of God" is followed by
the statement that Adam later "begot a son in his likeness, after
his image (*bidmuto k'ṣalmo*)" (5:3). Here the possibility of a
physical similarity, if not certainly present in the text, cannot
be ruled out. But in 1:26, the statement that man is to be made
in God's image immediately precedes his assignment to rule
the earth, from which it has been inferred that the image refers
to functional similarities or similarity of faculties with God, of
the sort that will enable man to perform his role.[13] This interpretation was suggested even before the Assyrian and Egyptian examples were brought into the discussion, and these

certainly enhance its credibility. Gen. 9:6 seems to lend further support to this interpretation, though I'm not sure this has been noticed:

Whoever sheds the blood of man,
By man shall his blood be shed;
For in the image of God was man created.

The statement about the image of God in the third clause of the verse has generally been taken as explaining why the shedding of human blood is a capital crime: The divine image implies that human life is inviolable. But if this were the point, or the only point, of the statement, the first two clauses of the verse could have read simply "Whoever sheds the blood of man, his blood shall be shed." The additional phrase "by man," appearing in the emphatic position at the beginning of the second clause, stresses that the punishment is to be executed *by man*. Since the statement about the image of God follows immediately upon the second clause, it seems quite likely that it is especially this clause which is explained by that statement: Because man is made in the divine image, *he* is to punish murder. In other words, the divine image implies a functional similarity of man to God as governor and executor of justice in the world.

The Flood

The passage just discussed, Gen. 9:6, takes on a deeper significance as the culmination of the flood story in the light of recent discoveries concerning the meaning of the flood story in Mesopotamia.

For almost a century since its discovery in 1872, the eleventh tablet of the *Gilgamesh Epic* remained the fullest version available of the Mesopotamian account of the great flood.[14] A few fragments of another Akkadian version, the *Atrahasis Epic*, were also known (as well as fragments of a Sumerian version), but it was not until 1965 that most of *Atrahasis* became accessible to modern scholars, and not until 1969 that a transliteration and translation of the Akkadian text were published.[15] It soon became apparent that *Atrahasis* was the source from which an editor of *Gilgamesh* had borrowed the flood story for his own composition,[16] and only the version in *Atrahasis* showed the significance Mesopotamians attached to the flood story.[17]

The *Atrahasis Epic* begins several thousand years before the flood. It is actually a history of mankind covering several generations, from the creation of man through the flood, offering many parallels to the first eight and one-half chapters of Genesis. This epic is especially important in that, unlike the version in *Gilgamesh*, it describes the reason for which the flood was brought about and the steps taken by the gods after the flood to ensure that the problem caused by mankind would be kept under control in the future.

The first part of the epic describes the creation of man to be the slave of the gods, providing the gods with food so that they may live a life of ease. But after about twelve hundred years, the human population has increased to the point that the noise of their daily life has become to the gods an unbearable racket:

The land became wide, the people became numerous,
The land bellowed like wild oxen.
(The storm god) Enlil became disturbed by their uproar,
Enlil heard their clamor
And he said to the gods:
"Oppressive has become the clamor of mankind,
By their uproar I am deprived of sleep . . ."[18]

In an attempt to silence this noise, Enlil suggests that a plague be sent against mankind to reduce its numbers and thereby its noise. The gods agree, and they bring about a pestilence to silence man.

At this point the human hero of the story, Atrahasis, appears. His name means "exceedingly wise."[19] Atrahasis turns to his personal god, Enki (also known as Ea), the god of wisdom and exorcism, to complain about the suffering caused by the pestilence. Enki suggests offering sacrifices to the god of plagues, and apparently this remedy works and the plague ceases. But after another twelve hundred years mankind has multiplied to the point where its noise is again unbearable to Enlil, who determines to reduce its numbers with a new plague. After this happens several times, with Atrahasis saving the day each time on the basis of advice from Enki, Enlil gets the gods to agree to put an end to the nuisance once and for all by completely destroying the human race with a flood (this is the point at which the better-known narrative in the *Gilgamesh Epic* sets in). Enki (Ea) surreptitiously warns the hero to build a ship in which to ride out the flood with his family and various animals. The details of the story, and its similarities and differences in comparison to the biblical account, are much like those in the *Gilgamesh* version, which has been summarized by Sarna and need not be repeated here.[20] What the new fragments of *Atrahasis* reveal to us for the first time, however, is the immediate aftermath of the story. The versions in *Gilgamesh* and *Atrahasis* run parallel until Atrahasis and his wife are granted immortality. This is the point at which the excerpt in *Gilgamesh* ends, because this is what is relevant to the theme of *Gilgamesh*. But in *Atrahasis* there is more. Enlil is determined to prevent mankind from ever disturbing him with its noise again. He therefore takes steps to control the size of the human race: Henceforth some women are to be incapable of giving birth and others not legally allowed to, and there are to be demons to snatch away and kill some newborn infants.[21] These decrees reveal the point of the entire myth. It is to explain why some women are infertile and others are not allowed to give birth, and why there is infant mortality. The myth explains these as divine ordinances designed as population-control measures with the aim of reducing the noise produced by humanity to levels the gods find bearable.

To the Israelites, who undoubtedly learned of the flood story from Mesopotamians directly or indirectly,[22] this explanation of the event was inconceivable. Israelites were convinced that God never sleeps (Ps. 121:4; I Kings 18:27), and that God had explicitly ordained the multiplication of the human race both at creation and after the flood (Gen. 1:28; 9:1, 7). The historicity of the flood itself was not doubted, but the Israelite view of the way God operates required that the event be understood in a way that was compatible with that view. And since that view held that God judges the human race for actions in the moral sphere, it followed that the human offense which led to the flood must have been a moral breach, not a violation of mythic divine repose.

In light of the *Atrahasis Epic*, covering the history of humanity from creation through the aftermath of the flood, Genesis 1:1–9:17 may likewise be understood as a single literary unit rather than a series of unconnected episodes.[23] In both Genesis and *Atrahasis* the account of the flood constitutes the climax of a series of episodes which describe the problem with humanity and the steps taken by, respectively, God and the gods to deal with that problem. In *Atrahasis* the problem with man is that he disturbs the rest of the gods with his noise;[24] the gods' solution is to reduce the population and prevent it from growing too much in the future. In the Bible, the problem of man is lawlessness, especially violence (the basic meaning of *ḥamas*;[25] note the killings in Gen. 4:8 and 23). God's solution is, first, to dispose of the guilty and then to establish laws against murder and to give man the responsibility for executing those laws (Gen. 9:6).[26]

Both of the issues we have been studying thus culminate in the same verse, Gen. 9:6. In light of the metaphoric usage of the image of God in the ancient Near East and the meaning of the flood story in *Atrahasis*, God seems to be saying the following in Gen. 9:6 "What I intended by creating you in my image was that you should rule the world as I would. You are to use your Godlike qualities—your authority, your status above the animals, your understanding—to limit violence by punishing it." Although a physical resemblance between God and man may also be part of the image, and although it may be the divine image which makes every person's life inviolable, the established metaphoric usage of the divine image suggests that to the ancients the primary implication of the phrase, when applied to humans, had to do with behavior, status, and function. The flood story testifies that man's failure to perform his Godlike role upon himself is what most disturbs God about man.

Seen in this light, it is no accident that the rabbis inferred that the Noachide laws required man to establish courts of justice in every human settlement.[27] To Judaism, law has always been an essential component of man's relationship to God. One of the great achievements of the Torah in this sphere was not simply the individual laws, many of which were paralleled in the ancient world,[28] but the teaching that moral laws were the command of God, not merely expressions of wisdom or good citizenship.[29] Judaism, as we have noted, expects each of its adherents to develop the judicial skills necessary to apply these laws in daily life. In the universal context of Gen. 1:1–9:17, the Bible implies that this is the obligation of mankind as a whole.

Notes

1. Thus Solomon Schechter's view of Judaism is characterized by L. Finkelstein in his introduction to Schechter's *Aspects of Rabbinic Theology* (New York: Schocken, 1961), p. xiv.

2. E.g., I Sam. 6:5, 11; Dan. 3:1; II Chron. 4:3.

3. A. R. Millard and P. Bordreuil, "A Statue from Syria with Assyrian and Aramaic Inscriptions," *Biblical Archaeologist* 45 (1982): 135–141.

4. Note the comment of M. Friedländer, *The Guide of the Perplexed of Maimonides* (New York: Hebrew Publishing Co., n.d.), p. 28, n. 2.

5. Vayyikra Rabba 34:3. To paraphrase Morton Smith: Hillel was not going to wash his intellect or his immortality. See Smith's comments, "On the Shape of God and the Humanity of Gentiles," in J. Neusner (ed.), *Religions in Antiquity: Essays in Memory of Erwin Ramsdell Goodenough* (Supplements to *Numen,* XIV; Leiden: Brill, 1970), p. 319, and especially his survey of midrashic texts on the subject, "The Image of God," *Bulletin of the John Rylands Library* 40 (1958): 473–512. Smith concludes "that the Biblical statements concerning man's likeness to God were interpreted in many different ways which were not thought to be mutually exclusive, and that among the interpretations was the opinion, held by some very important rabbis, that man's body was made as an image of God" ("On the Shape of God," p. 320).

6. What is denied in the Bible is not that God has a visible form but that man can survive seeing that form (Ex. 33:20; cf. Ex. 3:6; Isa. 6:5).

7. Philo, *On the Creation of the World* XXIII, §69 (in F. H. Colson and G. H. Whitaker, *Philo* I [Loeb Classical Library; Cambridge, Mass.: Harvard University Press, 1971], p. 55). In the Wisdom of Solomon 2:23 (in the Apocrypha) God's image is taken to refer to his immortality, as in B'midbar Rabba 16:15.

8. The latest edition of the Adad-shum-uṣur texts is in S. Parpola, *Letters from Assyrian Scholars to the Kings Esarhaddon and Assurbanipal*, pt. I, *Texts* (Kevelaer: Butzon & Bercker, and Neukirchen-Vluyn: Neukirchener Verlag, 1970), nos. 125, obverse 15–21; 143, reverse 4–6; 145, reverse 10–13; 144, reverse 2–7. The memorandum from Asharidu is from R. Campbell Thompson, *Reports of the Magicians and Astrologers of Nineveh and Babylon*, vol. I (London: Luzac, 1900), p. 49, no. 170, reverse 2, quoted in A. L. Oppenheim, "Divination and Celestial Observation in the Last Assyrian Empire," *Centaurus* 14 (1969): 116. The last text cited is quoted from I. J. Gelb et al. (eds.), *The Assyrian Dictionary of the Oriental Institute of the University of Chicago*, vol. 7: I and J (Chicago: Oriental Institute; Glückstadt: Augustin, 1960), p. 92. This dictionary is cited below as *CAD*.

9. W. G. Lambert, "Three Unpublished Fragments of the Tukulti-Ninurta Epic," *Archiv für Orientforschung* 18 (1957–58): 50–51, lines 8–10; P. B. Machinist, "Literature as Politics: The Tukulti-Ninurta Epic and the Bible," *Catholic Biblical Quarterly* 38 (1976): 465–466.

10. G. Meier, "Die Zweite Tafel der Serie bīt mēseri," *Archiv für Orientforschung* 14 (1941–44): 150–151, lines 225–226.

11. Cf. *CAD*, vol. 1: A, pt. II (1968), pp. 431–432, sec. 2'; G. Contenau, *Everyday Life in Babylon and Assyria* (New York: Norton, 1966), p. 291.

12. R. J. Williams, "Scribal Training in Ancient Egypt," *Journal of the American Oriental Society* 92 (1972): 221. Note also, with reference to the pharaoh: "Thou art the living likeness of thy father (the god) Atum of Heliopolis (for) Authoritative Utterance is in thy mouth, Understanding is in thy heart, thy speech is the shrine of Truth" (Kubban stele of Ramses II [1290–1224], quoted in Henri Frankfort, *Kingship and the Gods* [Chicago: University of Chicago Press, 1958], p. 149).

Another Egyptian text uses the image of god in connection with the creation of man:

Well tended is mankind—God's cattle
He made sky and earth for their sake,
He subdued the water monster,
He made breath for their noses to live.
They are his images, who came from his body;
He shines in the sky for their sake;
He made for them plants and cattle,
Fowl and fish to feed them

180

Jeffrey H. Tigay

(Miriam Lichtheim, *Ancient Egyptian Literature*, vol. I, *The Old and Middle Kingdoms* [Berkeley and Los Angeles: University of California Press, 1975], p. 106). Here a reference to the physical form of man is possible.

13. See Nahum M. Sarna, *Understanding Genesis* (New York: Jewish Theological Seminary and McGraw-Hill, 1966), pp. 14–16.

14. This version is translated by E. A. Speiser in *Ancient Near Eastern Texts Relating to the Old Testament*, ed. James B. Pritchard (Princeton: Princeton University Press, 1969), pp. 93–95, lines 11–296.

15. The cuneiform text was published by W. G. Lambert and A. R. Millard in *Babylonian Literary Texts: Cuneiform Texts from Babylonian Tablets in the British Museum*, vol. 46 (London: British Museum, 1965), nos. 1–15. The transliteration and translation were published by the same authors in *Atra-ḫasīs: The Babylonian Story of the Flood* (Oxford: Clarendon Press, 1969).

16. See J. Tigay, *The Evolution of the Gilgamesh Epic* (Philadelphia: University of Pennsylvania Press, 1982), pp. 215–217.

17. The following summary is based on several studies, including one which preceded the publication of the full text of the epic. See: J. Laessøe, "The Atraḫasis Epic: A Babylonian History of Mankind," *Bibliotheca Orientalis* 13 (1956): 90–102; A. R. Millard, "A New Babylonian 'Genesis' Story," *Tyndale Bulletin* 18 (1967): 3–18; E. V. Leichty, "Demons and Population Control," *Expedition* 13 (1971): 22–26; W. L. Moran, review of *Atra-ḫasīs*, by Lambert and Millard, *Biblica* 52 (1971): 51–61; A. D. Kilmer, "The Mesopotamian Concept of Overpopulation and Its Solution as Reflected in the Mythologies," *Orientalia* 41 (1972): 160-177; T. Frymer-Kensky, "The Atrahasis Epic and Its Significance for Our Understanding of Genesis 1–9," *Biblical Archaeologist* 40 (1977): 147–155.

18. Lambert and Millard, *Atra-ḫasīs*, p. 67, lines 352–60; p. 73, lines 1–8; p. 107, lines 1–8; etc. Although some have tried to interpret the noise as a metaphor for sin, the fact that the noise always comes with the increase in population shows that it is meant literally as referring to the hustle-bustle of human life. See Moran (above, n. 17), pp. 55–57, especially p. 57 n. 4, and other references to the characteristic noise of human life in Isa. 22:2; Jer. 51:55; Pritchard, *Ancient Near Eastern Texts*, p. 442, line vi, 1 and preceding line; pp. 612–613, lines 43, 46; *CAD*, vol. 6; Ḫ, pp. 15–16; vol. 7: I and J, p. 58, upper left. In talmudic literature the noise of Rome was proverbial, audible from 120 miles away and drowning out the noise of the sun sawing through the sky (Yoma 20b–21a; Makkot 24a).

19. The survivor of the flood is known from other texts to have been the king of his city. While he is called Atrahasis in the myth of that name, in *Gilgamesh* and elsewhere he is known as Utnapishtim, meaning "he found life," while in the Sumerian version he is known as Ziusudra, "life of long days."

20. Sarna, *Understanding Genesis*, chap. 2; see also W. G. Lambert, "A New Look at the Babylonian Background of Genesis," *Journal of Theological Studies*, n.s. 16 (1965): 291–292, and Frymer-Kensky (above, n. 17).

21. Lambert and Millard, *Atra-ḫasīs*, p. 103, lines 1–8.
22. See Sarna, *Understanding Genesis*, pp. 38–40; Lambert, "New Look,"
pp. 298–300; Tigay, *Evolution*, p. 215; cf. p. 119 n. 35.
23. The echoes of Gen. 1 (particularly vv. 26–30) in Gen. 9:1–17 (particularly vv. 1–6) form a literary frame marking off these eight and one-half
chapters as a unit. This demarcation of the first large unit in Genesis is
supported not only by the parallel of *Atrahasis*, which covers the same
ground, but also by the recurrent phrase "after the flood" which appears in
the succeeding sections of Genesis (9:28; 10:1, 32; 11:10). In ancient Near
Eastern literature the periods before and after the flood were the two main
periods into which human history was divided, and the phrase "after the
flood" was used to mark the turning point between these periods (see
Lambert and Millard, *Atra-ḫasīs*, pp. 15–21, 25–26). This division of the
material implies that the "universal history" at the beginning of Genesis ends
at 9:17, not at the end of chapter 11, as is usually thought. In fact the function
of 9:18 through the end of chap. 11 is to narrow the focus of Genesis from
mankind as a whole to Israel in particular by showing how humanity came to
be divided into separate nations. In this context 9:18–27 functions as an
introduction to this transitional section by foreshadowing the special status
which will be accorded to the Shemites, from whom Israel will ultimately
emerge.
24. The description of the divine response to man's behavior in both texts
invites comparison: in *Atrahasis*, "Enlil became disturbed by their uproar . . .
and he said to the gods: 'Oppressive has become the clamor of mankind, by
their uproar I am deprived of sleep' "; in Genesis 6:5–6: "The Lord saw how
great was man's wickedness on earth, and how every plan devised by his
mind was nothing but evil all the time. And the Lord regretted that he had
made man on earth, and His heart was saddened."
25. Though the broader meaning "injustice" is not to be denied, the
underlying meaning of "violence" is visible in the use of the verb *ḥamas* for
"tearing down," "knocking off," in Job 15:33 and Lam. 2:6.
26. The prohibition against eating blood is also technically a prohibition
against murder in that it removes the slaughter of an animal from the
category of murder to the permissible category of procuring food; see J.
Milgrom, "A Prolegomenon to Leviticus 17:11," *Journal of Biblical Literature* 90
(1971): 149–156.
   The new order established in Gen. 9:4–6 follows God's resolution in 8:21–
22 not to destroy the world again because of man's behavior, since human
sinfulness is to be expected. This implies that as a method of controlling sin,
eradication of the sinners is futile; note Josephus' observation on why God
punished the next generation of sinners (at the Tower of Babel) differently:
"God was not minded to exterminate them utterly, because even the destruction of the first victims [the flood generation] had not taught their descendants wisdom" (Josephus, *Antiquities* I, iv, 3, §117, in H. St. J. Thackeray,
Josephus IV [Loeb Classical Library; Cambridge, Mass.: Harvard University

Press, 1967], p. 57). From now on it is not expected that sin will be eliminated but rather that it will be controlled with punishment.

27. Though the requirement is not based on Gen. 9:6; see the discussion of the Noachide laws in Sanhedrin 56a(end)–56b.

28. Many, but not all. For characteristic differences even in laws which are superficially similar, see M. Greenberg, "Some Postulates of Biblical Criminal Law," in *Yehezkel Kaufmann Jubilee Volume*, ed. M. Haran (Jerusalem: Magnes, 1960), pp. 5–28 (reprinted in J. Goldin [ed.], *The Jewish Expression* [New York: Bantam, 1970], pp. 18–37).

29. Y. Kaufmann, *The Religion of Israel* (Chicago: University of Chicago Press, 1960), pp. 233–234; cf. Greenberg, cited in the previous note.

על זהות, תבונה ודת *

משה גרינברג

כוונתי להציע גישה לתכנים יהודיים שלא תתבסס על תורת התגלות מיוחדת, או על עקרונות אמונה המונחים מראש, ואפילו לא על הנחת ייחוד היהדות (שלא לדבר על עליונותה על שאר הדתות). את הגישה שאני מבקש להציע אימצתי ממחקר הדתות, המחייב את תופעות האמונה והראוה בהן יסוד שבטבע האדם והחברה התקינה.[1] גישה זו עשויה לעניין מחנכים במיוחד, כי יש בה כדי לאפשר למורה להגיע להבנה ואפילו לאהדה כלפי תופעות האמונה הדתית, מבלי לחייבו לקבל את תכניה כמאמינים אותו. והרי מה שדרוש מן הנוגע בתכנים דתיים הוא, קודם כול (ואולי גם סוף כול), שיבין ושייצג הצגה הוגנת את התכנים האלה לפני חניכיו, כי אלה הם המשותפת של כל ישראל.

א

מה צורך יש בטקסי הדת, בספרי הקודש, במערכת אמונות ובאורחות חיים הגדורות בגדר הלכה? למה לא ללכת אחרי מראה העיניים ותבונת הלב והמיית המעיים? לא רק הבנים שואלים שאלות אלה בדורות האחרונים, אלא גם אבותיהם. תשובה הראויה לשאלה ולשואלים חייבת להצדיק את קיומם של המרכיבים האלה של חיי הרוח כתכלית בפני עצמם, ולא כאמצעי לכל תכלית אחרת, כגון להשגת האושר או לתיקון החברה או לאחדות האומה (אף על פי שתכליות אל יכולות לבוא בעקבותם). שהרי המרכיבים האלה מוצגים — ומציגים את עצמם — כערכים מוחלטים וכאמיתות, וכוח השפעתם על האדם ועל החברה בא מתכונתם זו, עד שאין לדמות כי יפעלו את פעולתם אם ייתפסו כערכים מותנים ומועילים בלבד. קדושה, שאין שורשה אלא הסכמת בני אדם שהיא נצרכת כדי שהאושר יושג, או שהחברה תתוקן או האומה תתאחד, אינה קדושה אלא גינונים בעלמא. חוזרים אנו ומנסחים את

משה גרינברג פרופסור לתנ"ך באוניברסיטה העברית בירושלים.

נדפס בפתחים חוברת א–ב [49—50], אדר תש"ם (מרס 1980).

*הובא, תוך קיצורים אחדים, מתוך החוברת תכנים יהודיים בחינוך בישראל, שיצאה מטעם המזכירות הפדגוגית של משרד החינוך והתרבות בשבט תשל"ח (ינואר 1978) — העורך.

שאלתנו: מה ערכם המוחלט של טקסי דת, של ספרי קודש, של מערכת אמונה ושל
אורחות חיים גדורות בהלכה? מה אמיתתם?

יש בהוויה יותר מן הנראה לעין. בן האדם שממולי יש בו יותר מן הנראה לעין;
שלשלת המאורעות שהגיעתנו עד הנה יש בה יותר מן הנראה לעין; נושאי אחריות
— שופט, מנהיג או אם — אפופים דבר־מה יותר מן הנראה לעין; יחסי אדם עם
חברו טעונים מטען שהוא יותר מן הנראה לעין. ברור לכולנו, שאין ראיית שטח
הדברים תופסת את כללותם. יש בהוויות החיים מימד של עומק, מימד של "הַמֶּעֱבָר",
והמימד ההוא הינו מרכיב משמעותי של המציאות חלקה גלויה — נראית ומוחשת,
בת כמות ואיכות נמדדות — וחקלה מעבר לתפיסת־החוש הישירה. אם תעיין בדבר,
תמצא כי אין סדרי הקדימה והעדיפות, ובחינת הערכי והמשמעותי שבחיים, נקבעים
אך ורק על־פי מימד־הנראה־לעין, אלא נקבעים במידה לא פחותה בהתחשב במימד־
המעבר.

כיצד אפשר לצייר או לדמות את היבטיו של המימד ההוא, הנעלם? כיצד
להמשיג היבטים אלה כדי להרהר בהם? כיצד להביע אותם כדי לשתף בהם את
הזולת? רק באמצעות סמלים — חפצים או מונחים או סיפורים או טקסים או
התנהגויות, שכל־כולם לא באו אלא להצביע על מציאות שהיא מעבר להם. היכרויות
גולמיות של מימד־המעבר לובשות צורה רק באמצעות סמלים; ורק בהם אפשר
לטפח את ההכרה ולהגות בה, להביע אותה לזולת ולעוררה בלבו. כי לסמלי מימד־
המעבר יש סגולה לא רק לרמז וליַיצג אלא אף לעורר לפעולה. הסמלים הם כלים
המכילים את התפעלויות הנפש, ובאמצעותם אפשר גם להפעיל את הנפש.

יצירת הסמלים בשפע והשימוש הבלתי־פוסק בהם, הם ממהות טבעו של האדם,
הם מותר האדם מן הבהמה. לא נכזב אם נאמר, כי המשמעותי שבחיי האדם רובו
נתפס ומובע בסמלים — רמזים לחלקה הנעלם של ההוויה.

"אמר הפילוסוף: כבר התבאר תכלית הביאור, שהאדם מדיני בטבע, ושטבעו
שיהיה מתקבץ, ואינו כשאר בעלי החיים אשר אין לו הכרח להתקבץ" (מורה נבוכים
חלק ב, ראש פרק מ). והנה ממהותו החברתי־המדיני של האדם היא השאיפה ליצור
תחום של שותפות בערכים. שותפות זו קמה באמצעות סמלים — יותר נכון מערכת
סמלים — המתפשטת בקרב בני אדם מסוימים. תולדות האדם הן תולדות חברות
שהדבק המאחדן הוא מערכות סמליהן. השותפות בסמלים לא דיה שחיזקה את
החברה או קיימה אותה, אלא היא היא שיצרה אותה. בלעדיה לא דבק איש ברעהו,
לא שמח בשמחתו, לא עמד לו בעת צרתו, ולא חרף נפשו למות בעדו.

אם ממעיין היצירה האנושית שפעו סמלים שפיעה אינסופית, הנושאים
המסומלים משותפים לכל האנושות. מהם נצמצם את השקפתנו אל אותם סמלים
שנועדו להצביע על עצמיותו של המימד־שמעבר בהיבטיו השונים.

מקום נועד לסמל את המימד הזה, מקום הנאצל מן החיים היומיומיים החולפים,
המשתנים ומותני־המשמעות, כדי לסמל את הפכם — המציאות־בעצם והמשמעותי־
בעצם; הוא מקום קדוש. בני כל חברה הפרישו חלקה, אשר בעיני זרים אינה אלא
שטח בעלמא, ואילו בעבורם הוא תחום נאצל ומוקדש להוויה הנעלמת. בתחום זה
הקימו מבנה כלשהו כגון שער או בית. בעבורם את השער ובהיכנסם לבית, הם חשים
— לעתים בעוצמה רבה מאד — מימד אחר לגמרי של המציאות. אצל היהודים
מקום זה היה בית המקדש, ותחליפו היום — בית־הכנסת.

וכן בנושא הזמן. לבני כל חברה יש עתים מזומנות הנועדות להתעלות מעל
המימד התועלתי הגשמי המותנה והחולף — מימד החול — וליהנות מזיו של הקיים
לנצח, בעל הערך המוחלט. אלה עתים שבהן בא האדם במגע בלתי אמצעי עם
המשמעותי־בעצמו עם מקור הברכה והחיות, ומן המגע הזה הוא ניזון בשובו אל
עולם החול היומיומי. בשביל היהודי ששת ימי המעשה הם השרייה בחול — הדאגה,
ההתחרות והמאבק, ההצלחה והשמחה החולפת, והכבוד המדומה. **השבת** הוא הזמן
הנאצל והנפרש משאר ימי המעשה, הנועד לאפוף את האדם בזיו השבת (אשר גדריה
אינן אלא הקפת תחום נאצל). אין ימות החול יכולים להרחיק את האדם ריחוק גמור
מהתחום המחיה של ה„מעבר".

בדרכים שונות הסתמלה והתבטאה תחושת האדם במימד ה**מוסר**. אין האדם
מבחין רק במועיל ובמזיק, כי אם גם בטוב וברע. הוא חש בכוחו המושך של הרע
ובפיתוויו, וכנגדו הוא שואף לטוב. הוא מבחין בין המעשה הטוב לבין המעשה הרע,
ואינו אדיש להבדל שביניהם. איכפת לו אם הוא נוהג כך או כך: עשה טוב — יש לו
קורת רוח; עשה רע — נפשו עכורה עליו. ברוב החברות וברוב התקופות, הסתמלו
הבחנות ותחושות אלה בסמלים דתיים. ניגוד הטוב והרע הסתמל בישויות קוסמיות
איבות זו לזו — אלים ושדים. ויש אשר שדה־המאבק צויר כבנשמתו של האדם,
כמלחמת יצרי לבו — יצר טוב ויצר רע. תוקפם וממשותם של הטוב והצדק, האהבה
והרחמים, אף הם נסתמלו בישויות מתחום המעבר; בישראל נסתמלו במצוותה של
ישות־מעבר אחת מקיפת־הכול. במערכת השכר והעונש, שבדרך כלל הופקדה בידי
הישויות הללו, הסתמלה ההשתכנעות שבשביל האדם וחברתו העניין המוסרי הוא
עניין של חיים ומות, של קיום או כיליון.

אין האדם מכיר רק במצוי כי אם גם ב**רצוי**. בכוח דמיונו ובסגולת תקוותו אין
הוא מקבל את המצב הנוכחי, לא כתכליתו ולא כתכלית העולם בכלל. לעומת הרשעה
והמלחמה, הבדידות, העוני והצער הרווחים בעולם, הוא מעריך את הצדק והשלום,
האחוה, הרווחה והאושר, לא כהזיות מופלגות ובלתי מציאותיות אלא להיפך! הצדק
והשלום ושאר הטובות הנן, איכשהו, קנימידה שבהם הוא בוחן ודן את העולם; הנן,
איכשהו, ה**אמת**, שביחס אליה המצב הנוכחי הפגום מוערך כמשגה וכהחטאה. גם

הכרה זו הסתמלה. מסמליה — עולם טוב יותר במקום אחר (מעבר לסמבטיון), או בזמן אחר, אם בעבר (גן עדן), אם בעתיד (ימות המשיח), או בהוויה אחרת לגמרי (הישארות הנפש במחיצת האלוהים). באמצעות סמלים אלה תחושת הרצוי היא כוח המחזק ידיים רפות, והמשיב נפשות רצוצות מתלאות ההווה. משל לאור היום המציץ בקצה המערה הארוכה, והמשפיע עידוד על ההולכים בחושך לקראתו.

בין גדולי הסמלים בתולדות הרוח קיים מושג האלוהות. רבו מאוד ההבדלים שבמושג זה בין עם לעם, ובקרב עם מסוים — בין תקופה לתקופה. בכל זאת ניתן לקבוע כלל גדול ולומר, כי הסמל הזה, המחיש לרבי־רבבות בני־אדם את המבלול הרב־גוני והרב־משמעי של מימד־המעבר האופף אותם, העמיק והחדיר את הכרתו לתוך חייהם — ההוד, הסדר, המשמעות, היראה, האחריות, התום, התקווה ההתחדשות והתחייה. באמצעות מושג האלוהות ריכזו את כוחותיהם וטיפחו את הטוב והמעולה שבהם, וכפרטים וכציבור השיגו את עליוני הישגיהם. מושג האלוהות מבטא בצורה המלכדת והמקיפה ביותר את עוצמת מימד־המעבר המורגשת בחיי האדם. מי שיודע להבחין בין האלוהים לבין מושג האלוהות יאמר, כי באמצעות המושג חדר האלוהים לחיי בני אדם ועיצבם. לפיכך סמלי האלוהות הם קודשים — היינו אמצעים להמחשת המימד־שמעבר בחיים. אולם יש לזכור לעולם, כי ככל הסמלים לא הם האמת כי אם המסומל בהם.

אפילו סמל אדיר כמושג האלוהות יונק את משמעותו, בסופו של דבר, ממערכת שלימה של מושגים וערכים ומעשים, שהאלוהות היא אמנם היא ראש פינתה, אך לא כולה. אם נדבר ביהדות, למשל, מושג האלוהות שבה הנו חיוני, מעורר ומשפיע רק במערכת המשלבת את כל הסמלים. ואם כך ביחס לראש הפינה, שאר הסמלים על אחת כמה וכמה. המערכת היא בית יוצרה של המשמעות. הדת היהודית הנה מערכת סמלים כזאת, והיא בית יוצרה של המשמעויות אשר יהודים המחזיקים בה מגלים בעולם.

כעת מוכנים אנו להשיב על השאלות שבהן פתחנו את הדיון הזה. ערכם המוחלט של כל אביזרי הדת והנהגותיה הוא בסימולם את המימד־שמעבר ובהחדרתם את הכרתו לתוך חיי האדם. אין בזאת המצאת מימד שהוא טפל לעצמותו של האדם, אלא מתן ביטוי ולבוש למימד־הנעלם שכל אדם מכיר בו. בכך מתאפשר לאדם לחוש, להתעורר ולעורר אחרים למימד זה. אמיתם של אביזרי הדת היא לפי המידה שהם מבטאים ומרחיבים את המימד־שמעבר. היא אמת המוכיחה את עצמה למשתמש בהם על־ידי כך, שבאמצעותם הכרתו את המימד הולכת ומתגברת, הולכת ומעמיקה. ועם זאת, יסוד ההבנה הסמלי הדת הוא להכיר שהאמת אינה נבה אלא במסומל בו, וכי מערכת סמלים דתית רומזת לא רק אל מה שמעבר לאדם וגדול ממנו, אלא אל שמעבר וגדול אפילו ממנה. האמת שבדת אינה כלולה בה אלא

במציאות שהיא רומזת אליה בסמליה, ומעוררת באמצעותם להכרתה. לפיכך ניתן
לומר, שהדת מקנה לאדם תבונה להבין בתחומי מציאות שרק היא פותחת לו.

ב

תפיסה זו של הדת מובילה למסקנות מסוימות בעניין היחס שבין הדת לחברה
בכלל, וביחס שבין הדת היהודית לחברת היהודים בישראל בפרט; וכן בשאלת תפקידו
של החינוך הלאומי.

אמרנו כי חברה נוצרת וקיימת בזכות שותפות בניה בערכים. בתולדות האנושות
עמדה שותפות זו על מערכת סמלים דתיים המבטאים את ערכיה העליונים של
החברה. והנה קרה, שבתולדות גויי המערב — אירופה ואמריקה — נתהווה בעת
החדשה קרע בין הדת ושאר ערכי התרבות. במקום מקור ערכים אחד בא ריבוי
מקורות, כל מקור ותת־מערכת, בלי התאמה ובלי השלמה ביניהם. האידיאלים
המדיניים נובעים ממקורות־הגות ההשכלה, ששורשיה עולים עד הוגי יוון ומשפטני
רומי; האידיאלים הכלכליים נובעים מסברות מדעיות־למחצה, הבנויות בקצתן על
תורות התנהגות והסתברות, ובקצתן על חזונות תיקון החברה; ערכי הרוח נובעים
מצד אחד משיטות באסתטיקה ומתפישת האדם כ„משחק" בעיקרו (homo
ludens), ומצד שני מתורות סמכותיות — הדת (הנוצרית), המארכסיזם,
הפסיכואנאליזה. לפרט החי באווירת תרבות המערב, חסרה מסגרת המשלבת
והמלכדת את ערכיו הרבגוניים. הנצרות בחברה כזו היא, לכל היותר, הצד הדתי של
חיים חילוניים. אם הפרט מצליח ללכד את ערכי חייו בכלל, הצלחה זו היא אישית
לגמרי. פארה של החברה המערבית הוא דווקא פתיחותה למכלול „המשחק" האנושי.
והוא גם חוליה: „התמוטטות עצביה" של אירופה, חוסר יכולתה עמדות עקרוניות
ולהשתלט על פגמי־החברה, על קלקול מידות בתוך רווחה ושפע ללא תקדים. אלה
סימני החולי. כל עוד אין איום חיצוני על גויי המערב, ייתכן שאין קיומם בסכנה. גם
הפרט גם הציבור יכולים לחיות כשגופם משמש משכן לחיידקים הרסניים, והם
מתפקדים רק כדי לכלכל את קיומם. כאשר מתקיף אויב חסון מבחוץ, רק אז מתגלה
החולשה, והמנגנון הרעוע קורס בפני הגוף החזק המתקיפו. חוקר דתות החי במערב
והמשקיף על התהליך מתארו כך: מחלת רוח פושה בגוף החברתי. החיים מתרוקנים
ממשמעות; בני אדם מנוכרים זה מזה, בהיעדר חזון המפעים אותם יחדיו; לבסוף הם
מתנכרים לעצמם. מחזה נורא זה הוא המשכנע, אותנו, כי מערכת אמונה אינה
תוספת טפלה לקיום האנושי, קיום שביסודו הוא כאילו חילוני; אלא המערכות
השונות של אמונה הן הן הצורות המשתנות של הקיום האנושי. ההסתכלות בתולדות
האדם מעלה, כי טבעו של האדם הוא לחפש ולמצוא משמעות בחיים, ולבטא את
המשמעות הזו בסמלים — סמלי האמונה.[2]

אם זוהי השתכנעותו של חוקר המשקיף על התמונה הכלל־אנושית, לנו נקל להחיל את מסקנותיו על היהודים והיהדות.

היהדות אינה הצד הדתי של חיי היהודים; בתולדותינו, היהדות היא ממש צורת החיים של היהודי — מערכת המשמעויות השולטת והקובעת את מקומם של כל שאר הגורמים. סמלי האמונה — טקסיה, ספרות הקודש שלה וארוח חייה ההלכתיים — עיצבו את העולם כפי שנראה בעיני היהודי: חוויות הלידה, גידול בנים ובנות, יציאתם מרשות ההורים, הנישואים, הזדקנות, המיתה, הקבורה והנצחת שם המת — כל אלה עוצבו בדת. ברירת מקור הפרנסה, ההמודדות בקנאה ובשנאה, היחס להצלחה ולכישלון, בעיית רדיפת הכבוד, צורות הבילוי של שעות הפנאי, פיתוח הכישרון האמנותי — אף אלה עוצבו כלבוש לערכים דתיים.

התפוררות הליכוד התרבותי הזה אצל היהודים החלה במערב במקביל לתהליך החילון של גויי אירופה, והיא מגיעה כעת לשיאה בקהילות היהודית הגדולות במערב. תנועת התחייה היהודית הונעה בשאיפה להתחדשות המכלול התרבותי היהודי על כל גווניו. מעבר לצורך להמציא מקלט לנפשות יהודית שבסכנה, נהגה המדינה היהודית כבית יוצרה של הרוח היהודי בכל אותם תחומים שממעמד המיעוט המשועבד והתלוי סגר או צמצם בפני יהודי הגלות — עיצוב חברה בעלת חלוקת הון צודקת, מסגרת המעניקה חירות לפיתוח החינוך, מוסדות הדת והתרבות היהודיים, וכיו"ב. מנהיגי תנועת התחייה היו משוכנעים, כי באוצר התרבות היהודית היו קווים מנחים בכל תחום פעולה וביטוי אנושיים, והעוצמה הרבה של רעיון התחייה ינקה מהתפשטות הכרה זו (עמומה ככל שתהיה) בלבות המונים. העוצמה החברתית שנדרשה כדי להתגבר על הקשיים בדרך לתחייה, עמדה כולה על שותפות־ערכים וסמלי אמונה ממיגזר צר למדי של מערכת היהודית השלימה — אהבת ישראל, צדק חברתי, אהבת ארץ ישראל ומצוות יישובה. אולם מיגזר זה הספיק לשמש בסיס לליכוד המחנות בשעות חירום (ואמנם, במידה שלא היתה שותפות ערכים בענייני אמונה, כן לא נוצרה עוצמה ציבורית).

עם השגת הייעד המדיני הראשון — כינון המדינה — כבר הורגש שמשבר אידיולוגי ממשמש ובא.[3] אמנם, האיום הקיומי לא פסק מאז אף לרגע, והוא משמש עד היום כמכנה המשותף הנמוך לליכוד שורות העם. אולם מכבר התברר, כי ביצור רוחו של הנוער ומשיכת עלייה (אפילו מארצות מצוקה) תלויים ביותר מאשר פריטה על מיתר האיום הפיזי. היום מתבררת אמת יותר מרה כולל: בעיית פיתוח ארצנו (שלא לדבר על הגנותה) היא אמנם בחלקה בעיה טכנית וכלכלית, אך בחלקה היא בעיית ההתמסרות לתפקידים באמונה וביושר לב. ברור לעין כול, שלא נוכל להיבנות בלי תעשייה וחקלאות מתקדמות ומקורות אנרגיה חדשים. אך למבין ברור באותה מידה, כי מבלי להשכים לעבודה, לדבוק במשימה, לשרת בלב חפץ ולמאוס בשוחד ובבצע

קל, מבלי להתמסר לחזון, שלא אנו, כי אם רק הדורות הבאים, עשויים לראות בהגשמתו. בלי נאמנות לאידיאלים מהביעים את משמעות חיינו המשותפים — לא תהיה למדינתנו תקומה.

מאין תבואנה אותן מידות של נאמנות ומסירות אם לא מתחום אמונה משותפת — אמונה המכשירה את הפרט ואת הציבור לפעול ביחד, להתמיד בתוך הקשיים ולהתגבר על איבת עולם? ומהו כור מחצבתה של אמונה משותפת זו שתוכל ללכד אותנו, אם לא מערכת ערכיה וסמליה של היהדות? הרי רק כדי שהיהודים יוכלו להיות עצמם ולטפח את ערכיהם, נכנסנו למאבק גורלי זה שנמשך כבר דורות בארץ, ואינו אלא המשך מאבק בן אלפי שנים על קיומנו הסגולי מראשית לידתה של אומתנו.

וכי מה יוכל לשמש נס לקבץ סביבו את כוחות נעורינו ופזורינו — חזון שוויון המעמדים הכלל־אנושי? חזון חיים מסודרים נוסח שוויץ או הולנד? או אומנות ומוסיקה נוסח איטליה וגרמניה? או חזון השפע הוורווחה נוסח אמריקה? הרי אין צורך לבוא הנה ולהישאר בקלחת רותחת זו בשביל לרדוף חזונות כאלה. אחד הוא בלבד הבסיס שעליו תקומנה הדבקות והמסירות הנחוצות לקיים את עצמנו כאן: הרצון העז להשיג את התנאים שיאפשרו לנו לבטא את זהותנו היהודית בכל מכלול גווניה — זהות המיוסדת על הצורה (אם לא תמיד מתמצה בה), שבה סימלו היהודים את הכרתם המיוחדת של המציאות־מעבר.

בשביל שיהיה רצון עז זה, צריך להכיר את היצירה היהודית, את ערכיה וסמליה על כל מכלול גווניה, ולראות בה את המורשה הרוחנית הסגולית שלה. דבר זה הוא תפקיד החינוך הלאומי. אבל הכשרה רבה צריכים נושאי התפקיד עד שיצלחו למלאכה.

ג

תפקיד זה מביאנו אל שאלתנו האחרונה והעדינה — שאלת תקיפותם הנמשכת של סמלי הדת והתייחסותו של החינוך הלאומי אליה.[4]

אמרנו, כי טקסי הדת וסיפוריה וארחות חיי הלכתה הינם סמלים המצביעים על מציאות־שמעבר; כי האמת אינה הסמל אלא המסומל בו, וכי גם מערכת הסמלים כולה אינה אלא רומזת למה שמעבר לה וגדול ממנה. קביעות אלה נובעות בהכרח מתפישת פרטי המערכת הדתית הדתית כסמלים. מכאן, שאינם יכולים להיות גילומים שלמים וסופיים של אמיתות מתחום המעבר. מהותו של סמל היא, שאין דייותו אלא יחסית: יש שדיי יותר לסמל את המסומל ויש שדיי פחות, ובין כך ובין כך לעולם אינו יוצא מגדר סמל — מגדר רומז בלבד, שאין בו כדי להקיף ולהגדיר כל צורכו.

לפיכך יש לסמלי הדת היסטוריה; לאחר שנבראים, הם ניתונים לפירוש ולעיצוב מחדש במשך הזמן, עם השתנות נסיבות התרבות והתפתחותה. דבר זה מוכח יפה

מתולדות סמלי היהדות. קח, למשל, את מושג האלוהות: בתקופת המקרא הוא עוצב
בהיקש לדמות מלך רב, יושב על כיסאו בהיכל ומוקף פמליה, ושולח דברו לנתיניו
בידי שליחים; הוא בעל צלם ודמות, והאדם בדמותו. מסומלים בסמל זה הם, בין
השאר, היהוד והפקודה המחייבת שחשו נביא ישראל במציאות שמעבר-הנראה-לעין,
וכן הקירבה המיוחדת של האדם אל מקור היהוד והפקודה. מתקופת הגאונים ואילך,
כשטופחה החשיבה המופשטת, החלו לראשונה להבחין הבחנה ברורה בין משמעותן
הראשונה של מלים למשמעותן המושאלת לדימויים; התום הקמאי חלף. לשון
המקרא פורשה בבחינת "דיברה תורה כלשון בני אדם"; ומושג האלוהות זוקק עד
שנקבע כי "אין לו דמות הגוף ואינו גוף". אחר כך חזר ונתרכב במבוכי הקבלה. וכן
בטקסים: בראשונה היו כורכים את עשרת הדברות עם קריאת שמע, עד שבאו
המינים וטעננו כי רק אלה (עשה"ד) ניתנו בסיני, וחזרו וביטלו את אמירתן.

השתנות הסמלים או פירושם מחדש הינם הכרחיים בחברה שתנאי חייה משתנים,
אך שאינה מוותרת על המשך ייחודה. בישראל, האמצעי המוֹוסת, תהליכים אלה
במשך דורות של חילופי ממלכות, וכיבושים והגליות, היה התורה שבעל-פה. הלכה
שגיבשה ערך,[5] ובהשתנות נסיבות קיומה של ההלכה סתרה אותו ערך — באה תורה
שבעל-פה ופירשה אותה בהתאם לערך, עד כדי ביטול צורתה הראשונה מכול וכול.
"כשראה (הלל) שנמנעו העם מלהלוות זה את זה ועוברין על מה שכתוב בתורה
(דברים טו): 'הישמר לך פן יהיה דבר עם לבבך בליעל לאמר קרבה שנת השבע שנת
השמיטה וגו' — התקין הלל פרוזבול" (משנה שביעית י, ג) — הוא טכסיס חוקי
להערים על שמיטת חובות בשביעית.

כל זמן שכוח יצירה וביטחון רוחני שוררים בקרב עדת-המאמינים, תורה שבעל-
פה חיה וממשיכה לעצב, לפרש ולסנן את סמלי האמונה. אמנם, יש אשר נעצר
התהליך מחמת אסונות ודלדול כוח. אזי עלולים הסמלים להינתק מן החיים ולאבד
את סגולתם להורות אל ה,"מעבר", וליהפך לתכלית בפני עצמם, "מצוות אנשים
מלומדה". המופקדים על ההמשכיות מעלים ומשבחים אז דווקא את אטימותם,
ואוחזים בשיטה (עתיקת יומין ולכאורה מצויה כבר במקרא) שאין הלכות האמונה כי
אם גזירות-מלך חסרות משמעות כשלעצמן, ומכוונות רק לצרף בהן את הבריות —
היינו לנסותם אם יצייתו לגזירה ואם לאו.

במצב זה מוצא את עצמו היום רוב הציבור היהודי בישראל. הר' אליה שמואל
הרטום, בספרו "חיי ישראל החדשים", רמז לו בכותרת פרק כ"ב בלשון זה: "עכשיו
אין תורה במציאות". וכך הסביר את כוונתו:

"... שאין לנו הלכות שבעל פיהם אפשר להוציא לפועל במדינת ישראל את
החלק הנצחי של התורה. יש אמנם בידנו דברי התורה שבכתב ודברי שאר כתבי-
הקודש. ישנם בידנו יסודות מהתורה שבעל-פה מתקופת המשנה, והמקורות השייכים

לאותו הזמן, עד התשובות של הפוסקים האחרונים. אבל חסרה לנו עוצמה של התורה שבעל-פה, מפני שחסרים לנו אנשים שרוח התורה פועמת בהם, אנשים שירגישו את עצמם מוסמכים לקבוע את ההלכות הנחוצות כדי שתישמר התורה, ושייִדעו להביא את העם להכיר בסמכותם זו" (עמ' 127).

בכל מקום ובכל זמן שסמלים מתים נתבעים לשמש חברה, שתנאיה השתנו מאוד מאלה ששררו בשעת לידתם של הסמלים, קמים „שוברי צלמים" המבקשים לבער את הפגרים מן הבית. יש אשר המתקוממים מדברים בשם רעיונות נעלים יותר, ויש שהם מדברים מתוך בערות — והשניים עשויים לשמש בערבוביה.

כבר קרה, שמערכות סמלים חדלו לשמש את הציבור שלהן, ואז פשתה בו מחלת הרוח שתיארנוה למעלה. במצב כזה נמצאים המורים והמחנכים שליחי הציבור במצוקה ובמבוכה. לכל היותר אפשר לדרוש מהם שיורו את הסמלים על-פי משמעותם במערכת השלימה ההיסטורית — היינו לפי מה שביטאו בתפישת העולם היהודית בתקופת פריחתם ולפי גלגוליהם, כל עוד חיו ופעלו על הנפש. אי-אפשר לדרוש ממורים שיעשו את מלאכת היצירה הכבירה של פירוש ועיצוב מחדש, של סינון וביעור ויצירת יש מאין, שהיא תפקידם של אנשי רוח מחוננים.

מי מאתנו אינו חש העת „הרת-עולם", וכי מערכת חדשה ומחודשת של סמלי היהדות מבקשת להיוולד. בינתיים „באו בנים עד משבר וכוח אין ללידה". עם זאת פועמת בלבנו האמונה, כי הגישה למורשת היהדות כאל אוצרות בלומים של סמלים הרומזים על אמיתות המציאות-שמעבר ועל עושר של משמעויות — כי גישה זו תמשוך את הבריות אל האוצרות האלה להשתעשע ולרוות את הנפש בהם, עד שיווצר ציבור בעל אותה „מאסה קריטית" — מיצבור של יידע ותבונה של התלהבות וביטחון ועוז — אשר מתוכו יוכלו לצמוח ולשגשג כוחות רעננים אשר יחדשו את סמלינו לפי נסיבות ההווה.

1. שאבתי במיוחד מכתביו של חוקר הדתות Wilfred Cantwell Smith שמהם קראתי *The* *Faith of Other Men* (New York, 1963) (עיין מאמרה של חוה לצרוס־יפה בפתחים ב, כסלו תשכ״ח); The Meaning and End of Religion: A New Approach to the Religious Traditions of Mankind (New York, 1963);   *Encyclopaedia Britannica;* *Propaedia* (Chicago, 1974), s.v. "Religion as Symbolism."

משני הפרטים האחרונים דליתי הרבה, הן לניסוח הן למבנה, מפני שחכמתו של סמית נצרכת לנו ואין בידי לנסחה טוב ממנו: גרעתי והוספתי ושיניתי ועיבדתי לצורך העניין היהודי שאינו מעסיק את סמית בחיבורים אלה, אבל סוף דבר טבועים דברי במטבעו.

2. על־פי סמית, 1974, עמ׳ 500.

3. סימן ברור לכך, למשל, ספרו המרתק של ר׳ אליה ש׳ הרטום, **חיי ישראל החדשים**, שהושלם בשנת תש״י והובא לדפוס על־ידי בנו מ״ע הרטום בשנת תשכ״ו (הוצ׳ יבנה, תל אביב). מפליא תיאורו הישר והנועז של דת ומדינה של ימינו, אשר צפה אותן כבר לפני כשלושים שנה.

4. האמור בסעיפים הבאים בא להשיב על שאלה זו ברוח הגישה שתוארה לעיל. בוודאי יש בו משום עמדה אישית; אולם לא נקטתי עמדה לגבי מכלול השאלות הכרובות בגישה מבחינתה של עדת־מאמינים. הסבוכה ביותר מבחינתם היא שאלת הסמכות לדון ולהחליט בעניין שינויים בסמלי הדת, ובה לא נגעתי כלל, כי לא לעדת־מאמינים מועדים דבריי כי אם למחנכים. אלה הנם שליחיו של ציבור מגוון שאין בו דעה מוסכמת בשאלות חמורות אלה. לפיכך המורה הנאמן לשליחותו לא יערב בהוראתו עמדה אישית ביחס אליהן (העלולה להתנגש בזו של שולחיו), אלא ידבק בתפקיד ולמסור מורשת רוחנית ותרבותית. אם בתור אזרח רשאי ואפילו חייב הוא לנקוט עמדה וליהאבק עליה, בתור מורה במסגרת בית־הספר הציבורי, חובתו היא להעביר לחניכיו את המורשת המופקדת בידו כמיטב יכולתו, כמבואר להלך. מסגרות אחרות, פרטיות, כגון חוגי עיון הסמוכים למפלגות או לקהילות־קדש, הן המקום הנאות לליבון עמדה אישית וביטויה.

5. ליחס שבין הלכות לערכים עדיין חשובה מסתו של ח״נ ביאליק „הלכה ואגדה".

THE EDUCATIONAL PHILOSOPHY
OF LOUIS NEWMAN:
Selections from His Words and Writings

In this chapter of the *Festschrift,* the editors gave Louis Newman an opportunity to speak for himself. Unfortunately, Lou has never taken time out of his long and busy career to write a statement of the philosophy which underlies his work in the field of Jewish education. We have selected four pieces, none of them heretofore published. We would like to acknowledge the assistance of Dr. Steven Lorch, Shuly Rubin Schwartz, and Dr. Saul Wachs in helping us to obtain the materials contained in this chapter.

The first piece, "My Reflections on Counselorship," was written on the eve of Lou's assumption of the directorship of Camp Ramah in Wisconsin, in June 1951, and in it he outlines the role of the camp counselor in the setting of a Jewish educational summer camp. Lou Newman's work at Camp Ramah, and its impact, is described in a number of chapters of this work. Much of what he has to say to the camp counselor would apply to anyone working in an educational setting.

My Reflections on Counselorship

We must clearly recognize that camp is an educational situation. So is the street. But street play is haphazard. Its educational results may or may not be desirable. In camp we are expected to know in advance what kind of humans will emerge after they have been subjected to us. In camp we are supposed to know the effects of what we do, and we are supposed to know what to do in order to gain the ends we want.

If educational science has information for us and we don't know it, or know it and don't use it, we are abusing our responsibility. We have to know what should be done and we should be able to do it. At all times we should bear in mind a goal which we passionately desire, and a method, which, we are firmly convinced, will yield our particular goal.

Our campers come to us with interests and attitudes which we did not form. It is to be expected that most of them come to us with pre-formed preferences and aversions among the various activities which camp offers. When the camp staff schedules an activity for any particular group, what do those who prefer not to participate generally do?

They offer passive resistance. They go along complainingly. They drag. They say it's boring. They criticize the counselor's ability or his methods. They make a superficial attempt at doing something. Some do not dare to show their resentment to any person of the staff. They obey instructions. Among their peers they express their feelings. Rarely does one rebel outright. They "wait it out."

There are those who use "dodges" to get themselves out. They may get another staff member "to need them." They get stuck somewhere and so "have to be late." Some will disappear without permission—sneak away and hide. Some will "not feel well" and visit the infirmary. Some will even get themselves punished and put off activity.

On the other hand those who *want* to participate hurry to the activity. Some take the lead in organizing it. Others wait around to see what "we have to do today."

Usually a staff begins to cope with such a situation with "How do we get them all to participate—to hurry out of the bunk on time—to participate energetically?"

I'll begin, however, by asking why does one *want* them to participate? The words *"one wants"* should imply to us, as educators, some pre-conceived notions of desirable human beings.

My first question to you is: Have you *thought* about these matters? Can *all* the traits which you would like to see in people be integrated into one human being? Who, among all the people you know, embodies the ideas which you value in the abstract? Have you any hypothesis as to why this person developed as he did? What are you doing to make yourself the person you value in the abstract?

One who hasn't already given a great deal of thought to these questions is not yet ready to be a counselor, club leader, Sunday School teacher, or, in short, anyone who deliberately influences others' behavior. If one hasn't probed these matters deeply, hasn't selected some values and discarded others, but is merely going along on the momentum of childhood and adolescent habits, one has no moral right to be a teacher.

A person may challenge me and say, "You supply me with the goals which concern you and I will achieve them." If a person said this to me before the camp season opened, I would immediately answer, "You are honest, diligent and have many fine qualities. Find yourself a good job elsewhere." I would then put a few dollars in the JNF box in gratitude for having discovered early this dangerous value-less person. It is impossible for one person to successfully educate another to be a particular kind of human being, without a consciously and personally formulated philosophy. Robot-educators will not develop the persons we desire. As educators we dare not function on the sub-human animal level by force of unexamined habits and mental inertia. We dare not just behave and not reflect.

Here is what I've been thinking. In camp, we want (1) to create living situations through which all people, campers, counselors, and all workers, will become better human beings. By better I mean:

A. To expand one's ability to enjoy life, and to develop and use one's innate capacities.

B. To be sympathetic to other human beings, interested in seeing others enjoy life and capable of fulfilling such interests through proper action.

We want (2) to transmit to our campers the knowledge of traditional Jewish values. In a democracy each of us should become able, as one matures, to act less out of habit and unconsidered impulse, and more on the basis of independent reflective judgment and conscious deliberation. We believe that the experiences of our people as a whole, and of outstanding Jews individually, offer criteria to aid anyone in choosing among alternate ways of behaving. (3) To teach a working knowledge of the Hebrew language, both in reading and conversation.

These three goals with their suitable methods of implementation may not seem to be much. To me they are everything. Much is implicit in them and their ramifications are infinite.

Let us think about methods and goals.

"We want to create living situations through which people will *become*." The choice of words is deliberate. As I see the facts of educational science, the essence of method is this: to get young people to behave now as we wish them to behave as adults, the reward being intrinsic in the act, and extrinsic group approval being incidental.

Most civilized cultures in the world, in the education of their young, rely upon one variant or another, of the catechism method. Some children are forced to study paragraphs which add up to "I will be good." Some children learn proverbs. All children are expected to know verbally the correct responses, in hypothetical moral situations. And almost everyone believes that these words influence conduct positively and mould character. And almost all of those who know that it doesn't, go on teaching through words, hoping, against fact, that something good will come of it. Words may influence children but not in the way it is generally assumed. A 12-year-old girl last Passover won a Barton's chocolate prize with "Why I like to go to Hebrew School." She told me privately, and I believe, honestly, that it was all a lie. This child had learned a kind of behavior with the aid of the right slogan, namely, hypocrisy.

I believe that all thinking people are concerned with responses that come from the whole body, not just from the mouth or pencil point. We must discard all variants of catechism education.

To elicit behavior that is more than words, cultures, civilized and uncivilized, have used coercion. "The quality of coercion is twice cursed. It corrupts him who acts, and him who received." No matter what isolated habit is impressed upon a youngster by means of coercion, injury is done to the youngster.

A person is never coerced without being hostile as a consequence. Those who coerce frequently deceive themselves. They may use anger, glances which indicate lack of love or sympathy, and threats of loss of privileges, or status among peers. They believe they are clever, not coercive. But a person who acts against his will, or is restrained from acting, feels with his whole being this limitation of his freedom, and resents it. Someone, it may not be the powerful person, will at some future time bear the brunt of the hostility thus generated.

Our culture generally is hostile to criticism of prevalent methods. One hears slogans such as "You have to toughen em up," "A child must learn self-control," "You can't always have your way in life," "A child has to learn to pay attention to others," "What's wrong with memorizing?" These are, by implication, methods and goals contrary to our approach. This is false. These goals and proper steps to attaining them we accept. The conflict is elsewhere.

It is an old chestnut that not everything which pleases the

child is consequently good for him. We want to give this statement a new slant. How many counselors have said, "But they love the grades we give them for inspection." One camp director told me, "I don't care if 90% of the 'color-war' is done by the counselors. Do the kids get excited? Do they have fun? That's all that counts." Remember—some youngsters get to like opium.

Where do *we* begin?

Did you ever love anything? Really? With a love that is different from one's love of parents—there is generally too much dependence and fear in that love. A love that was all positive and not negative in the least? Did you ever love something that couldn't harm you, never harmed you, but gave you deeply experienced pleasure? A pet dog? A baby brother or sister? A little cousin? Perhaps you never really loved without obligation, without fear, without dependence?

If *one hasn't* then one's capacity for sympathy has yet to be developed. The capacity of getting out of one's own skin and sensing the world through another's desires, pains, pleasures, fears and anxieties. This is the basis of educational work. To influence an individual, not to deceive him or trick him temporarily—but to give direction to his life, one has to be able to perceive the world as the individual perceives it. Do that, and you will revolt at the glib, automatic, mass-production rules of education. You will resent the assumption that individuals are machines off the production belt which will react uniformly. You will experience within you emotions which will rebel at uneducational procedures, even before you can articulate in words why it is you are apprehensive.

Are you doubtful? There are scientific books in camp to prove it. But why should this thought be new to you? Didn't you learn the story of Hillel on human behavior, *"V'ahavta l'reacha kamocha,* and the rest is commentary"? Yes, to be an efficient educator one has to be a decent human being in the highest sense.

A recent survey, by the U.S. Bureau of Education, on the qualities of successful teachers in different areas of education offered the following conclusion:

A thorough knowledge of subject matter is absolutely essential but insufficient to produce a teacher. The excellent teacher was characterized by, either an intuitive or trained understanding of human beings, and an interest in the welfare of the human being. Subject matter was merely a tool for a more all-encompassing goal.

So we must learn to sympathize deeply with humans, every *one* of them.

Are you afraid? Are you being pushed? Are you going to be punished for something? Then take a vacation—because you cannot identify or sympathize with others. You have yourself to take care of.

It is important for each of us that we reflect about our personal situation in Camp, sense any feeling of threat to our personalities, put it into words, and do something about it. We should satisfy our doubts, remove our apprehensions, ask for changes, make suggestions, ask for relief, and do the things which will eliminate any sources of anxiety. One of my ways of coping with my personal anxiety is by communicating with you through this paper.

If we are worried about our personal status we will be alert and intelligent in its defense. All our energies will be mobilized in the service. What will be left for the service of the Campers?

Once our energies are freed from self-concern and self-protection we are ready to grow. And when we grow our campers grow.

Am I belaboring the obvious?

Let's each ask ourselves: How many new interests did I acquire within the last year, two years? What have I started to learn completely from scratch—something that even a ten year old can start?

Our specialty counselors have asked that members of the staff take advantage of their services. Have you ever put an Israeli "Chalil" to your lips? Have you wished you could tamper with some of the varied materials available in arts and crafts? Would you like to get a few counselors together and put on a short but polished performance in song, dance or drama?

(There's no law which says that counselors can't perform together with campers.) Have you wished to improve your swimming? You will have some free hours during the day or evening. You will have days off. *Do it.*

Can you imagine what will happen to our campers when they see a growing staffer, perhaps an excellent athlete, messing in clay, an artist struggling to coordinate breathing and hand movements in the water, a licensed graduate teacher asking the professor how to say something in Hebrew, etc., without end. If we sympathize with the campers they will like us and trust us. They will tend to identify with us. Our example, not our directive, will be the best teacher.

Eliezer

The second piece, "Memorandum for Hebrew and Sunday School Teachers," was written by Lou Newman in the summer of 1961, in his capacity as director of the Melton Research Center of the Jewish Theological Seminary of America. The Center had undertaken to utilize the religious school of Congregation Tifereth Israel in Columbus, Ohio, as its model school. In this memorandum Lou describes some of the "root concepts" which ought to be reflected in the learning experiences of the students in that school.

Memorandum for Hebrew and Sunday School Teachers

Every activity, formal or informal that we carry on in our schools must lead to behaviors, attitudes, and skills which will achieve or are in themselves the following objectives:

Everybody concerned with the school, student or parent, should know that the purpose of attending a Jewish religious school is to learn how to lead the good life, and how to go about defining the good in new situations that arise and which we have not met before as individuals or groups. The teacher must always be ready to defend his activity as one that leads to the good life. The good life may be that of the individual, the family, the city, or the world. Judaism and Jewish religion is a history of this search. Judaism assimilates from every source that it comes into contact with, those ideas and practices which lead an individual or a group to live better.

To lead to the good life we must question what it is that man wants, what is it that he needs, what are the ultimate valuable processes for him, and the ultimate valuable activities for him. What is the source of value? When we study and question in this way we are studying religion. When we teach Bible and history we are teaching the development of religious answers to these questions. The purpose of the entire educational process is to lead our youngsters to an "individual standing at Mount Sinai." By this we mean that the individual or youngster must continue to grapple with the world, the impersonal and the personal world until he concludes that he has a stable philosophy to live by. We can teach a child the ritual skills and their purposes; a religious conviction which helps one to live comes from a wide learning about oneself and the world. In this search he will be led to examine deep root concepts of our Jewish heritage. Here are some:

1. We must search for truth, be ready to accept truth, and build our lives as individuals and as communities on the basis of facts. Man cannot advance by blocking from his mind certain facts which may make him reorganize his way of life. The truths should be the truths about himself as he is, his deficiencies, scientific truths—with the known fact that they are limited by man's present knowledge.

2. In Jewish religion, God has been described negatively, that is, by what he is not. Man's constant search for meaning in the universe and the physical inconceivability of God is something that human beings must learn to live with. That which we believe God is, we infer from the history of the universe as we know it. Therefore, we think only of God's attributes.

3. Man in society is perfectable. Barriers between individuals, between communities, and between nations can be removed. People can learn to cooperate, and an individual's love can include every other human being in the world.

4. To achieve cooperation and not to give way to personal instinctual desires which rule out consideration of other human beings, man must discipline himself and establish a balance between personal satisfactions and that which he does for others. He must control his impulses. He must set himself reminders of his ideals. Self-gratification is not the highest ideal in life.

5. The child must be introduced to the eternal questions by word of mouth and by experience. Some of these experiences can be arranged, others he will have to wait for life to bring to him. Knowledge of science, the awe which the knowledge of nature induces, these can be arranged. The great tragedies and happinesses take place without our arranging them. History shows us how eternal questions are given tentative local shape

and color. Some have lasted for a long time and some have been given up. This item overlaps with the search for truth.

6. Man feels alone and needs help, hence, the cruelty of lethargy, of conformity to a status-quo, and the need for cooperativeness and sensitivity to the on-going needs of other human beings. Man needs self-encouragement and stock-taking of his strengths for which he offers thanks in the form of prayer, and assesses his deficiencies after which he tries to mobilize himself to overcome them in the form of prayer.

7. This leads us to symbolism in living. For most of us there is no avoiding the fact that the mitzvot are voluntarily chosen by us because they help us to lead the good life. Today mitzvot must have a rationale in terms of the good life. In individual personal life or in community living these mitzvot are either reminders of what we say we want to do, or are in themselves the things we want to do—enhancers of the good life.

8. In studying all of these we come to the root concept of change. Throughout Jewish history, in attempting to achieve the good life, and to live with consciousness that this is their God's world, Jews have changed their rituals, and their ideas of the cosmos. Whereas the fundamental impulses have remained the same, the change *process* becomes an important root concept to teach our children. At all times Conservative Judaism talks of historical Judaism. Historical Judaism means that we must study the situation in the world before the Bible was given and studied, then the period during which the Bible was developed, and finally the post-biblical period until today. From there the challenge must be thrown to the youngsters to develop the kind of Jewish life which will help them to lead the good life today.

9. The historical tie of the Jewish people to the land of Israel where as a people they will live the ethical and good life is important. The sentence in the Bible which says that if you do not live right you will be vomited up from the land must be repeated over and over again. Likewise, the peoplehood of Israel, the bond which exists among Jews everywhere when they accept the same spiritual outlook, must be stressed.

10. All of these concepts must so be studied, so that the

internal hindrances within ourselves and the external hindrances from society at large and the family around us are studied and we see what specifically prevents us from behaving in a disciplined manner and from carrying out the ideas which we are accepting. This means that our knowledge of the social situation in the world at all levels is indispensible for the religious school teacher. He must know himself as a human being, he must know the problems of the city, the state, the country and the world at large and constantly intertwine the ideals of which we are talking and what is going on and show how frequently they are relevant.

11. Throughout all of these learnings there must also be an awareness of the means-ends trap or, much ado without consequences. By this is meant the self-satisfaction that derives from practicing a discipline while forgetting the end to which the discipline is supposed to lead; going smugly through many rituals of learnings while being insensitive to the pains, hurts and needs of people around one, is a perfect example. Heretofore the idea-action combination took place *within* the isolated or enclosed Jewish community. There was little the ghetto Jew could do to influence the ethical outlook of those who enclosed him. The Jew worried about his own behavior and about his small Jewish community's assistance to any person in need. Today we must learn how to take our general principles of ethics for the society at large and convert them into ideas for improving everybody's existence; our concern for others through action stops only at the end of the world.

12. Within the Conservative Movement there is space for much intellectual maneuvering about theology, ritual and change. No code for all Conservative Jews has been established. *Two* principles are functioning among the leading thinkers of the movement: (1) We Jews have ritual forms which have helped us achieve our spiritual goals. Let us not destroy them wantonly. (2) Change in religious living does take place. Let us control the change process so that it does not destroy us.

This piece, "Address to the June, 1964 Graduates of Akiba Hebrew Academy," was written by Louis Newman when he was invited to give the address and received the Joseph Cohen Award at the June 1964 commencement of the Akiba Hebrew Academy. In his address he asked the graduates to carefully consider the challenges of modern life and what Jewish tradition has to offer in response. After a long tenure as principal of the Academy, Lou left the position several years prior to delivering these remarks in order to become director of the Melton Research Center.

Address to the June, 1964 Graduates of Akiba Hebrew Academy

Dear Graduates:

Tonight I want to warn you of a basic omission in college education and offer to you a Jewish solution.

Were you to do some research in college catalogs and among college seniors you would probably be surprised to discover that there is insufficient reason to assume that the college education which you are about to receive will be a good one. Of the 27 of you who are graduating tonight it is quite likely that more than 20 will not be required to examine in any systematic way the great goals to which man has dedicated himself through the ages. You will *not* be required to understand what great thinkers have said to each other across the centuries. You will *not* be asked to formulate for yourself that which would make life worthwhile and meaningful nor will you be given the opportunity and encouragement to compare your choices in a scholarly way with those of other students. You *will* be required to know, for a semester at least, many facts, and some interpretations of the facts. You will also be required to know some scholarly skills in some of the disciplines. With these you will be in a good position to earn a living. But as the cliché has it, there is little reason to assume that your full college course will have included a guided experience in learning what to live for.

All of this is so, not because schools have suddenly gone bad. Rather they are still growing and have not yet become good. You are right, of course, when you infer that I believe a college is not worthy of its name if it does not stimulate and competently help a student to search for worthy ends in living. At the conclusion of my remarks I will tell you that you will have to work this out for yourself. And I will have a suggestion.

I believe it is true of all but few major courses, that they teach you information or a skill which you can sell. And because this is so, and there is little if any force in most colleges operating to give to you a truly liberal education, you find courses like: (a) psychology for interviewing; (b) psychology for teaching; (c) psychology for business.

But you don't find: (a) the *implications* of psychology for ethics; or (b) the *implications* of psychology for religion.

You do find books on these subjects by scholars but rarely do you find any courses. Because there is so much knowledge in the world and it is departmentalized, special anti-educational forces are set in motion in the world of learning. You may have read recently about the absence of contact between the specialists in the humanities and the specialists in the sciences. Often within the humanities and within the sciences themselves scholars do not have much to talk about if they are not in the same special field. To overcome this, some small colleges have instituted a book-of-the-month program. Everyone on campus, instructors and students, reads the same book so that occasionally they can talk meaningfully to each other about something they have in common. What they lack is a common frame of reference or common concern about what is important. If they had one, they would be able to talk about the contributions of different scholarly disciplines to something which all would have in common.

If what I am telling you fits the facts, you will not find the campuses places where older scholars and young students have as one of their preoccupations the systematic pursuit of ultimate values, of how one applies them in real life, or how one resolves conflicts among moral dilemmas. You will find some students active in movements for needed social change. This is commendable. Far less often will you find students involved in needed personal change, i.e., change of themselves. And rarely will you find anyone engaged in either, who is acting in the light of carefully, systematically examined and deliberately chosen principles.

To be what I am picturing, the students would have to be permanent students of philosophy or religion, applying their selected principles to themselves, personally, i.e. *intra*-personally, and to others, i.e., *inter*-personally. And, of course, I am saying to you *that* is the obligation of every human being, no matter how he earns a living.

Nor does our valued off-campus pluralistic culture help us very much in achieving a deliberately chosen way of life. It is my conviction that in an odd sort of way we are becoming less and less pluralistic. Not because American culture is becoming monolithic. It is not. Nor because it is becoming increasingly uniform—which it is. But because to have any kind of meaningful pluralism you must have as participants a number of self-respecting, serviceable individual cultures. *And individual cultures are coming apart.* Whether the cultures are ethnic groups, religious groupings or synthetic groupings like the Marxist, or humanist groups, they are not serving their purpose, namely, they are not being used by people. They are not being lived out with their implicit value choices, their ritual teaching forms for maintaining group solidarity and for stimulating personal courage. It is increasingly difficult to find people—people who live according to an organically whole, inwardly coherent outlook. We do live, instead, with parts of different cultures. Sometimes these parts are in harmony. More often they are in conflict. Let me illustrate simply the strain which we put on ourselves, or, as the New Englanders say, the mishmash of principles, with which we function daily.

I. One example is the conflict between any form of religious Judaism and our business sub-culture. It merits the name, *sub-culture*, because it takes in the greater part of most working men's lives. Immediately you will think of a variety of possible contradictions—of people functioning with a mixture of principles—some from the business world and some from the religious.

II. A second example has its origin in the fact that religion teaches the need for a stable family, of seeking a mate of good personal qualities. Our *sub-sub*-culture, advertising, whose goddess is Aphrodite (sexual stimulation, in plain English), entices people and conditions them to the gaudy, the superficial, disregards the youth in our community and the dangers of unceasing over-stimulation.

You get the idea. Tension-creating combinations of behavior from different cultural sources operate in disharmony. Think of the monstrous combinations of religious ceremonies and conspicuous consumption; of Hanukah lamps and Christmas trees in a Jewish home, of valuing the use of intellect and inquiry in general and limiting it in religion; and conversely, of valuing ritual in general life and repelling the ritual of religion under the force of the anti-religious sub-culture which exists in our society. Briefly, one would be hard put to learn from the life of people at large what a thoroughgoing Judaism would be like, or, for that matter, a humanism or a Christianity.

And now back to college. I want to point to two kinds—there are many others—of campus sophisticates, instructors and students who avoid coming to grips with the problems of a person's responsibility for his behavior. One plays God—let's call him the pseudo-rationalist. The other plays Child—let's call him the unarrested adolescent. In any school where the pursuit of the enduring values and their implementation does not play a key part in the curriculum and does not affect the intellectual climate, an intellectual vacuum develops into which "pseudos" make their way. When specialists, who have not had very much of a humanizing education, face problems of the meaning of life, many tend to commit the sin of particularity, substituting the part for the whole, or seeing the whole universe through the lens of their particular competence. It is not what the specialist knows that is dangerous. It is what he does not know. It is the unwarranted assertion on matters where the specialist has no competence that endangers you when you drop your critical faculties. When a scientist is the one who commits such errors we call it scientism—the embellishing of unwarranted assertions with a halo of scientific or rationalistic terminology. But this may be an error of any specialist. What is most treacherous in their approach is the artificial elimination from life of areas where pure fact-finding and rationality are insufficient to guide us. Put another way— they would have you believe that they act only on fact and restrain their actions when the facts are not in.

Man is a probabilistic animal at his intellectual best. That's a fancy way of saying he always acts on faith. In matters which concern him very deeply, like falling in love, deciding how he shall encourage his children to behave, sacrificing his personal pleasures for others, the facts are never completely in for man. Then why would our sophisticate put on a pseudo-rationalistic show? The answer is: to avoid having to make explicit their principles of choice, *which they assume on faith,* consciously or unconsciously, with more or less rational elements. By avoiding such explicit statements, you cannot criticize them with their own principles, they may be all saint or all jungle animal, or a mixture of both. They will deride *you* for being a person who candidly declares an explicit faith. And faith was not a flattering word on the campus until recently.

At their worst, the pseudo-rationalists, following no consistent pattern, for they chose none with deliberation, may be the most irrational of people. Through self-deception, they avoid responsibility for their behavior.

The opposite side of the coin is the *unarrested* adolescent. He may be 40 or more. But he has not yet made up his mind as to what actions, people, institutions he shall commit his loyalty. He is spiritually amorphous. Daily he acts—he has to—and these actions involve choices. But he doesn't know that he chooses. He is not aware that he is either helpful or not; charitable or not; consistent or not. However, to hear him, he doesn't know what life is *really* like. In contra-distinction to the pseudo-rationalist he knows very well that all the facts never come in, in vital personal decisions. But he is still waiting for more information. This attitude, which made sense when you as high school students displayed it, in an adult is a sign of childish self-deception. In any case it permits one to vacillate from day to day without any internal pressure to any consistent rational pattern. Thus our permanent adolescent also can avoid recognizing himself.

No! You, too, will never get all the facts. But you can, you must, if you are to attain your humanity, formulate for yourself the guidelines by which you are going to live that will be your religious faith. That formulation, and its implementations, are the most important tasks which you face in life.

I am suggesting that you learn about comprehensive cultural systems and ideologies. Study those which exist in writing, those of the Jewish tradition or of Plato, for example, and compare them critically. I plead with you to do on an adult level what we could not do at Akiba, to become deeply informed of our Jewish tradition and seek its guiding principles for personal and social living. Unfortunately, Jewish thought developed over 3000 years and is not organized for you in a currently popular frame of reference, in current philosophical terms. You will have to work hard first to translate its thought from the styles of different times and places. You will have to remember that it was never written for outsiders who would examine its merits, test its internal consistency, etc. It was always directed to the young and old who lived within Judaism and took its major premises for granted. You will have to learn to extract those major premises which transcend time and place. The premises concern questions, such as: (a) What is worthwhile for a person? (b) Among what kind of people, in what kind of situations, under what rules, shall a person live in order to achieve what is worthwhile? (c) Specifically, what is the proper kind of family life? (d) What is the right kind of community in which families should live? (e) To whom should authority be given? and (f) How shall authority be used?

The word "democracy" is not sufficient. It is a safeguard to let us work out what we want, a method, but it doesn't in itself aid each individual to sensibly make his choices. Each of us must take his stand in this world so that he will use the democratic process to achieve what *he* considers important.

I urge you to examine Judaism for its clinical approach, for its guidance to individuals, i.e., what an individual shall value and how one should train himself to be able to value what is worthwhile. I urge you to examine its sociological approach—what should a community be like so that individuals can achieve what is worthy of value?

You will discover a religious philosophical system of thought about God and man, about faith, that is in harmony with all modern knowledge and offers principles of living which the "facts" alone never supply, because a faith to live by always transcends facts. You will then have a set of personal and social ideological tools to achieve a ממלכת כהנים וגוי קדוש, which I like to translate freely for educational purposes: "A government of citizens who are so aware of their self-transcending obligations and so disciplined in their mutual interaction that they constitute a holy nation."

I urge you to discover how modern life challenges you and what Jewish tradition has ready in response.

The final selection from the words of Lou Newman is taken from a speech made at a Hebrew College open board meeting (March 14, 1983), honoring him on the occasion of his retirement from the position of executive director of the Boston Bureau of Jewish Education. In it he discusses three areas which need to be addressed in order to significantly improve the quality of Jewish education in the United States: (1) the need for the community to take Jewish education more seriously, (2) the need for Jewish educators to grapple with the question of how one educates for religion in a nonauthoritarian mode, and (3) the need for the development of a long-range plan to provide well-prepared teachers for the schools of the Conservative and Reform movements.

Speech to a Hebrew College Open Board Meeting

. . . It is superfluous to tell this audience that the organized Jewish community must have larger concerns and different criteria from those which often prevail. The community has reason to be concerned with the holding power, the strength, of much of Jewish education that takes place today when that education will be tested in the future under adverse circumstances. My first additional comment to the Report, therefore, is this: The serious side of Jewish education is often neglected by satisfied schools, and they are not even aware of what they are omitting. Leakage in the schools is taking place and people don't know it. What we do educationally for children from ages four to eighteen should be guided by *clearly understood Jewish goals.* Formal classroom study, curricular experiences, and the school environment should be shaped by these goals. But too often they are not. The late Dr. Heschel spoke of the "trivialization of education." He said what young people need is not religious tranquilizers, not religion as a diversion, not religious entertainment, but spiritual audacity." He also said, "While the climate has never been particularly favorable to either Judaism or any attempt to serve God, Judaism must learn to survive in spite of, and because of, adverse spiritual conditions. It would be suicidal to live by the maxim that unless the climate favors our principles, it will have to be discarded." In my judgment, Dr. Heschel's strictures apply today even more than they did some twenty years ago.

In my view, the most basic goal from which guidance should be derived by any program claiming to be Jewish education is this (I will read to you from something I wrote a few years ago with Susan Shevitz):

Every eighteen year old should know about the basic challenge of existence. It is that the world does not appear to us with its meaning or purpose as given. It is an ever-continuing, challenging puzzle. Humankind, however, is irremediably limited in its capacity to solve this puzzle. Every way of life, therefore, every religion, every philosophy, and every articulated "style" that is at all appealing, is a subjective imposition of some meaning upon the universe. Because there are always the unknowns behind the beginnings and the ends of life and of the world, no solution to the problem of meaning is complete. Yet, for the thinking person who would rescue existence from alternating absurdity and tragedy, it is an absolute necessity to make a considered, subjective choice.

Whether called philosophy, religion, or life-style, the choice is what a person bets his life on. The end of the choice may be the self and its particular mode of satisfaction, or the welfare of self and others in a tranquil community, or the will of God as it is believed to be known, or a combination of these. The Jewish educator's task is to make clear, with the purpose of convincing, how Judaism enables one to respond to the unceasing challenge of being alive.

My second observation is this: The task of educating for religion in a non-authoritarian mode has not been addressed by professional educators either in the professional literature or in the schools of education. This idea may not be readily grasped. It refers to the fact that non-orthodox religious teaching encourages or tolerates many different views in important elements of religious thought and practice. And while these different·ideas are bound in print and in lectures for adults, and occasionally find their way into children's texts, the academic educational leaders have not offered guidance to teachers that includes this goal: Teaching for openness of mind and the possibility of making choices in religious ideas and practices.

On the adult level, we hear rabbis outside of the Orthodox tradition who, as they preach, recognize that their audiences may or may not observe a particular ritual, may or may not be committed to a particular belief, and may attend synagogue essentially to pray or essentially to socialize. In short, the rabbis take account of the different commitments to Jewishness by which their members live.

The rabbis' audiences, we must remember, send children to religious schools and by acts of commission and omission, influence the Jewishness of their children at home. The Reform Movement *de jure* and the Conservative Movement *de facto*, interact with their adult adherents on the basis of free choice among the elements of Jewish commitments. The rabbis respect individual differences. They inform, teach, and try to persuade. I do not know of a Reform or Conservative synagogue that gives a commitment test to any applicants for membership.

Now, it is important to note that although the openness in intellectual, theological, and religious ritual observance has been with us for a long time, the professional educational arms of these open Movements have not focused on this characteristic of their respective ideologies. They have not analyzed nor responded to the special task of Jewish open-ended religious education for the young in the schools. They have not delineated what characteristics the curriculum must reflect, what professional skills the teachers must acquire, and how one should offer common experiences as educative, trial experiences rather than as authoritarian compelling ones. In short, this mode of education has not yet been perceived as a challenge by the philosophers, administrators, and curriculum makers of the schools of education in Jewish life. This openness and its assurances are no small matter. There are at least three points of view which are the basis of Jewish commitment: first, the Jewish supernatural view of revelation, second, the Jewish religious humanistic view without supernatural revelation, and third, Jewish secular humanism without a theology. I do not mention Zionism here because when Israel is considered not only a place of refuge, it is an ideal that must be integrated with one of these views. Now, consider what effect holding each of these views has in one's understanding and commitment to each of these elementary school subjects that I will mention. This may sound technical to you but I've got to point at least to the problem that is involved for the working teacher today in a non-authoritarian school.

You are the teacher—you, sitting here, are the teacher in a school with families representing the three views that I have mentioned. What do you say about prayer? So many questions immediately come to mind. The choice is not easy for the teacher to make without guidance. Should every child be urged to pray? Does God answer? The child is asking: "Does God answer?" "What do you think?" "How does He answer?" "Does He listen to me?" Should a student pray if he or she doesn't feel like praying? The teacher needs help to convey choice in an intellectually honest way, and yet the teacher needs to devise at the same time a common prayer experience for all the children in the class.

Consider ritual. Ritual is a reminding and instructional mechanism. It is also an experience as a comforting and ennobling or joyful life experience. In a school where there are no musts, no "you have to's," should the teacher put a value on the traditional ritual? Should the Reform teacher encourage the putting on of tefilin? I know some who do. Should the Conservative teacher talk about the choices of halakhic behavior? The split decisions of the Conservative Law Committee say in effect, "Take your choice."

Consider ethical imperatives in the tradition. Every ideology in Judaism is concerned with ethical imperatives. Why be good? Did God instruct us? How did He instruct us? Are non-believers good people? Can they be good people?

Take God. Do you teach authoritatively that God exists? Do you say that God is in every person? Why do people believe in God? Why does God make the little baby's teeth hurt?

Consider the Torah. Did God give the Jews the Torah? How? When? Did men write it? What does it mean when one says, "God inspired men to write the Torah"? Does God inspire people to write the Torah today?

At this point, you may have concluded that I am belaboring a point unnecessarily. My only answer is that my experience with tens of teachers and thousands of students in a specially structured situation showed that children learn to suppress their questions and curiosity. They do this either because of authoritarian put-downs or because of silly evasions of the gravity of their questions by the teachers. Over and over again, when they were encouraged by teacher prodding and intellectual honesty, children ten years old and older, have let loose a flood of basic existential questions about the universe in general and Judaism's response in particular. The children have questions—even the younger ones, with whom we didn't deal. Show them that you respect them and then they will ask you their questions, and the questions will be about the most basic existential elements of living.

The Long Range Study emphasizes the need to upgrade teachers with knowledge and skills. Now, in the light of what I have said, add to the teachers' assignments the task of conveying respect—subjective, religious affirmations and negations in basic areas of the Jewish school curriculum—then remember again, professional, academic education has not offered help. I've now pointed to two areas—(1) seriousness in Jewish education, which is *not* dominant, and (2) the unreadiness of the educational profession, and consequently the working, face-to-face teacher, to deal with freedom of choice in the Conservative and Reform Movements and other non-orthodox situations.

I want to focus what I have presented from a different perspective. The Jewish school teacher's main task is fundamentally different from that of the general studies teacher in a public school or a private general school. It is more difficult. The general studies teacher is content- and skill-oriented. The ideal Jewish school is, or should be, concept- and ritual-practice-oriented. Most general school learning is immediately practical and useful. Interwoven in general schooling, especially today, is the notion that what is learned will ultimately pay off. In the Jewish school there should be emphasis on mutual concern; on giving rather than earning; on sensitivity to others rather than on a concentration of self. In general schooling, the content is recognizable from the student's environment. The reading ritual skills learned in the Jewish school often have no place to function.

The Jewish school has to be counter-environment, and whether we like it or not, from its earliest opportunity, philosophically oriented לעשות את הטוב והישר "to do that which is right and good." And all of this, the knowledge, the reading skills, and the ceremonial habits, has to be imprinted and become permanent life cargo for all the students through the work of our teachers.

Now, if my perspective fits reality, then in many schools, much of what Judaism offers will not be available to students. That's the point I'm getting at. There is an urgent need for personnel upgrading and a need to overcome a professional lag in delivering non-arbitrary modes of religious thought and practice. One can predict there will be gradual change within the community processes, local and national, moving at the current rate, but a significant jump upward, a significant ascent, will not be made until Boston and other communities find ways to employ teachers full-time. Only full-time teachers will prepare themselves, or can be prepared, to serve Judaism and Jewish children as they deserve to be served. Only full-time teachers will do that job and will invest. Nobody else will. And all schools which do not employ full-time teachers, well-prepared teachers, are doing less than they could for the children. And the great tragedy is that the well-intentioned, trusting families do not know what they are missing. Only when we have full-time teachers, will they come prepared from training schools to overcome the obstacles which currently exist. Most communities without a substantial number of teachers have given up on the idea of providing full-time work with respectable salaries. (I can say as an aside, apart from my stream of thought, that the Bureau's Long Range Planning Committee is studying this problem intensely and is seeking ways to establish at least a substantial number of full-time positions in Boston.) But for the long-range welfare of Jewish education, which means the positive survival to live Jewishly and not only Jewish self-protection against every kind of antagonist, American-Jewish communities must recognize the gap between what is and what can be, and devise ways to provide teachers with full-time positions.

I ask myself, who has the greatest influence on religious education in the United States?

- Not the school professionals
- Not the university academics
- Not the Bureau staffs

I submit that it is the leaders of organized religion: the leaders of the rabbinical seminaries who guide the rabbis and synagogue lay people and set priorities for service to their constituencies.

And here I will take a real long-range jump. The seminaries are the only ones who have the power to get their constituencies to realize how much educational opportunity is being sacrificed through inertia. The seminaries, therefore, are the only ones who can turn things around and, in the long run, stimulate the creation of full-time positions.

The seminaries are involved in education, but not enough. The *first* task of rabbinical seminaries is to produce rabbis. In concert with their lay leadership from synagogues, they also offer educational services, often on a grand scale. The most recent large educational enterprises in both Movements deal with current curriculum development. Nothing near these investments in thought and finances has been devoted to the task of providing competent teachers.

I question whether curriculums are the wisest investment at this time. Having worked both in curriculum development and teacher training I now conclude, that in a forced choice, I would go for the development of a long-range plan to provide well-prepared teachers, as against a plan to develop a national curriculum. This is my reasoning: well-prepared teachers know something; teach something, and learn on-the-job. A well-prepared curriculum without teacher training teaches neither the novice teacher nor the children. I am puzzled by the discrepancy between the lofty goals and inspiring statements in both Movements' educational literature for young and old and the silence on the proper preparation of teachers who will be able to communicate these ideas and deliver the programs. I read Rabbi Eugene Borowitz's *Reform Judaism Today* and am moved by its openness and religious conviction. I read the Conservative Movement's recent curriculum (four from the United Synagogue and one from the Melton Research Center) and am impressed by their depth and applicability. Yet, I often wonder how the powers that be—these Movements in the seminaries—expect that teachers who can do justice to the religious views and practices will ever emerge. One-, two-, and three-day workshops through the Bureau or at a CAJE conference will not substitute for the learning investment necessary to teach Judaism properly and effectively.

Because I cannot believe that the gap between what Judaism can be and that which is delivered to the students will be forever carried on, will be accepted with a sense of resignaton by the local people, because of my inability to believe that, I have one hope. It is a big, long hope—that concerned local lay people and rabbis will start to influence their parent bodies to do some fresh reorganizational thinking about how schools are run, Conservative and Reform; thinking that will make it possible to provide a maximum of full-time prepared teachers.